Pra.

Not the Son He Expected

Tim Clausen has written a wonderful book to help gay men explore the powerful and emotionally-laden terrain of their relationships with their fathers. But it is so much more than that. This work could really be for all men; the variety of relationships the men in this book have had with their fathers mirrors that which any group of men have had. By sharing his own story Tim gives a powerful example of what is possible in creating and sustaining a loving relationship with one's father. I would give anything to have had the experience that Tim and some of the other men in this book have been able to have with their fathers.

The powerful journey that Tim tells of is quite touching. He was able not only to connect with his father but to be of service in one of the most profound and loving ways a child can be there for their parent—as they pass on from this world. Tim's story of his relationship with his father shows the power of forgiveness and the power of detachment from our own parents' humanity to be able to see them and love them in all of their imperfections. As I read Tim's story I couldn't help but imagine what it might have looked like had my father ever gotten sober. What it would have looked like had we ever had a chance to sit down and truly connect. Like too many other fathers and sons, our story is one of missed opportunities. As sad as it is for me reading stories like Tim's and some of the other men's in this book, it gives me a sense of hope and a much more positive sense of fathers in the lives of their children. It gives me hope as a father myself.

There is no question that due to the vast amount of homophobia in our culture, so many wonderful gay men are still walking around carrying deep and painful wounds from how their fathers reacted to their being gay. In my work I talk about The Man Rules, those ideas that we have internalized from a very young age about what it means to be a real man. These ideas live inside of our spirit and our minds, unconsciously driving our behavior and our relationships. One of the biggest Man Rules, sadly, is *Don't Be Gay.* Connected to that notion are so many of the horrible things that we do to males, particularly in prohibiting any true intimacy between men. We have pathologized the love between adult men as only being able to be about sex and lost sight of the much broader and beautiful experience of intimacy and connection. Sadly, gay men serve as a massive projection for all of that fear and internalized shame in our society. But it is books like this that help change that.

What is beautiful about this book is that it shares the incredible hope and healing that is possible. I especially enjoyed reading the narratives of the men whose fathers simply didn't care that their sons were gay because they loved them unconditionally. These fathers were not restricted by the Man Rules and their own internalized homophobia.

I highly recommend this book to every gay man. In these pages you will be able to see glimpses if not a full depiction of your own story. For those gay men walking around with deep wounds from how you've been treated and marginalized by your fathers, you will experience hope and an opportunity to let go of some of the pain that is limiting you and your life. Any man, whether he is gay or not, can find an incredible amount of hope and healing in this book. What Tim has provided is a collection of journeys men have walked in their relationships with their fathers. It is in hearing our stories through the experience of others that we feel less alone and more connected. It is in reframing our stories that we not only get to have a different life in the present but we also get to change our past. Every man deserves that.

Dan Griffin, MA

Speaker | Trainer | Author of *A Man's Way Through Relationships: Learning to Love and Be Loved* and *A Man's Way Through The Twelve Steps* For more information, visit www.dangriffin.com

Not the Son He Expected

Gay Men Talk Candidly About Their
Relationship With Their Father

Tim Clausen

Published November 19, 2017

ISBN-13: 978-1539697909
ISBN-10: 1539697908

Contents

Foreword by Brian McNaught 7

Acknowledgments 10

Preface 13

Dedication. 19

Befriending My Father 21

Introduction to the Interviews. 55

The Question List and A Reading Suggestion 58

Chapter 1: Mark Rinder. 60

Chapter 2: PJ Painter 69

Chapter 3: Mark Matousek 80

Chapter 4: Sean Smedley 86

Chapter 5: Stuart Gaffney. 94

Chapter 6: Danny 106

Chapter 7: Luke McAvoy 113

Chapter 8: Jay Larson. 122

Chapter 9: Ron Brunette 137

Chapter 10: Charlie Skinner-Waters 150

Chapter 11: Bobby Levithan 154

Chapter 12: Chi Chi La Rue 163

Chapter 13: Jim Bopp. 167

Chapter 14: Justin 173

Chapter 15: Jesse Ehrenfeld 184

Chapter 16: Mike Kygar 190

Chapter 17: Maurice Monette. 197

Chapter 18: Jesse Torres 206

Chapter 19: Matt 213

Chapter 20: George Morris 223

Chapter 21: Darrell Schramm. 234

Chapter 22: Dale 242

Chapter 23: Johnny George 249

Chapter 24: Dennis 257

Chapter 25: Matthew Shurka 262

About the Author 277

Foreword

By Brian McNaught

In the 1994 Australian film "The Sum of Us," a middle-aged widower is more embracing of his son being gay than makes his son comfortable. Ray and I, who had far less enthusiastic responses from our fathers, were deeply moved, but a wee bit skeptical. We had never heard of a gay man's father being so cool about his son's homosexuality.

When Ray and I met in 1976, his parents in Kansas had finally ended their long silence of rejection of him. But they weren't fully embracing of him or me. Once during grace, as we held hands around the table, his father prayed that God might send two good women into our lives. The comment did not go unanswered by us, and he never said it again.

I've been told that my father called the President of Marquette University wanting to know how I became gay while a student there. I suspect he is the one who stopped The New York Times from publishing my "Dear Anita" Bryant open letter. He felt I was squandering my talents by my work as a gay speaker and writer. It was only when I started working with major corporations that he got his arms around my profession as a diversity trainer on lesbian, gay, bisexual, and transgender issues. He did, in fact, agree to read my manuscript for "Gay Issues in the Workplace."

When I finally identified myself as gay, my father told me that everyone has some homosexuality in them. I later concluded that my father was probably bisexual, and was trying to get me to understand that every man puts that part of himself in a box, and does the right thing by getting married and raising a family.

Ray also surmised that his father was bisexual, and that he married and raised seven sons because it was the right thing to do.

The father-son relationship has long been tricky. The dynamics of this relationship have provided for great drama in the Bible, and in classic literature and art. Psychologists write at length about the feelings of sons toward their fathers, and vice-versa, including admiration, disappointment, love, competition, power, and subjugation, among others. Most straight and gay men I know describe their relationship with their father as "complicated."

I spoke at my father's funeral about the difficulty I had getting him to express his feelings about me. I would tell him I loved him, and he would deflect the emotion with humor. He could write, "Love, Dad," in a letter, but not say the words. After the funeral, a few men came up to me to say that I had described their fathers too. I wanted to be my father's friend, but he wasn't interested in being my buddy. He was the father, I was the son, and I was to respect and defer to him.

"Do you really want your father to be your best friend?" my therapist at the time asked me. I had written my father many long letters in which I asked for a closer friendship. None of them were answered directly.

I know there are some men, even those who are gay, who had terrific relationships with their fathers. There are a lot of factors that influence the feelings of fathers for their sons, and sons for their fathers. What was the father's relationship with his father? What religion are they, where do they live, what do they do for work, how old are they, are there other sons, who made the most money, does the father like children, was the son expected and wanted, what's the relationship between mother and son, and between father and mother? Add to this mix alcohol, drugs, infidelity, abuse, divorce, and death. And what is the impact, if any, of sexual orientation, when Dad is straight, bisexual, or gay, or when the son is bisexual, or not gay?

I don't have the answer to those questions. What I know is what I experienced. My being gay didn't seem to impact my father's feelings for me. In fact, he and my mother were very welcoming of my romantic partners. They had the most difficulty with the spotlight I put on them when I came out publicly.

Before he died, Ray's dad announced that I was one of his sons, a welcomed member of his family. My father had love and admiration for Ray, and I know he privately felt the same for me. After his death, we found in his desk all of the letters I had sent him over the years, those alone, and none from my siblings.

In this fine book, you will find a number of stories of gay men and their relationships with their fathers. None are exactly the same, and some the complete opposite of others, because of all of the variables that influence our relationships with our fathers. I trust that you will find, as I did, that the common theme is a desire for acceptance and closeness. I suspect that many straight men would tell similar stories, hoping for their father's acceptance and closeness. And some of them fared less well than the gay men in this book.

This collection of stories was the idea of Tim Clausen, who sought out, interviewed, transcribed, edited, and placed each chapter. This is the second project on which I have worked with Tim. In his important, and most informative, first book, *Love Together: Longtime Male Couples on Healthy Intimacy and Communication*, he interviewed me on my relationship of more than forty years with my beloved Ray.

I come away from both experiences believing that the most successful relationships between fathers and sons, or with one's spouse, entail mutual respect, open and honest communication, loving kindness, patience, commitment, and a good sense of humor. Having shared values makes a big difference too. My father being a Republican, and me a staunch Democrat, made communicating lovingly during any election season more difficult. And yet, we endured.

Brian McNaught is an author and educator on lesbian, gay, bisexual, and transgender issues. For more information, go to www.brian-mcnaught.com

Acknowledgments

My gratitude and special thanks to:

My Creator, who keeps giving me these book assignments to do. They are a mountain of work, but I love the work.

To Lindsay Foster Photography for the magnificent cover photo.

To BJ Barone and his son Milo, our handsome cover boys.

To Steven Franzen for my new author photo. I'm finicky about such things and I really like this one.

To Toby Johnson, my editor, for so many great and helpful suggestions throughout the course of putting this work together. Thanks to his wise guidance, this book is far better than it might otherwise have been.

To Diane Weymier-Dodd for her solid design expertise with the cover art and jacket design.

To my interviewees, for baring your souls in sharing your father stories with me. Each of your stories was powerful and touching and further confirmed my sense that this book is both timely and needed.

To Brian McNaught, for the terrific foreword and for his consistently constructive feedback on my creative works.

To Gregory Maguire, Dan Griffin, Brett Jones, Fred Hersch, Daniel Helminiak & Steven Snyder-Hill for generously reading the manuscript and for their thoughtful and incisive words about this book.

Acknowledgments

To Harry Banzhaf, June Kurzon, Steve Franzen, Mary Lutz, Mark Modic, Eric Marcoux, Kerry Benedyk, John Shaughnesy, Bob Barzan, Jean Bottorf, Gail Tschanz, Brandon Best, Laura Cavosi, Jeremy Avner, Rosemary Kolodziejczyk, Tom Hornby & Angelique Johnson for reading portions of the material and providing helpful feedback, suggestions, and encouragement along the way.

To Judy Wolkenstein, for her proofreading eagle-eye.

To Byron R, Eric M, Ron B, John S, Fred H, Kevin C, Caroline D, Robert F, Michael J, Bob P, Tom O, Jim M, Rick L, Robert P, Ursula R, Jim D, Mary L, Daryl B, Sue C, Keith S, Peggy G, Mike S, Kevin S, Terry Z, Jeremy A, Greg T, Brandon B, LuAnn M, Dennis P, Christian C, Ron K, Sally B, Bill H, Danni M, Kenneth M. Carl H, Risa G, Harry B, PJ P, Louise B, Eric C, George H, Bill B, Eugene R, Keith R, John C, Duane S, Robin F, Stuart G, Evan S, Hillary C, Fred W, Karl R, Tom H, Mary Lou L, Lori Ann S, George M, Rhea G, & M.K for their kind and generous support of this work.

To Eric Marcoux & Rob Kallmeyer for introducing me to several interviewees whose stories appear in these pages.

To Robin Filipczak, reference librarian, for being especially helpful to an out of state writer needing assistance with some non-local geography questions.

To Pepper, my cat, who often snoozes pressed up against my leg while I write. Her warm and affectionate presence has been deeply appreciated throughout the long, solitary work of writing both this and my first book.

To Bob Clausen, my father. What a journey we had. How slow I was to recognize that I had one of the great dads in the world. This book is my love letter to you.

Preface

Any substantial exploration of the relationship between gay men and their fathers might well take into account the powerful social factors which shape, define, and constrain us as males. Whether we were consciously aware of them or not, each of us grew up steeped in limiting social constructs, and they have shaped our lives by informing us just exactly how we are expected to be and to conduct ourselves as boys and men. In the insightful book *A Man's Way Through Relationships,* men's issues writer Dan Griffin, talks extensively about the omnipresent and unwritten, yet very real, "Man Rules." These rules are extremely narrow and restrictive, and there is a high price to be paid for not following them, which many of us learn— painfully—very early on. Dan writes:

At the heart of the Rules is an attempt to be safe in the world, to not only be validated as men but to feel truly safe and fit in. Every young boy learns that when he follows the Man Rules he is safer in that he is less likely to be made fun of, criticized, beaten up, and so on. The majority of us did not learn the rules in peaceful conditions. Maybe your home had a more enlightened approach to gender, but no boy escapes the brutality of the schoolyard. In fact, I would say that given how much the process of socialization cuts us off from core parts of our humanity, there is a degree of trauma experienced by every man. For some of us the trauma is severe. To make matters worse, at the heart of any attempts we make to be intimate and truly known to others is a degree of vulnerability that we may not be prepared for or have the ability to navigate. This experience can touch our trauma, triggering it constantly in our most intimate relationships, and when it happens we have no idea what to do and end up sabotaging our relationships as a result.

Exactly what are the Man Rules? A list of them would include "don't show your emotions," "don't be weak," "don't ask for help," "don't cry," "don't care about relationships," "don't be effeminate," "don't talk about your issues," "handle your problems yourself," "be tough and independent," "always be in control," "have all the answers," and especially "don't be gay." The Man Rules are often spectacularly effective at quashing a boy's sensitivity and straitjacketing his emotional life and natural expressivity. Boys soon learn that any qualities perceived as being feminine will be acceptable in females only, and many males grow up jettisoning—for safety's sake—their innate human wholeness for a socially sanctioned psychological one-sidedness. The rules too often impoverish males emotionally and blunt us as full human beings. They isolate us from each other in deep and intrinsic ways. We are not asked at any point while growing up which of the rules we agree with or don't agree with and which ones we will accept or refuse to accept. If you happen to be of the male gender, your compliance with them is fully expected—or else.

For boys who are gay the demands of the rules can be especially oppressive and problematic, since they are designed to socialize developing heterosexual males and do not acknowledge other orientations. It is common for boys who are perceived as not being "all boy" to experience severe trauma in their growing up years at the hands of classmates and others, and it is certainly no coincidence that four out of every five suicide attempts—tragically—are made by LGBT youth. For some boys this nightmare continues or even worsens at home and, instead of being a source of support, his father may be one of the worst oppressors in the boy's life. For sons who are luckier, having the support of an understanding father makes all the difference as they navigate the struggles of growing up gay in a predominately straight world. Some boys have had the good fortune to have had a stepfather, grandfather, teacher, or counselor in their life as a caring and steadfast male mentor when their birth father was physically or emotionally absent. It would be nearly impossible to overstate how profoundly important a father or father figures' presence and character is to the emotional, physical, social, and spiritual development of his son.

It is probably not a stretch to say that most fathers take it for granted that their sons will grow up to be heterosexual. It is also likely that very few dads, if any, are schooled in how to effectively raise and nurture a gay son. Since having a gay child often introduces a unique set of dynamics into the father-son relationship, it is not surprising that these relationships can become rocky or problematic and offer special challenges for both father and son. The father may feel bewildered and frustrated by his boy, who appears to be anything but a chip off the old block. Dad may wonder if he has maybe not tossed the football enough or played enough baseball with his son or has somehow failed to provide a sufficiently strong and masculine example. He may question if the boy's relationship with his mother is too close and somehow to blame. Having been influenced by the homophobia which is inherent in the Man Rules, Dad may consciously or unconsciously distance himself from his son or even reject him altogether. Joe, one of the men I interviewed for this book, spoke about how profoundly shocked and hurt he felt when, as a young boy, he tried to kiss his father, and his dad angrily pushed him off, saying, "Boys don't kiss their fathers." Such experiences are devastating to young psyches and can leave deep and lasting wounds.

Oftentimes the son's sexual orientation may not emerge or become apparent until he is in his teens or twenties or older. For safety's sake, he may have learned early on to hide his gay feelings from others and even from himself and may have dated plenty of girls and married and fathered children before finally coming to terms with his true feelings and deciding what to do with them. Quite a few of the men I interviewed for this work came out to their fathers as adults. Sometimes their father's reaction was exactly what they had anticipated, while often it was not at all what they were expecting. Danny, whose story is in the following pages, had just come out to his dad and was bracing himself for a punch as his father stood up and walked toward him. Instead he was completely surprised when his dad extended his arms and embraced him. Other interviewees have found themselves disowned or estranged from their fathers after coming out to them. Some fathers do eventually come around, and it is encouraging to know that a father's initial reaction is often not his only one. Just as learning to accept ourselves and our sexuality is often a long, slow process for many of us, our fathers and families often need a period of time to process and fully come to terms with this new information. There are more than a few fathers who reacted negatively to their sons coming out who have since become their staunchest and most outspoken allies. It is also not uncommon for a son's coming out to cause his father to examine—maybe for the first time—his own sexuality. John, one of the men in the gay fathers group I ran, came out of the closet a year or so after his teenage son came out to him. John found himself connecting especially well with another group member and the two have now been together for twelve years and married recently. Coming out always changes things, and impacts everyone in the family in not always predictable ways.

As we mature as adults, psychological growth asks us to meet our fathers on an equal footing, man to man. The difficult task of coming out to our dad in painful self-honesty is both a powerful self-affirmation as well as a clear declaration of our equality and independence as a man. Coming out often signals a turning point in our relationship with our father. Many dads gain a newfound respect for their gay son for simply having had the balls to take the risk of coming out to them. Coming out is never an easy thing to do, and more than a few sons opt to never discuss their sexuality with their dad, often at a significant psychological cost to themselves. Nonetheless, it is up to each of us to determine if and when and how we want to come out to our father. It is an entirely individual matter which each of us must find our own way with.

As our fathers get into their later years, our relationships with them may undergo a shift. Dad may have retired and now has time for reflection and soul-searching. He may realize just how important his relationship with his son actually is to him and may let go of some of his old attitudes and become more loving and accepting overall. Understanding that his gay son may one day soon become the elder of the family, he may desire to make things right if there has been discord and estrangement between the two of them. Positive relations are sometimes restored in even the most difficult father-son relationships during this time. For various reasons, some relationships are never mended, and regrets may continue to linger on one or both sides if things remain unresolved. For fathers and sons who already have a good rapport, Dad's later years can bring about an even deeper and closer relationship between the two.

If a father's health begins to decline, it is not uncommon for sons to find themselves stepping into the father role, particularly if Dad is now a widower. Gay men often make great natural caregivers, and though this role reversal might take some getting accustomed to initially, it can be extremely gratifying to be able to help one's father out in this way. When my dad had a stroke sometime after my mother died, I made a commitment to spend as much quality time as possible with him as an active participant in his recovery. He and I became much closer through this process and forged a strong and vital friendship which continued to improve and deepen throughout the last years of his life. I know that I was extremely fortunate to be able to experience this.

The death of one's father is a profound life event for any son, whether the two were close or not. Sigmund Freud himself said that the death of his father was his most poignant loss. Regardless of the son's age at the time of his father's passing, the loss typically brings with it a strong sense of being orphaned, especially if the mother has preceded the father in death. Several of the men I interviewed for this book were able to be present with their dad at the time of his passing. A couple of others were traveling to be there with their father but were not able to get there in time. Some were able to see or talk with their dad prior to his passing while others did not get to see their father until his funeral. At least one interviewee was undecided if he would even want to attend his father's funeral or not. Others who for various reasons were unable to attend their father's funeral wished that they had been able to.

Every son experiences the loss of his father in his own way. The abrupt finality of the death of one's father means that any unresolved issues or leftover unexpressed thoughts and feelings now remain for the son to come to terms with on his own. A good therapist or counselor can be invaluable in addressing and healing father wounds and related issues while helping the griever journey through the grief process. Grief support groups are becoming increasingly prevalent and can offer needed and ongoing support. A father's passing will often bring surviving family members closer together, and being able to share feelings and thoughts candidly with a brother or sister or mother who is also mourning the same loss can be especially helpful and comforting. As has been observed, shared sorrow is half-sorrow.

A wise therapist once told me, "People die, but relationships continue." In a subtle and very real way I feel that my father continues to live on, and I sometimes find myself introspecting and listening for what he would advise me to do in a particular relationship or situation. I realize how very fortunate I was that my father and I got to say everything we wanted to say to each other, that there was no unfinished business between us when he died. I know this is not every son's experience. Although I'm not a therapist, I passionately believe that no matter how difficult or traumatic our relationships with our fathers may have been, each of us deserves to have peace in our life and freedom from past hurts. Some of the men whose stories appear in this book share how they were able to find and make peace with their living or deceased father, and it is my hope that readers will find their experience, insights and hard-won wisdom to be especially helpful. Whether we were ever told so by our fathers or not, each of us has always been lovable and deserving of respect just exactly as we are. Acknowledged or not, gay men always have and will continue to bring special gifts to the collective table which help enrich our families, our workplaces, and our world.

In this work, twenty-six gay men speak openly about their relationship with their fathers. In the Introduction you will find my own father story, which I had the opportunity to write and refine over a three month period. The remaining twenty-five narratives were shared by a variety of men I interviewed for this book. These interviews generally ran anywhere from fifty to ninety minutes; all were recorded and later transcribed and edited. Even though my interviewees did not have the luxury of writing and fine-tuning their father stories over time as I did, their sharing is uniformly powerful and compelling. We have all bared our souls more than a bit here in these pages. May our stories be helpful to sons and fathers everywhere.

Not the Son He Expected

Dedicated with love to my late father, Robert Clausen.
Becoming your friend was one of the greatest experiences of my life.

Age five, happy with the steady progress of the silver maple tree I'd planted in my grandparent's backyard.

Befriending My Father

As my friend Eric Marcoux recently observed, seeing into the hearts of men is not easy in this society. This can be especially true for gay men who long for a better relationship with their father. Getting to know and understand your father's inner, emotional life and his private struggles, joys, disappointments, hopes and regrets is, for many of us, not an easy matter. With some fathers it may be practically impossible.

I was extremely fortunate to be able to experience the type of close and loving friendship with my father late in his life that I would have liked to have had all along, though that relationship did not happen by chance. As two males who seemed to have been cut from radically different cloth, my dad and I did not get around to understanding each other until he was in his mid-seventies. I had stubbornly pushed for years to make him accept me. Being equally stubborn, he refused to be pushed. It was the death of my mother in 2001 which significantly altered the dynamics between us, and it was at that time that I intentionally set about getting to know my dad and to actively pursue a deeper and closer friendship with him. There were things I learned and did along the way which proved to be especially helpful in building this new bond between us, and the chief reason this book exists is because I want to share what worked for me with other gay men who seek a better relationship with their fathers. You may find these practices useful. It is certainly worth the effort, and even if you don't end up with a closer relationship with your dad, you'll always have the satisfaction of knowing that at least you tried.

What follows is my own story, which charts my father's and my relationship from the atypical circumstances of my birth to the time of my father's death in 2005 and its aftermath. The narrative is by nature intensely personal. After my dad died, I felt an urgency to journal the events of the year or two preceding his passing, not knowing at the time that the material would prove invaluable in assembling this essay twelve years later. Of paramount importance to me was that this essay be both true to events and the emotions associated with them as well as a worthy tribute to my father, whom I grew to love and admire more deeply than I ever thought possible.

According to family lore, my dad and I did not get off to the best start. The third of three children and the only boy, I was born, rather festively, on New Years Day during the Rose Bowl Game, when our home team happened to be playing. In order not to miss a single moment of this football spectacular, the delivering physician and my father snuck a portable radio into the delivery room, and the two were happily glued to its play-by-play broadcast throughout my birth. In later years my mother always half-jokingly insisted that my dad was more interested in what was going on in Pasadena than in her labor pains and my eight-pound debut. As it turned out Wisconsin ended up losing the game and—worse—two twin girls had been born several hours ahead of me, hogging up all the gifts, prizes, and adulation my hometown lavished annually on the first newborn of the year for themselves.

Birthing guru Frederick Leboyer championed the notion that children should always be born into a quiet, darkened environment in order to make their emergence from the womb less traumatic. This makes great sense. In reflecting back upon the conditions I was born into—you just KNOW that radio was turned *WAYYYY* up—it's no coincidence to me that I've never been able to bear the sound of sportscasting. I've never had any love for football or organized sports either. But I do love my father.

Like his dad before him, my father was cordial, outgoing, hardworking and conscientious. A World War Two veteran, he joined the Navy directly after high school and worked as a baker on a ship in Guam, turning out delectable coconut cream pies and fresh daily bread for his legions of fellow Seabees. After the war he returned to the states where he met my mother, who was then studying to become a registered nurse. The two married and gave birth to two daughters, two years apart. By the time I came along, my parents had purchased their modest first house. Dad was already well established in a career in sales, where his integrity and strong work ethic made him both quite popular with his customers and increasingly successful.

In photos from my earliest days, my father appears happy and proud of his new son. One black and white snapshot, dated just weeks after my birth, shows him sitting thoughtfully in a straight-back chair, tenderly cradling me as I slept contentedly against his chest. One of my earliest conscious memories is of being upset and crying in the car as Dad drove our family some distance back to where we had been visiting to retrieve an old teddy bear I was intensely attached to and which had been accidentally left behind. A favorite childhood memory also involved riding in the car: I loved our Sunday night car trips home as our family returned from visiting my aunt and uncle near Milwaukee. My sisters and I would happily doze against each other in the back seat of our station wagon, enjoying the darkness outside and the comforting hum of the wheels hugging the road, feeling utterly safe and content with Dad at the wheel. My father was handsome and generally good-natured yet he also had a definite temper as well. The family disciplinarian, he would not hesitate to use the bottom of one of his leather slippers to administer our spankings when we'd gotten out of line.

An artistic boy, I spent lots of time drawing monsters and trees, writing poetry, and creating and illustrating my first simple books. I was intensely aware of the beauty of nature, where both God and a spiritual realm were very apparent to me, as they were—to a lesser degree—in the ELCA Lutheran Church our family attended on Sundays. I recall always feeling particularly close to my mother. Though I liked being male, I identified emotionally with her and was comfortable joining in her world of relationships and cooking and reading and shopping and conversation. I very much enjoyed pulling up the occasional cup of coffee—mine loaded with sugar—with her and our comical neighbor, Bobbi G. I identified with my dad also but to a lesser degree; he seemed in many ways to be "the other" to me. My father was a man completely at home in the world of men. A talented golfer, he had gotten a hole-in-one on a course in Green Bay in his early thirties. I admired my dad's strong mechanical abilities, and he seemed to know how to handle most any situation and how to fix pretty much everything. His attention to detail in keeping the house and cars in good mechanical order and the yard and shrubbery in tip-top shape was exemplary, and I can still smell the scent from the tinned polish he would use to shine and buff his dress shoes. I generally felt inept and out of my element in the realm of mechanical things, especially when Dad would ask me to help him with certain tasks. I recall intensely disliking helping chain saw wood for the fireplace; he'd ask me to hold and steady a long section of branch or tree trunk while he cut it into segments, and sometimes the branch would spin unexpectedly in the saw blade and scrape my hands, which irritated me greatly. Sometimes I just thought my father oafish and insensitive and I felt that as an artistic sort I should be exempt from having to help with such menial and stupid tasks. I felt put upon and generally resented being asked to do simple things like cutting the lawn. This was evident in my sometimes sullen attitude, and I wouldn't make any efforts to hide my unhappiness about a situation. How nice it would have been to have had a brother who was more traditionally masculine who could instead have been roped into doing all of those dreary chores I felt were beneath a person of my talents! I'm not sure exactly where that attitude came from but I do know it was very much present.

Dad and I did connect well on certain things. Early on he taught me how to play Cribbage, at which I was a quick study and frequently lucky, and we enjoyed countless trips around the Cribbage board together. The two of us had a favorite Saturday lunchtime ritual; many weekends we would split a can of olive oil-packed King Oscar sardines. He liked his on saltine crackers, while I preferred mine straight from the can. Dad was generally encouraging of my drawing and writing pursuits and he laughed at my jokes. My childhood favorite: "A cop pulls this guy over and says, "Sir, your wife fell out of the car three blocks back…" "Oh thank God, I thought I'd become deaf!"

When I was about ten it became clear to my parents that my passionate, ongoing interest in playing the piano was more than just a passing fancy, so Dad took me to try out a piano a family had advertised for sale in our local newspaper. I liked it, and he paid them $350 for it. I was thrilled to finally have my very own instrument, a sturdy 1937 Gulbransen console which I still own and play today. After giving piano lessons a try, it quickly became apparent that those were not my cup of tea. I had little patience for practicing scales and reciting beginner's ditties over and over again. Fortunately my parents were wise enough to let me drop the lessons and find my own way around the keyboard picking out pop and blues and jazz tunes by ear.

Reflecting back on my early years I did not feel unloved by my dad yet I also wasn't at all sure that I was fully acceptable as I was. Intuitively I sensed that there were parts of myself that were not or would not be welcomed and somehow weren't pleasing or worthy, and even though I may not have been able to articulate it I had deep questions about how lovable I truly was. I knew that I would never be able to easily fit in or to measure up to the unspoken standards and codes of the world of men which my dad and other males seemed to so effortlessly inhabit. I did feel a part of our family yet I also had a strong sense of being an outsider too, some difference which saddened me and often occasioned a deep and private loneliness within me.

I have an old snapshot Dad took of me when I was about six, wearing his car coat and hat, crossing my eyes and making a goofy face for the camera, and another photo he took of me and a neighbor friend, Judy, both of us dressed up in long dresses, parading around the neighborhood waving American flags. I don't recall my father outright trying to dissuade me from doing such atypical-boy things or ever giving me a bad time about it. I think he knew well that I was never going to grow up to be a star quarterback, and, to his credit, I think he tried his best to accept and encourage me to just be myself. My Grandpa Clausen, his father, had been something of a playboy back in the '20's before he married my grandma, and he always called me "Tiger." From about the time I was in second grade he would often ask me if I had a girlfriend yet. Grandpa clearly envisioned me growing up to be a major ladies' man, and even then I somehow knew that would not be my path in life, but I didn't want to disappoint him by saying so.

From a very young age I was dazzled by male beauty. I recall being wowed by Robert Conrad's muscular chest and shapely butt on *The Wild Wild West*. On *Lost in Space*—one of my favorite shows—handsome and dark haired Don, though he seemed like kind of a jerk, was really good-looking and filled out his spacesuit in a compelling way. (I was jealous of Judy, who I assumed he was regularly making out with behind the Robinson family spaceship.) My two sisters—five and seven years older than I—both had some hot boyfriends over the years. I had a crush on a few but intuitively understood that it would probably be wise not to mention this to anyone.

In my adolescence I recall my dad dutifully sitting me down to give me the birds and the bees talk, while he read to me and showed me the generic illustrations from a pamphlet entitled, *"A Doctor Talks to Ten to Twelve Year Olds."* I remember one page had three drawings of the male body, the first a young boy's body, the second one showing the bodily changes at mid-puberty, and the third a grown man's body with well developed pecs and a larger penis dangling from a nest of pubic hair. The next page had three drawings showing the female body's transformation from girl to teen to woman. This rite of passage talk was likely awkward for both my dad and me, and I wasn't about to tell him that the man's body interested and excited me the most.

It was during my early teen years that a trio of major events happened which turned my world completely upside down. For some time the atmosphere around our house had become increasingly and inexplicably tense, and I recall it coalescing into a very heated fight one night between my parents in which it finally it came to light that my father had been having an affair with a woman he had met in Milwaukee. I remember Mom being nearly hysterical and yelling at him to leave the house, which he did. My sisters and I were stunned. Dad was at the time the chairman of the congregation at our Lutheran Church; how could this *BE*? Mom was completely devastated and—understandably—an emotional mess. Dad moved out after this and was not at all a pleasant person to be around when he would visit. I sided completely with my mother and quickly learned to hate him through this time. I made myself scarce when I knew he'd be around. This went on for quite some months and my parents divorcing seemed to be where things were clearly heading. I was one-hundred-percent in favor of that, and the sooner the better too. I was incredibly angry at my father and just wanted him out of my life for good.

Friends and relatives were sympathetic and offered support and encouragement to us during this difficult time. One Saturday summer night an older friend of the family stopped by and he and my mom and sisters and I sat and chatted breezily. Out of the blue Al suggested, "Hey Tim, why don't you come spend a night at my place, and get away from the girls for a while?" Mom thought this would be OK, and I was thinking, "Cool... Maybe I can go and drink a couple of beers...," so I took him up on his offer. Al's place was on a small lake somewhat out in the boonies, and when we got there he did break out some cold beers and we each had a few. Afterwards he wanted to wrestle, which seemed odd to me, but we did for a while, and then he wanted to shower together. Though a bit buzzed, I was feeling pretty uncomfortable with things by then, and when I suggested that I would just sleep in the guest room, he said, "Oh, there's no sense messing up two beds. You can stay in my room with me..." It was a large bed, and I remember lying as far away from his side as humanly possible. When I felt his hand suddenly creep in between my legs I froze. It didn't ever occur to me at the time that I could ask him to stop; I was just too stunned and afraid. Things happened from there, and when I woke up in the morning I felt instantly sick to my stomach. On the ride back to my house Al told me, "Let's just keep what happened last night here..." I remember walking in our house with Al, and Mom cheerfully asking me, "How was your night, Tim?" I said, "Fine," as normally as I could muster, and after she and Al chatted for a while, he finally left. I eventually ended up telling my oldest sister what had happened but told her, "*DON'T* tell Mom. She has enough shit to deal with already with Dad being gone..." Of course my sister told her, and my mother ended up calling the police. I just wanted the whole thing over and done with. As it turned out I was supposed to have to go to court and testify against him but thankfully didn't have to. Al ended up getting probation for a couple of years, and I always wondered if there would be some payback for having told. Needless to say, this whole situation messed my head up in a major way, and I was more or less left on my own afterwards to try and deal with things or to forget about them as best as I could. It was quite surprising to me to learn later on just how prevalent sexual abuse is among young males and how common it is for those who were sexually abused as kids to find themselves feeling—against all logic—guilty, ashamed, and somehow responsible for the abuse. I know that I felt like damaged goods where sex and sexuality was concerned and I pretty much just shut down in that area of my life for a long time.

Several months after that both of my sisters were nearly killed in a horrific car crash. The driver, my oldest sister's fiance, died instantly. My sisters and their boyfriends had been out partying on a Sunday night, and the police later estimated that the car had been flying along at about seventy miles per hour in a twenty-five mile per hour zone when it missed a turn in the road, hit two trees and wrapped around a telephone pole. My second oldest sister, who had been ejected through a back seat window, was not expected to make it through the night but miraculously pulled through. (The heavy transformer from the telephone pole had landed just feet from her head.) If my mom was already on thin emotional ice, this event all but pushed her over the edge. In the hospital chapel that night she prayed and had a powerful spiritual experience which gave her renewed strength and hope. After the accident it was a long, painful recovery for my sisters, both of whom still live with permanent damage they suffered in it. Frankly it was a miracle that anyone survived that crash, and I remain deeply grateful that their lives were spared.

This trio of heavy events took a significant emotional toll on me as a fourteen-year-old kid, and I turned to drugs and booze as a way of finding relief. In a strange way, this probably saved my life. Drugs and alcohol brought me up out of a dark and lonely depression. I started to hang out with a group of cool new friends who liked to party whenever possible and I quickly fell in love with these magic pills and substances and how wonderfully they made me feel. They allowed me to let go of all the heaviness that was weighing me down and to have *fun* again. I recall one day out of the blue during this time seeing my dad and his girlfriend get out of his car at a local store and feeling this enormous wave of anger flare up seeing him with her. The asshole.... I loathed him for all the hurt and pain he was causing my mother and my sisters and me. I had no understanding then of what a midlife crisis was or of the fact that he might be going through one. I just saw him being incredibly selfish and not giving a crap about his family.

My sisters' car accident and nearly losing his two daughters for good turned out to be a turning point for my father. He and my mom began talking again and over time she forgave him. I was outraged to learn that the son of a bitch was going to be moving back home again and living with us. *REALLY?* After all the grief he caused us? Mom…are you out of your *FREAKING MIND???* She was convinced that he was genuinely contrite and had experienced a change of heart, but I remained skeptical and inwardly angry and rebellious toward him for a very long time. Dad joined her in her new Pentacostal religious groups and activities and prayer meetings. My parents became fans and supporters of Pat Robertson, which galled me no end, and there would be times they had people over, some of whom would be walking around speaking in tongues… I found it all ridiculous and distasteful and tried my best to steer clear of it all and focus on my primary interest, getting high. I was not a pleasant person to be around, and my parents and I had our share of conflicts and difficulties. My grades in school slipped. Knowing he'd messed up with me during the period he was gone my father did try to connect with me where I was, but I was not about to be forgiving and just write off all the difficulty and genuine heartache he had put us through.

At age sixteen I went through my first thirty-day drug and alcohol rehab and stayed sober for eighteen months. When Pink Floyd's *Animals* tour came to town, I attended the show, got high, and was back off to the races. After a huge fight with my father I was thrown out of the house for a number of months and lived with friends while finishing up high school. Post-high school there was a brief attempt at college, where I felt completely out of place and miserable. Through the constant clouds of pot smoke, my attractions for other guys were asserting themselves and I just didn't want to deal with them at all. My father, who had not long beforehand moved me up to UW Eau Claire, begrudgingly drove up and brought me back home. I was at a loss to explain why college hadn't worked out and became something of a hermit back home. Dad would give me lists of tasks to do and rightly wanted me to be out looking for work, which I resented. He and my mother were understandably frustrated and a bit bewildered by me. I just wanted to be left alone. There followed years and years of nothing and floundering around and bouncing from one housing situation and one job to another.

At twenty-five I met a woman through a jazz radio fundraiser in Milwaukee I'd volunteered at. Melissa and I liked each other and I was upfront with her that I wasn't sure where I was at exactly but that I knew I was sexually attracted to guys also. She was then living with a gay male couple in Milwaukee and, to her credit, was pretty open-minded about such things. Early in our relationship I had a random fling with a male friend of a friend of hers which she knew about. Before long she and I were living together and I recall how horrified I was when I learned she had become pregnant. Nine months later our son was born and I was privileged to be there for his birth. (I made sure there were no radios or sportscasts present.) Though my parents would have preferred that we were married before having a child, they were pleased and proud of their new grandson. I recall both Dad and Mom coaching me at various times on the nuances of things like changing diapers and feeding my son as I was in fresh and uncharted territory, as most new fathers are. My being high 24/7 didn't help either.

After a brief hookup with an adult movie store clerk one afternoon I knew that my insistent attractions for men could no longer be ignored or denied. My drug use was out of control and my relationship with Melissa had gone from bad to worse and I knew that something had to change. When my son turned a year old I put myself back into the treatment center I'd first gotten sober at and began the scary task of facing myself and of coming out of the closet to others. I discovered, to my surprise, that most others didn't seem to have as much of an issue accepting my sexual orientation as I did. After treatment Melissa informed me that she was moving back out of state to her hometown and taking my son with her, and although I was very opposed to her doing so there was nothing I could do to prevent this as we weren't married. It was during that time that I put pen to paper and wrote a coming out letter to my mom and dad and with some trepidation, mailed it off to them. Their 40th wedding anniversary was fast approaching and we were all going to be meeting at an area restaurant to celebrate the occasion with them. Walking into the place I recall how nervous I felt, not knowing how I would be received after they had read my letter. Dad and Mom were cordial and the meal went well but we did have some difficult years going forward.

I moved into Milwaukee and founded the Milwaukee Gay Fathers Group, which I facilitated twice a month for the next decade. Like many others who came in and out of the group, I had felt like I was the only gay dad out there, and it was an enormous relief and a pleasure to be able to share stories, compare notes, and identify with other fathers about our respective struggles, joys, and concerns. Pretty much every dad in the group had been or was in a straight marriage and was going through the roller coaster of coming out to his wife and kids, moving out of "the big house," divorcing, and starting a new life. I talked about my struggles with being a long-distance dad, and the guys were great about being supportive and offering helpful suggestions. Most all of the guys were exemplary fathers and set great examples for me to try to emulate. I felt that even if I might not be the world's greatest dad, I enjoyed being the father of the group and connecting regularly with all of these wonderful men. Laughter was abundant in our meetings and many lasting friendships were formed. Nothing was off the table for discussion, and many members talked about their relationship with their father; those relationships spanned the gamut from the textbook wonderful to the absolutely terrible. Every man strove to be at least as good as or a better father than their dad was to them. I continued to grapple with being a long-distance dad. Though I'd call regularly and visit my son once or twice a year, the reality is that I missed most of his growing up and I simply wasn't willing to move out of state to live closer to him. The decade I spent in the fathers group was one of the best experiences of my life and helped me to become a better and more conscious father and man than I had been before.

From my Dad and Mom's point of view, Al had made me gay. They told me that I was always welcome at their house but only if I was alone. They did not wish to meet or see anyone I might be dating or to discuss such matters with me. It was the "love the sinner but hate the sin" nonsense that their very conservative religion touted, and the "gay lifestyle" I was now—regretfully from their perspective—a part of. They did not or would not see that the signs had been there since my childhood: how many straight grade school boys were dressing up in costume dresses and parading around the neighborhood waving American flags on the 4th of July? I told them that Al had NOT made me gay and that the only choice I had made was to finally be true to myself and the feelings that have been a part of me from as far back as I can remember. Trying to talk with Dad and Mom about all of this I was often reminded of Timothy Leary's wonderful saying, "My chess set communicating with your Monopoly board." I felt frustrated attempting to communicate my truth to them, and I'm sure they felt similarly frustrated as well. I'd still visit and call them and we'd get together for holidays, but this uneasy alliance went on for many years.

Being especially strong-willed, there were times I really tried to push my folks to accept me, feeling like, "Damn it, if you love me then you need to accept me as I am," conveniently overlooking the fact that by doing so I was not accepting them where they were at. I had dated a guy named Vic for several months, and we broke up sometime in the fall. My parents were then wintering in Arizona and living in northern Wisconsin the rest of the year, so it was traditional for our family to meet at some Milwaukee restaurant in November to celebrate Christmas early as they were passing through town, getting ready for the long drive west. Dad had written me a postcard saying when and where we'd be meeting this time and that they'd like me to be there. Although Vic and I had broken up, and wanting to push the issue, I wrote him back and said, "Sure, Vic and I will be happy to attend," thinking that then when I showed up alone at the family gathering I could just say, "Oh, Vic couldn't make it. He had other things he needed to do today," which of course would have been true. I was determined to make them accept me. Dad wrote me back a very angry letter saying that they would never be able to condone or accept my gay lifestyle and that I would only be welcome at the family holiday gathering ALONE. Irked by his reply I didn't respond, and a week or two before the get-together I called the restaurant we were supposed to meet at to verify our reservations, and was surprised when they said there were no reservations listed for our family. When I dialed up my oldest sister to find out where we were going to be meeting, she told me, "I can't tell you unless you promise to show up alone." I was outraged to hear this and told her how ridiculous I thought it was. She said she sympathized but could not tell me where the restaurant was. As furious as I was I didn't stay on the phone very long. I certainly was not about to promise anyone that I would show up alone, even though I had planned to do so all along, with my story about Vic being busy that day. Screw *THEM*, I thought. That they would even do such a thing just really hurt. I did not attend the Christmas gathering and I kept my distance from my family for some time.

Years rolled by. In September of 2001 Mom and Dad were going to be celebrating their 50th wedding anniversary, and the entire family was invited up to northern Wisconsin for the weekend occasion. Even Melissa and her new husband and my son drove up from out of state to be there. It turned out to be a truly wonderful time. Harmony and good spirits and laughter prevailed throughout the weekend and my parents were in their glory having all of us there together with them for this very special occasion.

Several weeks after their 50th, my mother became gravely ill and was taken to a hospital, where after a series of tests a diagnosis of pulmonary fibrosis was made. Largely untreatable, pulmonary fibrosis is an auto-immune disease characterized by a hardening of the lining of the lungs. She was placed on a ventilator and given heavy painkillers. Dad encouraged me to make the drive north to Marshfield to see her, and although I was initially reluctant to do so I finally made the trip. As I walked into her room, Dad announced to her that I was there, and she craned her head slightly toward me though her eyes remained closed. She had clearly been waiting for me. Mom wasn't able to speak but she was able to squeeze my hand as I sat next to her and held hers. I had been doing some self-examination and was very aware that I had not exactly been an angel across the years and I had caused her and my dad some genuine heartache. I knew that I had an important window of opportunity here and I didn't want to find myself regretting not having made amends with my mother while I still could. Holding her hand I moved in close and asked her forgiveness for all the harm I had caused her and also told her that I forgave her for any harm she had caused me. She squeezed my hand in response.

Two days later the doctors wanted to meet with our family so I drove back up to Marshfield to be there. The physician in charge informed us that with her condition there was nothing more they could do to make her well and asked if we wished to keep her on the ventilator which was keeping her breathing. My mother had been a nurse for many years, and we unanimously agreed that, given her medical condition, she would not want to be kept alive on life support. Having always been in many ways the black sheep of the family, it was an incredible honor for me to sit with her and hold her hand during the last few hours of her life. I told her all the many things I was grateful to her for. Mom's breathing was gradually becoming more shallow and erratic, and a small tear began to form in the corner of her left eye. I watched as the woman who had ushered me into the world took one last breath and then, silence. The stars shone extra brightly in the cold November sky that night as I drove back to Milwaukee, so very grateful that I had the opportunity to be present and to share in the immensity of that experience with her. Being able to accompany to the threshold the woman who had ushered me into the world as she left us for the next one was a profound honor.

When the pastor of my parent's church in northern Wisconsin told me he didn't want me to speak to the gathered during Mom's funeral service because, "You know your mother didn't approve of your lifestyle, Tim," I really had to restrain myself from punching his ignorant, bigoted lights out. Later Dad accompanied the driver who drove Mom's coffin down to my hometown for the burial. Dad was kind and gracious to all and he and I bonded naturally in our mutual grief over her loss. As it turned out, Mom's death ushered in a new season in my father's and my relationship, in which we at last began communicating man to man and building a true friendship.

We began talking more frequently by telephone, and I'd call him often at my parent's place in northern Wisconsin or at their winter digs in Arizona. Dad was doing his best to adapt to life without my mother but it was clearly a struggle for him and he missed her deeply. The following spring when he drove to Milwaukee on a business matter, the two of us went for a walk along Lake Michigan and sat and talked for a long time on a park bench overlooking the water. It was wonderful to be talking much more openly together than we ever had before about our hopes and sorrows and joys and dreams. Mom's death had—understandably—taken something out of him and he seemed somehow gentler and more reflective than I remembered him being before. I offhandedly mentioned to him that I had always wanted to record interviews with both Mom and him individually and ask them all sorts of questions about their growing-up years, their hobbies as kids, recollections of their grandparents, etc.... I had always assumed I could do those interviews at any time and now I very much regretted having missing the chance to do so with my mother. I definitely did not want to miss my chance to interview Dad and asked him if he'd be open to be interviewed. He asked a few questions about it and then said he would be open to doing so sometime.

The phone interview I did with my father several months later turned out to be a real turning point in our relationship and brought us much closer together. I think he was honored and flattered that I would be interested and curious enough to want to know something about his early years, about who he was before he became my mother's husband and my father. Though I had some general ideas of things I wanted to ask him I didn't make out a question list, preferring the interview to be more of a free-form, spontaneous experience. Some of the questions I asked were: What are your recollections of your grandparents? Did you have any pets while growing up? What were your hobbies as a kid? Did you grow up attending church and what was that like? Did you have a job while in high school? When did you start dating? Did you have your heart broken by anyone? Were you drafted into the Navy and if not why did you pick the Navy? (His dad, my grandpa, had been in the Navy in WW1 and advised him to join the Navy because "you always know where you'll sleep at night.") What was it like in Guam? Did you make any good friends in the Navy and did you stay in touch with them? What was it like coming back to the States after the war? How did you get into sales? How did you and Mom meet? How did you pick our names? Overall are you satisfied with the course of your life? Do you have any regrets? Dad replied that he had one main regret. "It was the time that I left your mother and you and your sisters. I caused a lot of hurt and pain, and it could have been avoided." I told him that I had forgiven him and so had Mom and my sisters, but he clearly still felt burdened by it.

Interviewing my father was both a revelation and a turning point in our relationship. It was fascinating to learn so much about his life journey which had previously been unknown to me and—without having interviewed him—would have likely forever remained a mystery. I loved learning about his grandparents and what they were like as people. It was touching to hear him choke up a bit as he recounted returning home from the war and seeing his dad for the first time in several years and their reuniting with a tight bear hug. He talked about the heartbreak he experienced in high school when a girl he cared deeply for dumped him for a different guy. I was able to see my dad as a human being, as a boy, as a teen, a young adult, a newlywed, a new father, a man finding his way through a midlife crisis, a husband trying to patch things up with a wife he betrayed, a retiree, now a widower adjusting to life after losing his companion of half a century. The questions and the sharing flowed easily between us, and the ninety minutes just flew by. It was a beautiful experience which was powerfully bonding for him and me. I am SO glad I taped it. I cannot recommend highly enough to others how important it can be to do an interview like this with your father while he is still here. Tell him you'd like to learn more about him and his life and background and that you would be honored to interview him. Do it in person. Tape it, camcord it; whatever works for you. Write down the questions you want to ask in advance if that's easier for you. The experience will almost certainly open up a significant new door and deeper level of communication between the two of you. If you take the time to record it you will have a priceless keepsake to revisit any time you like. After your father has passed on, you will still be able to hear him speak to you. Trust me; you will be very glad you did so, for very many reasons.

Almost three years after my mother's death, I received a phone call one afternoon that Dad had just had a massive stroke and was in the hospital. I drove up to northern Wisconsin as quickly as possible to see him. We'd both been enjoying building this new father-son friendship between us; was this the end of the road for us already? Please God, no…. After arriving I was told that the stroke had mostly affected his right side, and that he was having difficulty speaking. I was happy to see him, impaired and foggy as he was, and did my best to be cheery and upbeat, as did my aunt—his sister—who had flown in from Pittsburgh. The doctor was somewhat encouraging when we spoke to him, pointing out that, while it was never a speedy process, stroke patients can regain functionality and even sometimes most or all of their prior abilities. That was good to hear and a relief.

As soon as it was practical to do so we moved my father down to the nursing home in my old hometown, where I had worked as a dishwasher during high school. Dad was put into a rehabilitation program, where he began to make slow but steady progress. Being able to see him now entailed just a quick forty-minute drive from Milwaukee, and I made going to spend time with him a top priority. I wasn't at all sure how many days, months, or years I might have left to spend with my dad and get to know him better but I was NOT going to squander this window of opportunity I was being given, for however long it might be there. On my twice a week visits I found that it felt very natural stepping into the role of helper and caregiver with him, helping pick things up, helping him cut his food for dinner, helping with a shirt or a pair of socks. It was wonderful to see him slowly gaining strength and regaining his speech abilities. In a very real way, Dad's stroke also became a gift for him and me because it brought him back in geographic proximity where we were able to spend a lot of quality time together, face to face. The two of us could never have become as close as we did if he had just lived out his days in Rhinelander and Arizona and we'd had to content ourselves with phone calls and postcards, though I would have called him often.

Although at first I had to help him a lot with counting and pegging and choosing cards, Dad and I started playing Cribbage again, which I knew would help stretch his brain and give us something fun to do which we had long enjoyed together as father and son. The primary goal was for him to keep progressing and regaining functionality and independence, and once he could achieve certain benchmarks, we would be able to spring him out of the nursing home and move him into a more pleasant environment at a newer assisted living facility across town. As focused as I had been on cheerleading him on in his recovery I was finding it increasingly wonderful just to be hanging out with him, enjoying the simple pleasure of his company.

The happy day arrived when Dad had regained sufficient independent functioning to graduate from the nursing home's rehab program and be discharged. My sisters and my brother-in-laws and I moved him into his own cozy apartment at the assisted living facility on the south end of town. Here he could live on his own and do as he liked but also would get one meal a day with the other residents and have nurses and staff to help with medications and laundry and whatnot. Wilkinson Woods was a very nicely appointed place in a wooded setting, and Dad seem to take to being there and to the other residents quickly and with ease. With his gentle charm it didn't take him long to make a number of friendships among the other residents and staff.

I would drive out there on Wednesday and Saturday nights to see him and we'd hang out at his apartment and play Cribbage and talk. On weekend visits I'd usually bring a pizza or sandwiches for us to enjoy while we talked about what was going on in our day and our week. My father and I were becoming closer and we very much relished spending regular time together. I was purposely being more open about my love life and talking with him about someone I might be dating, and it was indescribably wonderful to find that he had somehow shifted to a place of complete acceptance of me. When my nephew Ryan graduated from high school sometime during this time, Dad was very cordial and warm to Evan, the guy I was seeing, who had come along with me to Ryan's graduation party. What huge progress my father and I had made from that terrible lost Christmas some years beforehand. It seemed like a miracle, and I was quietly grateful.

How amazing it was to be able to talk freely with my father about sex. He told me he'd lost his virginity with a neighbor girl at age sixteen. When I asked him what his sex life was like with Mom, he said they enjoyed a good and active sex life but that they were "no acrobats." One night as we sat in his apartment playing Cribbage I asked Dad what Lillian—the woman he'd had the affair with—had been like. I was truly interested and curious. He told me that she had worked as a hostess at a Milwaukee area Holiday Inn where he liked to lunch sometimes. A nice rapport developed between the two of them which had ultimately turned into more. Dad said that she was a genuinely nice person and he really enjoyed her company. He said that when he informed her that he had decided to go back to his wife and that he wouldn't be seeing her anymore, she was deeply hurt. He said he had very much regretted causing her pain but knew he was making the right decision in returning to his family. He added that they spoke one more time after that but that was the last he saw or heard of her, and they necessarily each went their separate ways. This brief conversation gave me an entirely different view of the woman I had made out to be a selfish home-wrecker and I found myself feeling sad for her and for the heartache she'd experienced. I even looked her up name up in the phone book sometime later and tried to contact her but her number was no longer in service. Perhaps she had moved away or married or passed on by then, but I really would have liked to have had the opportunity to speak with her. In an interesting twist of cosmic irony, my only granddaughter's name happens to be—you guessed it—Lillian.

Wilkinson Woods offered a church service every Sunday, but my father did not attend. When I attempted to bring religion and spirituality up in conversation, he never had too much to say about his beliefs. It always seemed to me that Mom had been the one taking the lead in the religion department, and once she was gone, Dad was free to maintain his own relationship with his Creator and he seemed very content and at peace with whatever it was. We didn't talk about politics much either, but when John Kerry lost to Bush in 2004, I expressed my great disappointment about the election results to him during one of my visits. My parents had always leaned toward the conservative end of the spectrum, so I was quite stunned and delighted when he told me that he had voted for Kerry too. I was so proud of him!

Though my father had been using a walker regularly for some time, he had a pretty bad fall out of the blue one morning in June. Dad was admitted to the local hospital where he was in rough shape; confused, feeble, upset. He didn't look well, and tests were being run to find out what was going on medically with him. Unfortunately falling and being able to remain in assisted living don't mix well, and we were informed that he would not be able to return to assisted living. After a mad scramble to find a suitable nursing facility we found one in a nearby town, where Dad was given a shared room. After the relative freedom and independence he had enjoyed in assisted living it felt like a large defeat to be moving him there. Physically weakened and still somewhat foggy, my father settled slowly into the rhythm of the nursing home. I continued visiting twice a week and would bring meals and play cards with him and always strove to be as upbeat as possible. I loved being affectionate with him and liked to rub his back, which he enjoyed. I had graduated massage therapy school some years before and started spending time rubbing Dad's feet for him every time I visited too. Sometimes he'd nod off while I did this. It was really nice to connect with my father in this way and express the deep love and affection I felt for him.

It was a pleasure to bring hot meals en route on Saturday nights for the two of us to enjoy. At the new place Dad and I took to having our dinner in the physical therapy room downstairs, which was never in use at that time and had a nice table we could eat at. He'd take his walker or I'd take him in his wheelchair and we'd sit and eat together. Sometimes we would talk, other times not. I liked getting his commentary on whatever current events happened to be going on in my life and seeking his reasoned and seasoned perspective. Occasionally we'd play a round of Cribbage after dinner or if he was too tired to play I'd take him outdoors and wheel him around the large parking lot where we could take in some fresh evening air and the colors of the sunset sky. Then it was back to his room, where we had recently started a new routine: my parents had an address book full of names and addresses and phone numbers of friends of theirs from all over the country, and I would randomly flip to a page of names, some known to me, some not, and ask him, "Who is so and so?" He would tell me, and then I'd say, "Would you like to talk with them?" If he said yes, which was about half the time, I'd dial up the person and hand him the phone. As a result of these impromptu Saturday night phone calls my father got to talk with a lot of people who had been important in his and my mom's life over the years and I know that many of these conversations brought him a great deal of pleasure. It was most always a surprise of course for the people we'd call to be hearing from him too, and often it had been many years since they had last spoken. Sometimes I would initiate "phone-hour" because I had run out of things to talk about or was simply tired, but it was genuinely fun to just sit out for a while and help coordinate Dad's reconnecting and conversing with old friends of his and Mom's across the years.

In January he came down with pneumonia and ended up in the hospital. Dad had already been diagnosed with congestive heart failure, and now coupled with the pneumonia, he was in bad shape. The gut-bacteria, C-diff, was raising havoc with his digestive tract at the same time, and his situation became quite dire. They were pumping him full of antibiotics, and Dad was coughing terribly and would float in and out of consciousness. I was worried and praying a lot and asked others to pray for him. Thankfully he did slowly rebound. Though my father never did completely bounce back from this episode he did recover to a large extent and returned to a now single room at the nursing home, which he would occupy for the rest of his life.

It was clear to me that my dad's energy level was ebbing and that he was losing ground. Gradually the walker went away and he spent most of his time either in bed or in a wheelchair. At the urging of his doctor, my sisters and I got Dad signed up with hospice. The hospice people were amazingly compassionate and helpful. As usual I would call my father daily and check in with the nursing staff to see how he was doing. Dad, who had long since become a priority for me, was the overarching focus in my life, and since there weren't all these other large emotional entanglements going on in my life then and no significant other, I was able to devote my energy and free time to him. I loved being my father's watchdog and buddy, and my oldest sister and my brother-in-law and I were all deeply devoted to his care, making sure that he was being properly cared for. We couldn't be there 24/7 but due to our attention to detail and assertiveness my dad ended up getting probably the best care of any resident there.

One Saturday night about two months prior to this when Dad and I were having dinner down in the P.T. room I said, "There's something I want to ask you." "OK." "You know it really meant a lot to me to be able to be with Mom during the time of her passing. I was able to be very present with her during her last few hours and that was incredibly meaningful for me and I believe it was very meaningful for her too. Now whenever it might be, and I hope it's a long, long ways off, but whenever it comes your time I would very much appreciate being able to be there with you in that way too. How do you feel about that?" He said that he wouldn't have a problem with it. I added, "I also realize that with my living fifty miles away, that may or may not turn out to be possible. But my wish is very much be here with you. The staff here and the hospice people know that this is my wish too, but I just wanted to let you know that this is something that is extremely important to me." It seemed to me that he was quietly pleased by this, though he didn't really say a whole lot more either. That was an important conversation for my father and me to have, and I'm glad that I spoke up so he knew where I was coming from. This was a tricky subject for me to bring up with him too: I didn't want him to get the sense—ever—that I thought he was on his way out, though he surely had to know where his path was leading. I don't believe he had any particular fear or misgivings about dying, especially being confined as he was in a nursing home with his abilities and quality of life systematically declining. I also had something of a superstitious belief that to talk about his death would somehow be to hasten it or bring it on, and I was not at all ready to lose this wonderful man whom I'd grown to love so dearly and admire so profoundly.

Eventually the Cribbage went by the wayside. Dad's shoulders pained him too much to play any more, so we stopped. Despite these and other setbacks, he dealt with the decline of his health with tremendous grace. I was so often struck by my father's simplicity and his gentleness, his serenity and basic acceptance of things as they were. I loved walking into Dad's room and seeing his smile and hearing his "Hello Timmer," as he greeted me. He always seemed happy to see me. I loved walking in and giving him a big hug and a kiss on the cheek and taking in the warm, masculine scent of his skin as I greeted him.

Dad was coughing a lot, especially during meals, and on the second to last meal we had together I had stopped to pick up Chinese for us on the way over. I brought his favorite dish, shrimp with cashews and black mushrooms. The restaurant's shrimp were large and sweet, and I think Dad tried to swallow part of one without chewing it well first, and suddenly he was in crisis. His color became quite red, and I couldn't tell if it was a breathing or stomach issue, but he was gagging like he was about to throw up, so I grabbed a nearby pail and put it in front of him. It was a very scary moment, and thankfully he coughed up the offending morsel moments later. I did not know how to perform the Heimlich maneuver and since we were eating alone in the P.T. room this could have been a major crisis. After finishing the rest of our dinner uneventfully I don't recall if I took him for a wheelchair spin around the parking lot to enjoy the warm June air or if we just went to the lobby-lounge and I played a couple of tunes for him. They had some older dual keyboard organ there, and although I'm no organist I was somehow able to coax a tune or two from the thing, which my dad always seemed to enjoy. Feeling tired, he soon wanted to go back to his room. Once there it was always the task of finding an available nurse or aide to help him to the bathroom and back. Big Teri, one of the p.m. nurses, was not usually very helpful in this regard—Dad had privately nicknamed her "Waddles"—but she would typically defer to one of the aides. Our favorite was a vivacious nineteen-year-old nursing student who was extremely cute and sweet. By her own admission, Dad was her favorite resident, and he would always kiss her on the cheek when she visited. One night after she had helped him into the john, she and I were talking while we waited for him to finish up. She was telling me about the boyfriend-from-hell she'd been seeing for some time and about how difficult it was to find a good boyfriend, which I agreed was so. Suddenly Dad chirped up from inside the bathroom and said, "I'll be your boyfriend!" We all laughed.

My father and I had our last dinner together on the evening of Saturday, June 4, 2005. Dad was soon to turn seventy-nine on June thirtieth. There were big storms in the area on that day, with very dramatic skies. I walked into the place, pizza in hand, and headed to Dad's room knowing that I'd see his bright smile and hear his wonderful "Hello Timmer" greeting along with it. I wasn't disappointed; he was sitting in his wheelchair, catnapping as he often did. We talked for a minute, and I asked him if he was hungry and wheeled him down to our favorite dining spot, the P.T. room. Upon entering we discovered that they'd just re-carpeted the room, and the whole placed reeked of new carpet chemical fumes. We decided it would be far more pleasant for both dining and breathing in the chapel next door, so we moved over there. I, of course, had no idea that this would be our last meal together, which was probably a good thing. Dad seemed somewhat tired and low energy, which wasn't unusual. What was unusual was that he seemed especially grateful for my bringing dinner—not that he wasn't normally—but several times during the meal he very deliberately thanked me for bringing it, maybe for all the dinners I had brought. Perhaps he knew his time was running out. My father was certainly his usual mellow, gentle self, if anything more so than ever. I told him that he was more than welcome, that it was a pleasure for me to do so. I added that he was my favorite person in the world and that there was no one else I'd rather hang out with, which was true.

Back at his room I gave him a good foot rub and got a nurse to come and ready him for bedtime. After she left, I helped tuck him in and leaned over and hugged him and kissed him on the cheek, and he would kiss me on the cheek too. This tradition began in the Wilkinson Woods days, and I loved being affectionate with him and happily soaked up the affection he gave me as well. Afterward I'd usually try and coax a chuckle out of him before I left by telling him a blonde or a Polish or a lawyer joke, but always told him as I left for the night, "Love you, Dad. See you soon." I'd finish up every phone call to him the same way. I wanted to make SURE he knew it, which he certainly did. I left and went off to my Saturday night A.A. meeting in my hometown, which was on my way back to Milwaukee.

On the way to my Sunday restaurant brunch piano gig the next morning I called his room, and a nurse answered and then gave him the phone. Where my father had been completely lucid the night before, now he seemed anything but. He sounded confused and his speech seemed more than a bit slurred. "Are you coming to my party?" he asked. I played along. "Sure, Dad, of course." It was clear that something—another stroke?—had occurred since I'd seen him the night before. I was concerned and spoke to the nurse, who didn't convey any alarm or sense that things were not well. As I headed off to play my brunch gig with a heavy heart I wondered what this all meant.

When I called his room during my lunch hour the next day, the nurse I spoke to said he'd eaten pretty well at lunch. I asked if she could put him on the phone. Dad's speech was very slurred and he kept drifting out of focus. The nurse would tell him, "Bob, it's Tim on the phone," after which he would come to and say, "Hi, Timmer," and then zone off again. After two or three rounds of this, I didn't want to tire him out further and I told him I would talk to him later. The nurse told me at that time that he was having involuntary tremors in his limbs too. It wasn't sounding good at all.

When I called after work, my brother-in-law answered and said, "You better get up here right away. Your dad's color is terrible, he's non-responsive, and he seems to be having some type of seizures. I don't think he's going to make it through the night. How fast can you drive?" He added something about my driving fast enough to just hit the tops of the hills. I headed right over there as fast as I could. Dad looked bad and he was having these jerky, spastic movements in both his arms and legs. He hadn't been at all responsive when my sister and brother-in-law talked to him and he wasn't responding to me when I tried to rouse him either. The nurses were administering Ativan rectally, and he was not able to take nourishment. Along with the involuntary arm and leg spasms, Dad would grimace periodically with a pained expression which would then slowly fade. He was clearly having a difficult time, and the nurses were giving him the muscle relaxer every two hours. Hospice had been called and morphine was suggested. I wasn't shocked or startled to see my father like this; I knew this is where things had been building toward for some time and that his health had been inexorably winding down. It appeared that my dad was laboring intensely to wrest himself free of captivity in a nursing home and of a body that had simply become worn out.

Neither my oldest sister or brother-in-law had a chance to have dinner yet that evening so they excused themselves to go get supper and head home. I hadn't expected to have this private time with my father but was glad for the opportunity. I sat and held his hand. His limbs would thrash in fits and starts, very randomly and jerkily, and his breathing seemed erratic too, punctuated by gasps and long exhalations. I had the sense that he was deeply engaged in some kind of inner dialogue—talking with his Maker or my mother or someone—but he clearly was very busy and preoccupied. This was definitely *WORK* for him, the last work this good, hardworking man would have to do in this world. I told Dad I was glad to be with him while I sat there feeling utterly helpless other than to just be present with him.

I had arrived around eight p.m., and they had just given him another dose of Ativan. Now it was getting upwards of ten, and the tremors were increasing in severity and frequency as the medication was beginning to wear off. His grimacing increased and he would groan or puff air out of his cheeks, just like one might during deep sleep. His hand was hot and clammy. I told him, "I will go get a nurse to give you some morphine, Dad. It will help you to be more relaxed." Out at the nursing station I asked Marsha to bring him some Ativan and morphine, and she said she'd be along in five minutes, which she was, with an assistant. Gloved, they walked into the room, all business-like. Marsha put on the light above Dad's pillow and said firmly in his ear, "Bob, we're here to give you your medicine and we're going to have to turn you on your side to do it." To my surprise and delight, he came to at this, and I told them I'd be back in a minute, after they had done their thing, which I really did not want to watch.

Two minutes later I walked back in his room, their task now completed. Marsha was chatting with Dad at the head of his bed commenting, "There's that beautiful smile I love." I walked up towards his pillow, and she said to him, "And look who's here...," and I got into his line of vision and smiled at him. "Hi, Dad!" He got this very surprised, delighted expression on his face like he was just astonished to see me, which was wonderful, and he even gasped a little bit. "Hi, Dad. Yes, I've been here for a while." Marsha and the other nurse waved at me as they left the room. Dad spoke to me in this very, very thin voice, "Hi, Timmer." I sat down right next to him. He asked for some water, so I reached over and grabbed his styrofoam cup and held the straw up to his lips. He took several swallows. I'd never seen my dad look so lovable, innocent, and completely vulnerable before. Some of the words he said I could make out and some I couldn't. I told him how wonderful it was to be here with him, that there was nowhere on earth I would rather be and no one I'd rather be with than right here with him and that I loved him very much. What he did next was entirely natural but yet surprised me all the same; he puckered up his lips for me to kiss him, which I only too gladly did, the first and only time I recall kissing my dad on the lips. It was a moment of incredible sweetness and the pinnacle and summing up of all that we'd built up together over the last couple of years. It was my father's exquisitely tender parting gift to me, offered spontaneously, freely, magically. Then the morphine took hold, and he closed his eyes and drifted off. His limbs slowed their movements. My dad had shown his unconditional love and regard and acceptance of me, the son who had felt that he could never really fit in or be fully accepted and loved or welcomed into the world of men. It was the most beautiful moment of my life.

Afterwards I stayed a while, holding his hand and basking in the warmth of that remarkable exchange. It had been a long day and I told him I needed to go home and get some sleep but that I would see him again tomorrow. As I drove back to the city I was very aware that I had been given a great gift in those unforgettable moments together, and yet how fitting it was that we should have had that too, a sweet coda to the loving friendship we had built and nurtured through all our visits together over the past many months. Even though I knew my father was dying, I felt humbled and blessed.

Although my brother-in-law had thought that Dad's demise would be soon, I didn't think it would be within hours, and the nurses didn't think so either. They commented that many of his vitals were still strong. My workday the next day dragged on and on, and I made numerous calls to check in with the nurses and with Gloria, the hospice nurse. I debated whether I should even be at work or not but saw the day through. When I arrived at the nursing home after work, I was again grateful to have the place and Dad basically to myself. There was a machine by his bed suctioning fluid out of his lungs. He had also been put on a morphine drip, and unlike the previous day, he was quite still. Dad was propped up by pillows and bedding into a stationary position. His breathing was labored, and you could hear the moisture in his lungs with every breath he took. I felt, as I had with Mom during her dying process, that he had gone way down deep inside himself, and he was completely unresponsive. I rubbed his feet and talked to him and sat next to him and held his hand. How I would miss these visits with him… After a few hours at his bedside I was feeling very tired, and I debated just crawling in on the spare bed in his room but decided it would be better to go home instead. Remembering my request to him I knew it was important to speak to him about it before I left. "Dad, I know I told you that it was my wish to be able to be with you when your time came. But it's late and I'm tired and I need to go home and get some sleep for work tomorrow, and I want you to just do whatever you need to do. Whenever you are ready, you just go ahead. There's nothing holding you back here, no responsibilities or duties or concerns and you're totally free to do whatever you need to do. If I'm here with you, fine, and if not, that's OK too. I love you very much and you and I will always be connected, no matter what. You just go on home when you're ready to." I kissed him and left for the night. It was amazing that here just four days ago we'd had a pleasant dinner together, and now he was preparing to depart. How fortunate I was that we had been able to spend so much quality time together and that I'd had the presence of mind to make our relationship a priority. As I said on more than one occasion to people, "There will be plenty of days/months/years when I will want to see him and cannot."

After getting home I got to bed around twelve and was careful to put my cell phone on ring mode and place it right by my pillow before nodding off. The hospice nurses knew to call me right away if anything happened. I was roused by the phone ringing at approximately 3:30 a.m. A nurse told me that Dad had just died and asked if I wanted to come and be there with him. I told her I'd get there as soon as I could and not to move him please. I called my sisters and told them what had happened and that I was going to head over there to be with him for a while, then showered, called work to say I wouldn't be in, and drove back to the nursing home.

The morning of June 8th was exceptionally beautiful, with dawn coloring the early morning sky and birds starting up their morning songs. Beverly Terrace was dark except for a few lights on. I slipped past the nurses station and went directly to Dad's room. The door was closed, and I took a deep breath and entered. My father was lying on his back, arms folded gently across his abdomen, his mouth slightly open, with the comforter pulled up to his waist. He was the picture of peacefulness and appeared to be sleeping. This impression was further amplified, strangely, by the fact that his automatic air-bed was still hooked up beneath him, and every minute or so the mattress would inflate up, making it look like he was breathing. I was grateful to have the time alone again, just him and me, hanging out together one last time. It was now about 5:30 a.m. and the sun was beginning to brighten the window in his room, so I opened the drapes and the window and let in the soft morning air. The sunshine was streaking across the corner of his pillow as I hugged him, kissed him, held his hands and feet and talked quietly to him. Dad's skin still had his wonderful scent that I loved so much, and I inhaled it to store in my memory. He had a slight growth of beard which I knew the funeral home would shave off in preparation for the funeral. I sat in the chair next to him and made calls to family and friends. I recall his skin cooling off as the heat slowly left his body. After another hour or two I gave him a last kiss and left to go meet my oldest sister and brother-in-law at the funeral home to plan the service and burial for him.

A wide variety of people, including coworkers of mine, fathers group members, and old friends showed up at the funeral home to pay their respects. Dad looked great in his suit and he'd set out very specific instructions for his clothing and for the service itself. He had wanted his shoes shined, twice. During the service I was undecided until the last minute about speaking about my years with Dad but finally decided to get up and talk. I spoke openly about our long journey as father and son and about how very far we had come; my coming out to the folks in 1991 and all the difficult years afterward, about Mom's death and she and I making peace beforehand, and then working with Dad on building a strong and loving father-son relationship, which we did, and about what a gift that was for both of us. Though my candid share may have been challenging for some, everyone was very receptive and respectful, which I appreciated. I'm glad I got up there and spoke my truth and shared my gratitude for having had such a wonderful and life-giving relationship with my father.

After the service we made a slow motorcade over to the cemetery for the graveside service and burial. I was one of Dad's pallbearers and helped to move his coffin from the hearse onto the burial platform. It was an unusually hot, humid, sunny afternoon. There were smallish clouds drifting across the sky and a nice breeze stirring the early summer air as we gathered around the grave for the brief service. Pastor Don spoke and did a nice, concise job of characterizing my father and his life. Since Dad had been a World War Two Navy veteran, seven impeccably dressed, older VFW's were on hand to do the traditional twenty-one gun salute, with each man firing his rifle three times. Afterward two of them folded up an enormous American flag into a compact, tight triangle and with great formality presented it to me, the oldest son. One of the VFW's followed this up by playing *Taps*, which made for a wistful moment. The pastor said a quick closing prayer and adjourned us, and just then something most extraordinary happened: I suddenly felt something on my skin, and it took a moment to register what was happening, as it was so startling and unexpected. For about a minute and a half it rained on us. Oddly, there were no rain clouds around anywhere, and it didn't rain anywhere else besides on the small spot we were gathered together on. Then just as soon as it had begun, the rain stopped and the sun reappeared. It was a beautiful moment of benediction. I felt that my father was giving us his blessing, letting us know he was still there with us.

Losing my father left a large hole in my life, unsurprisingly. Fathers Day 2005 was coming up just eleven days after the day he died, and it promised be an empty and bleak occasion unless there was some way to make the day special, even memorable. My father had grown up in a modest two-story house on Grove Street, just a few hundred yards over the wooden bridge across the river from the cemetery. I had seen the house many times, though I had never been inside it. A few days after the funeral I drove out to the grave site, and as I was planting a few perennials next to my parent's grave, an idea popped into my head: Wouldn't it be fitting on Fathers Day to plant a bush or a tree in the yard of the house my Dad had grown up in? I liked the idea so much that after the flowers were planted I walked over to the house on Grove Street and went up to the door and knocked. As luck would have it, the owners were home and opened the door. They were a pleasant younger couple named Kurt and Jen, and they had purchased the house recently from a family who had lived there for many decades, and in fact in all the years the house had been there they were only the third owners of the place. I told them who I was and that my dad had grown up in the house and that he had died earlier in the month and that I had this crazy idea about planting a bush in their yard on Fathers Day in his honor. They invited me in and showed me around the house, which they had been busy remodeling and doing a fine job of too. As we were sitting in the living room chatting, Jen told me they had taken the old original paneling off the walls in the room. Suddenly she excused herself and said she needed to find a photo album. She returned two minutes later with the book and as she flipped through the pages she said, "It was funny… When we removed one of the sections of paneling we discovered these four handwritten signatures underneath it written on the wall, and I took a picture of it…" She flipped a page and said, "Here it is," and took the snapshot out and handed it to me. Here my dad, my aunt, and my grandma and grandpa had each signed their name on the wall, one name atop the other, along with the date, apparently just before the then new paneling had been put up. Dad would have been about sixteen years old at the time, in high school. She asked if I would like to keep the photo, and I said, "YES. PLEASE!" I was so incredibly glad I had made the trip over and had taken the chance to come and knock on their door and tell them of my dream to plant a bush there on Fathers Day, which I did, with their blessings. Doing so made for a wonderful Fathers Day, and whenever I drove past the house after that the bush always looked taller and fuller than it had been before. I planted it right in front of the house, just under the second floor window of what had once been my dad's boyhood bedroom. I like to think it pleased him to have the bush planted in his honor right there.

Today marks the twelve-year anniversary of my father's death. He was on my mind all day long at work and after dinner it was good to go for a long walk along the lake, taking in the bright sparkle of the full moon dancing across the water. My father has been gone for a long time now yet he continues to occupy a place deep in my heart. Sometimes I ask him for advice and listen inside for what he would say. I'm looking forward to hearing our interview on Fathers Day and enjoying once again the sound of his voice and wonderful laugh. So much has changed in the past dozen years. The house across from the cemetery that Dad grew up in was sold and the new owners removed the bush and re-did the landscaping in front of the house. My son is now a grown man and has two sons of his own.

I've now been sober for more that two decades and still enjoy attending 12-Step meetings and the fellowship of other recovering people. I am sure Dad would have been pleased to see same-sex marriage become legal across the land, and how wonderful it would have been to have him be best man at my wedding, if and when I meet a man I love and want to spend the rest of my life with.

Several years ago I chanced to read a piece about a New York matron whose beloved husband of many years was on his deathbed. Deeply distraught, she confessed to him that she honestly did not know how she would be able to carry on without him. He thought for a minute and then told her, "Take the love you have for me and give it out to others." His wise reply gave her just what she needed to carry on. Those of us who grieve the loss of any loved one can benefit from the man's insight. I do remember that after my father died, the world for a time seemed a bit colder place overall. I understand that my daily task is to try to give to others some of the love and acceptance my father showed to me. Some days I do reasonably well at that; other days, not as much. I strive for progress. I also understand well what Helen Keller once wrote: "With every friend I love who has been taken into the brown bosom of the earth a part of me has been buried there; but their contribution of happiness, strength, and understanding to my being remains to sustain me in an altered world."

Several years ago a longtime friend told me how impressed he was by a psychic he had been to, so out of curiosity I made an appointment to see her. During the session Carol surprised me by telling me something very obscure about my mother that she could not possibly have otherwise known. When I asked her about my dad she was quiet for a minute, then said that she saw him coming forward with a big smile. His message for me was not to always take life and things so seriously and to remember to lighten up. He then told her the same thing, which made her chuckle. Carol said that she and my father could have a good talk, and she seemed to be charmed by him, which would have been apropos. He said that he was always proud of me and my accomplishments. He added that he had sometimes found it difficult to understand or connect with me, but that even though he occasionally thought I was too sensitive he always knew that I had a beautiful heart. He told her that he loved me very much and he would have bled for me if necessary, adding that he is with God now and that I shouldn't worry a bit. He closed by saying I should never, ever be afraid and should also never be shy about using my strength; that I should be forthcoming and assertive with others and never withhold my opinions. I thanked Carol and told her that she had been both enlightening and helpful.

For Christmas in 1995 my father gave me one of his Navy dog tags, which he had strung on a thin silver chain. On the back of the tag he'd etched into the metal the words "I love you son. Dad - 10/95." I like to wear it and I give the dog tag a quick kiss when I take it off at night. I am aware of how incredibly fortunate I was to experience the deep friendship my father and I shared late in his life, even if it took us a long time to get there. Today I am blessed to love many people but I don't think I've ever loved another human being as much as I loved my dad. Getting to know him and to become as close as we did really opened my heart and allowed me to not be so guarded with those I care about. I feel deep down that my father and I and the strong bond we forged continues to exist in some vast, mysterious continuum which encompasses both of us, as part of the universal "love that moves the sun and the other stars," that Dante wrote about.

Thank you, Robert Clausen. What an honor and privilege it has been to get to know you and to be your son. Even though you insisted on listening to that godawful sportscast during my birth, I love you more than words can say.

Christmas 2003 at my father's assisted living facility. My brother in law was taking family photos and suggested that Dad and I take one together. Just before the shutter snapped I rested my head on his shoulder. My favorite photo of the two of us.

Introduction to the Interviews

The twenty-five interviews in this section are a diverse group. Selected from eighty-two interviews I conducted with a wide range of gay men between 2015 and 2017, these candid personal stories shine a compelling light on the great variety of bonds which exist between modern gay men and their fathers. In these pieces you will find violent, alcoholic dads, fathers who are unconditionally supportive, sons who were disowned, missing fathers, dads who grew to accept their sons over time, fathers struggling with their own sexual orientation, and others.

To highlight the great diversity between these pieces, I have sequenced them for maximum variety. While each is unique, the interviews share a basic structural similarity. All were very much shaped by the list of questions I asked each interviewee, and they follow a basic chronology from the individual's childhood through his growing up years and on through adulthood. The questions I asked sometimes varied from person to person, depending upon such factors as whether the interviewee's father was still living or not and whether the son had ever met and known his dad.

The men I interviewed range in age from their early twenties to late seventies and hail from all walks of life. They include men with primarily Asian, Hispanic, African-American and Caucasian heritage and backgrounds. One interviewee lives in Puerto Rico, two reside in Canada, while the rest make their homes throughout the United States. A number of the interviewees are now fathers themselves, having had children through a prior marriage, through surrogacy, or via adoption. Many non-fathers spoke of their interest in being a dad.

Interviewing the men for this book was a powerful experience. While the emotional tone and substance of the interviews I conducted for *Love*

Together, my first book, were in no way light or without gravity, the interviews for this project were, overall, emotionally weighty across the board. More than a few interviewees experienced significant trauma in their relationship with their father and strong emotions sometimes colored their sharing with me. Talking about the death of a father was quite emotional for many men, and it was not uncommon for tears and grief to well up as they spoke about it. When I was just beginning work on this book I asked a couple of area men if they would be open to interview about their father, and it was immediately apparent from their reply that this was a deeply painful topic for them, one which they had no interest whatever in revisiting.

The reader will find these pieces to be consistently heartfelt and emotionally stirring. Along with conflicted relationships, you will discover an abundance of inspiring stories, great father-son connections, and relationships mended, sometimes in situations where one might least expect it. I was repeatedly impressed by how resolutely many of these men have worked to recover from sometimes terrible childhoods, by how loving and forgiving some have been to fathers who were anything but loving to them. Throughout the two years of conducting these interviews it was humbling for me to hear other men's pain, hurt, and sorrow, as well as their joy, resiliency, and their great love. I was reminded over and over again just how profoundly powerful the father-son relationship is and how far reaching and lasting its effects are upon the psyche of every gay son. With all of their shining qualities, foibles, and deficiencies, our fathers remain a part of us.

For this work I offered to every interviewee any level of anonymity they preferred. Many men were fine with having their full name included, while others asked that I list only their first name. For various reasons some interviewees chose to be completely anonymous. As a member of a 12-Step program where anonymity is considered sacred, I understood the importance of offering anonymity to the men I interviewed, and was glad to honor each person's preference in this regard. Offering anonymity gave a comfort level to some who might otherwise have chosen not to participate and gave them the freedom and safety to talk candidly about their father and their life experiences.

Introduction to the Interviews

Every effort has been made to keep these interviews completely authentic to the voice of each narrator. In the process of transcribing the interviews I remove myself and the questions from the piece, resulting in a conversational, stream of consciousness piece on the part of the interviewee. To help improve narrative flow and clarity, editing has been employed judiciously throughout, and always as minimally as necessary. The reader will find that even though the questions have been removed from these pieces, it is not difficult to discern where they occur in the narratives. You will also find the complete question list included immediately after this section.

One of the most difficult aspects of writing this book was choosing which twenty-five interviews from the original eighty-two to include. As was the case with the interviews for *Love Together*, there was an overabundance of great material to choose from, making the selection process especially challenging. While certainly tempting, it was not feasible to include more interviews and still keep the book at a reasonable length. One factor was especially key for me in determining which pieces I included: Since the coming out experience is so profound and life changing for gay men, I tended to favor those interviewees who had at some point come out to their father. For most of us, coming out is a huge and daunting step to take, one which offers no guarantee of a positive reaction. The stakes are incredibly high, and gay people continue to be disowned by their parents after coming out. Coming out of the closet always changes our relationship with our father—for better or worse—and requires profound courage and a real commitment to being honest, chips fall where they may.

Although it was not easy to write, it was very helpful for me to write about my father and the sometimes arduous journey that we shared. I hope readers will find both my and the other personal stories in this section to be of value in their own relationship with their father. What was especially gratifying for me while interviewing the men for this book was how often someone would say, "You know, I haven't thought about or talked about my dad this much in years. It really did me a lot of good to do this. Thank you." It seems only fitting that the men whose stories will help others in the following pages were helped through the very sharing of them as well.

The Question List and A Reading Suggestion

Here is the main list of questions I asked my interviewees. As noted earlier, not every question applied in every case, so the list was freely tailored to each person's circumstances. I strove to ask what I considered the most important questions while remaining flexible in my approach and open to whatever spontaneous directions a given conversation might move in. Additional questions would arise naturally during the course of each interview as well and were often helpful in clarifying and expanding upon a particular point or aspect of the interviewee's sharing.

1. When and where you were born? Do you have siblings?
2. What are your earliest recollections of your dad and what sort of work did he do?
3. Did you and he connect easily? Were you closer to your dad or mom?
4. Was your dad affectionate with you or more distant? Did he hug and kiss you? Tell you that he loved you?
5. Did you feel supported by him?
6. Did you feel you were a disappointment to him?
7. If your dad was not supportive, was there a supportive adult male who filled that role during your younger years?
8. Was your difference as a gay kid apparent all along, and what was your dad's reaction to it?
9. Did you feel free to be and express yourself or that you had to hide and be closeted to be accepted and safe?
10. Did your dad ever have the birds and the bees talk with you and what was that like?

11. Did you ever officially come out to him and what was that experience like?
12. What's your communication level like with him and what activities did or do you enjoy together?
13. How has your relationship changed and evolved over time?
14. How has your history with your dad influenced your desire to be or not be a father yourself?
15. Are you a better father to your kids than your dad was to you?
16. Did your dad ever surprise you? This could include presents, trips, showing up at a school event, etc…
17. Did you ever see your father cry?
18. How are you recovering from childhood wounds related to your dad? Have you forgiven him and how did you do so?
19. What do you admire about your dad?
20. In what ways are you like him?
21. Is your dad still living and what is your relationship like today?
22. If your dad is deceased, what was your last conversation with him? What would you most want to say to him now if you could?
23. Do you have any regrets regarding your dad? What would you like to have done differently?
24. What regrets do you think your dad had or has?
25. If he's deceased, do you think of him often? Do you visit his grave? Have any keepsakes or mementos of him?
26. Has he shown up in any of your dreams, etc, and have these been positive and helpful experiences?
27. Did you ever tell your dad that you love him?
28. Do you have any advice for other gay men regarding dealing with their father?

I would like to offer a suggestion as you make your way through the interviews in this section… Like the interviews in *Love Together*, these are substantial pieces which are best read a few at a time, preferably taking time away afterward to reflect on the material before returning at a different hour to read another set. You will likely find that you will get the most out of this material by approaching it in this way.

Chapter 1
Mark Rinder

Mark lives in Atlanta with his partner of nearly twenty years. He works for an area corporation as a COO/CFO.

I was born in Cristobal, Panama in November 1956. My family was living down there from 1950 to 1957, when my father was an executive with the shipping company Grace Lines, and we were on an expatriate assignment. I have one brother and three sisters, all older than I am. As far back as I can recall, my relationship with my dad was troubled. He wanted me—in the worst way—to play in Little League and football, and I wasn't cut out for that. He was vocal about his unhappiness with me at family dinners, where he'd call me a sissy, while the rest of the family would sit in silence. It was uncomfortable and unpleasant for most of my childhood with him. My father wanted me to go to Little League and play baseball and football not because he was really enchanted with baseball or football, but because he figured that it would be a *remedy.*

He had a membership at a club down in New York City, in Manhattan, called the Downtown Athletic Club, and he announced that he was going to bring me down there on Saturdays to butch me up, so he took me down there and introduced me to the coach. So here I am with fifteen other kids from wealthy families in Long Island, and the coach is making us exercise and swim and wrestle and so on and so forth, and I'm thinking, "This has got to be the stupidest thing for me to do all day long on a Saturday..." I told my father on the way back, "I'm not going there anymore. It's a waste of my time." He says, "I'm your father, and you're going there next Saturday." I said, "I don't want to go," and he says, "Well, too bad." So sure enough he wakes me up the following Saturday morning and drags me out to the car and we drive down to Manhattan. Now I have been told that I'm a stubborn person, and so I stood there on the steps of the Downtown Athletic Club and waved at him as he drove around the corner, and as soon as he did I went down the steps and started walking around downtown Manhattan. I'm nine years old and I'm walking on my own around downtown Manhattan for about four hours. I knew to get back to the club by 1:00 lunchtime, when my father was going to come meet me in the dining room. So I was back there promptly at one, met him, sat down, had lunch, and he goes, "How was your day?" I said, "I don't want to come back next week," and he said, "Well, you're going to." So he took me for probably six weeks in a row, and for five of those weeks I toured downtown Manhattan as a nine year old on my own.

Then one day we were in the dining room, and the coach came in and said, "Hey Reg, how are you doin'?," and my father said, "Well, how is Mark doing?" The coach goes, "Mark?" And my father points to me across the table and says, "My son, Mark. How's he doing?" The coach says, "Oh, hi Mark." He says, "Well, you haven't brought him back since that first day," and my father goes, "What are you talking about? I've been dropping him off every Saturday for the past six weeks..." The coach goes, "No, he was only in our class for one day. I don't know where he was but he wasn't here." Needless to say, my father was furious and says, "Where were you?" I said, "I told you I didn't want to go and that I wasn't going to go and I didn't. As soon as you drove around the corner, I went off walking around." I knew he was never going to punish me because he'd have to admit to my mother that I had been walking around downtown Manhattan for five weeks on my own. He said, "I'm going to ground you," and I said, "And how are you going to explain this to Mom?" He goes, "What?" I said, "That I was walking around on my own for five weeks, for four hours each time, unchaperoned, in Manhattan?" So we just went home and he never mentioned it again. We did have a combative relationship.

I think my dad was affectionate when I was very young, and he definitely loved all his other kids. He wanted to love me, but I was damaged goods in his eyes. He was generous with me certainly. He built a beautiful swimming pool and we enjoyed that. He was really into gardening and he'd do a lot of landscaping on weekends on our four and a half acre property, designing it to his liking. I did enjoy puttering around with him doing that kind of stuff. Our relationship did get much better way, way later, but it was definitely troubled back then.

When my brother got married in 1967, I came home from school a few months later and my mother was in the living room having martinis with her girlfriends. So I went and sat on a stool off to the side, and they were chatting away. Mrs. Rakow said to my mother, "So Leonora, I understand there is news about Susan"—my brother's wife—and you may as well have just struck my mother with lightning, because she looked over at me, just horrified. Her eyes were the size of plates, and she looked at Mrs. Rakow and she looked back at me and she said to Mrs. Rakow, "Yes, there is." And Mrs. Rakow said, "Well, what is it? Tell us." My mother looked at me again and she said, "She's.... P.... G....", and Mrs. Rakow said, "Mark, I think you better go for a walk and play outside..." So I went down the hall to my sister's room and said, "There's something *really* wrong with Susan." And Joanne said, "What do you mean?" I said, "I don't know, but Mom looked terrible. When Mrs. Rakow mentioned this news about Susan, Mom looked awful. She looked horrified." I said, "She's got something. I think she's sick. It's something with letters..." Joanne said, "It isn't TB is it?" I said, "Yes! That's it. She has TB!" My sister goes, "OH *NO!*" and started crying and ran down the hall to talk to my older sister and tell her Susan has TB. Well, of course we found out later that she didn't have TB. She was P.G.—pregnant. But my mother could not bring herself to say the word pregnant in front of me because it was such a "bawdy" term. So needless to say, neither my father or mother ever had the birds and the bees talk with me either.

My dad surprised me one Christmas when he got Joanne and me a horse, which I was not expecting. But I was thrilled because I was an equestrian and a pretty good one. My equestrian friends couldn't understand why my parents didn't buy me a horse, and I had told them, "That's not going to happen." But it did. Ostensibly it was for Joanne and myself, and she rode it some, but it was really for me. I was about thirteen at the time. My parents had gift-wrapped a saddle in a big box, so when we opened up the box, I said, "Well, what are we going to do with a saddle? We don't have a horse." And my father said, "Well, maybe you should go down to the stables and check…" So I ran out of the house and all the way down to the stables, and sure enough, there was a new horse in there, a beautiful, beautiful thoroughbred. The horse was probably my father's idea.

My father's dad was a captain in the Royal Navy in England. It's really bizarre: his ship went down in a storm about five weeks before my father was born and he was washed overboard and was never found. So I never knew that grandfather, and then my father's mother died when she was like forty-three, so I never knew her either. My father talked about his father, but frankly I thought it was such a bizarre story that I truly thought he was making it up. I thought he had made up these stories about his father and the family because he wanted to canonize them. He told me that his father and his family had this great big estate in England with thousands of acres and dozens of people working there, and for the longest time I thought, "This is a bunch of baloney. He's just making this shit up…" Apparently Reginald Sr. married an American woman, and his family thought that he had gone "down market" in choosing her, so when he died they just gave her a small settlement relative to the value of the estate. She then bought a house on Long Island, and my dad grew up there. I did find out years later that, in fact, there is a place called Bowthorpe Hall, and Bowthorpe Hall is the name of the estate, and it's in the town of Bowthorpe. And Bowthorpe Hall is not named that because it's in Bowthorpe; the town is named after Bowthorpe Hall. It's right outside of Norwich, England. But all my life I had thought that he was just making this up. I didn't believe him.

My father and I used to go sailing on Long Island Sound, and there are plenty of times when we'd be just sitting there and there was nothing to do; we didn't have the internet or cell phones or anything back then. That's often when he would tell me about England and his father, and I'd think, "He's spinning this tale, and I have to give him credit: he does remember the tale correctly each time and he tells me the same thing. He's got this firmly memorized. But when he would talk about his mother he would get all choked up.

I was in the closet for a long, long time. My mother passed away when I was twenty-one, so I never told her. Then I got married and had children, and I have two really awesome girls who are smart and funny and successful. After eleven years of marriage I separated from my wife, and it was at that point that I decided I was going to come out. I started coming out to my sisters and brothers, and the following year I came out to my dad. He was fine. He was actually fine about it.

The week before I came out to him he sent an email, the title of which was "The queer pastor in Nebraska." There was some news item in 1995 about a minister who announced to his flock that he was gay, and there was a big brouhaha nationally about it, and seeing my father's email, I was like, "OK, this is not going to bode well for our conversation this week…" But in point of fact he just said, "Well, you're my son and we're going to figure this out. It's not going to prevent us from seeing each other and talking to one another and loving one another." And from then on he actually was very good. When I introduced him to my new-at-that-time partner—whom I've been with eighteen years now—he was always very nice to Dennis and respectful and never said anything untoward ever again. It's a lesson about the importance of coming out, because it absolutely shut him down in terms of homophobia.

After coming out to him, my relationship was much better with him than it had ever been before. I would call him a couple times a week, and he was always very interested in what was going on with my job. He was very proud of me and my accomplishments. I'm without a doubt the most successful of all my siblings, and he was very proud of that. At that point I had just been appointed the chief financial officer for Air-Trans Airways in Orlando, and he was retired and living in Vero Beach. So we were about two hours apart by car, and Dennis and I would go down there and take him out to brunch on Sundays and then come back Sunday late afternoon to Orlando. Things were absolutely fine between us from then on.

He did have a massive stroke in 1998, about three weeks after I'd had the talk with him. Of course, my siblings were like, "Did you *HAVE* to tell him? Look what happened…" I'm like, "Oh, for God's sake, he did not have a stroke because I told him I'm gay. Don't be ridiculous." But my father got another place for him and his second wife right on the beach, and they stayed there for the whole summer while he was doing rehab. So Dennis and I were down there more frequently at that point to see him.

I think I always wanted to be a father. When I first got married I said something about it to my wife, and she said, "Well, I don't want to have kids…" I said, "What? That would have been useful information for you to have shared with me before we got married?" She answered, "You mean you wouldn't have gotten married to me if we didn't have kids?" I said, "Well, it's an important issue. Really important." But anyway she changed her mind and she loves our daughters as much as I do.

After coming out and leaving the marriage I was living in Orlando, and the girls were in Annapolis, Maryland, so I was flying back and forth to Annapolis for my weekend visits, and I was flying them down to Orlando, which they loved. I joined the Gay Fathers Coalition in Washington, D.C. when I first came out, and they were extremely helpful to me because I couldn't see how to marry what-I-perceived-to-be these two mutually exclusive things: being a good father and being a gay man. Marrying those two seemingly opposite states of being successfully together was something I worried about a lot, and the fathers group was enormously helpful for me in that regard.

I did talk about the early years with my siblings but not with my father. My siblings held my father on a pedestal, and I understood why. When I told them about my experience growing up in the family, they were horrified. They were like, "How can you say that about Dad?" I said, "Well, I can say this about Dad and frankly I can say it about you, because you sat at the dining room table in silence looking at your hands when Dad was saying these terrible things to me." So I did have that conversation with my siblings but I didn't with him. I was able to forgive my dad. He was a product of his environment at the time.

My father had the stroke in 1998 and he died in 2004, so he lived a good six years, and he traveled to Spain and California and went up to Canada a few times. In late 2003 he was living with my middle sister in Vermont, and Dennis and I went up and spent a weekend there in October for his birthday. He clearly had declined substantially. We had a very nice weekend, but there weren't any significant conversations between us. My dad's dying the next year was a bit of a surprise, even though I knew he was struggling more than he had been. But then my mother suffered from cancer for six years, and I was completely shocked when she died. To this day I haven't quite gotten over the shock of her death.

I had my dad's family Bible. The head of the household from each generation signed the inside page of the family Bible, and the first signature went all the way back to 1604. So I kept that family Bible, and I sat my father down one time in Orlando when he came up to visit and said, "We're going to have a ceremony tonight," And my father's like, "What? What are you talking about?" I said, "Well, I've made drinks here and I've got some cheese and crackers. We're going to have a ceremonial signing today," and I went over and got the family Bible. I said, "It's time. You should be signing this as the head of the family for this generation." His father's signature was the last one in there, so I had him sign and date it. I had been in charge of this Bible since probably 1980, and this was now in 1997 or 1998.

When my father died, I brought the family Bible with me up to Vermont for his funeral, and something of a humorous twist occurred. When I gave my talk at the funeral service I mentioned the thing about the queer pastor, and I said, "OK, now besides the ceremony of the funeral we're going to have another ceremony today," and I'm sure everyone thought I was going to say, "Dennis and I are going to get married right now..." People were buzzing and looking at each other like, "This is ridiculous. What is he gonna do?" I said to my older brother, "Reg, please come up to the altar," and he came up. I announced to the crowd that I had this Bible that had been in the family for centuries, and I said, "Each head of the household's oldest son is supposed to sign this," so I had Reggie sign it in the church during the funeral. Then Reggie took the Bible and said, "I want to thank my brother for keeping this all this time, and I promise you I will take great care of it and pass it on." And he walked off with it. I thought, "That wasn't the way this was supposed to go down..." But anyway, it's fine. He has it and he did put it under glass for protection, which is good, because it needs protection.

The big important piece of advice I have for gay men is to tell your dad you are gay, not to hide. Even if you suspect that he already knows, the whole notion of saying, "Well, I don't really need to tell him because he knows already" is a barrier to your communication and your relationship. Because while that may be true, the fact is that your father is sitting there saying, "Well, OK, he's not talking about it to me. I'm not going to bring it up, because he has to come out in his own time and he's obviously not comfortable enough telling me about this yet…" So it inhibits conversation and, in my experience, it inhibits full, honest relationships.

It was a similar thing with my kids. The Gay Fathers Coalition that I joined had a lot of awesome, really smart professionals in it, and one of the members was a psychologist who said, "Look, you should tell your kids early and often, in an age-appropriate way. And you can't just say it once and be over with. It has to sink in. So maybe every couple months when you're sitting down to dinner, you just have that conversation." And I did that with my kids, and it's worked out very well.

When I went off to college, my father drove me to the campus. He drives into the university, pulls up to the student hall, gets out of the car, puts the bags down on the sidewalk, gives me ten dollars, and he says, "Alright, well, I gotta head home now…" I was like, "What? You're just going to leave me here on the sidewalk?" He goes, "Well, look, you're supposed to be a grown man. You ought to be able to figure this out. You have to figure it out. I'll see you later. Study hard." And he literally got in his car and drove off. I'm standing there going, "I can't believe this…" and also thinking, "Ten dollars? What am I going to do with ten dollars?" So I immediately went to a pay phone and called my mother and said, "Mom, Dad just left. He left me on the sidewalk here. I don't even know where I'm supposed to go or anything. But more importantly he gave me ten dollars and he said not to worry, that he's going to send me ten more dollars next month…" My mother goes, "I know, dearie. I got the same phone call from your brother when he went to college. Don't worry. I've got a check in the mail to you, and you'll be fine. And don't tell your father that I'm sending you money."

When her envelope arrived I opened it, and she had sent me two hundred and fifty dollars. This was in 1974 and that was a princely sum, so money became not even an issue and I was fine all through college. When I graduated, my father was taking a picture of me and my mother in front of my apartment in Charlottesville, so I reached over and put my hand in her pocket and said, "I'm putting a check in your pocket. You sent me far too much money, and I'm returning all the extra." She said, "But you're going to need that money. You're moving to New York. Why don't you keep it?" I said, "No. No, I'm graduated. I have a job. I'm going to be fine." So I gave her the check, which was for about thirty six hundred dollars.

I moved to New York and had this apartment with these soaring ceilings and this huge blank wall, and I said, "I've got to get something to put up on that wall. I went to Greenwich Village to look for something big and striking. I went into this gallery and was talking with the owner about what I was looking for and I looked over his shoulder and pointed way back in the gallery and said, "That. That back there would be perfect. How much is that?" He said, "Six hundred dollars." I said, "Six hundred dollars? I'm looking to spend ten or fifteen. I'm looking for a poster. That looks like a poster to me…" He said, "It's actually a lithograph from a very important, upcoming artist, and it would be a very good investment." I was like, "Yeah, well that's not happening." So I left the store but I thought about it all day and I called my mother up and told her the whole story. I said, "Mom, can I borrow six hundred dollars from that money I gave you? I will pay it back. It's not a gift." She said, "Oh, yes… It's Mark, honey." I said, "No. No. NO! Don't let Dad get on the phone." "Hello." I was like, "Oh, hi Dad…," and my mother announced, "Mark is on the phone. He found a lovely piece of art for his apartment and he wants to borrow six hundred dollars…" My father went ballistic. "*SIX HUNDRED DOLLARS*? *Have you lost your mind*? You've only been in New York for six weeks and you've already lost your mind…" He said, "Do you know I haven't spent six hundred dollars on all the artwork in our house?" I said, "Yes, I'm very aware of that, Dad," and he goes, "Don't smart-mouth me, son." And so I did not buy Andy Warhol's *Tomato Soup Can*.

To give credit where credit is due, that experience caused me to become an avid art collector. For the past forty years I have bought art that I really like and enjoy and I have an absolutely fabulous collection of art. The artwork in my house is probably worth as much as my home. But to me it doesn't matter. It's not a business. I've never sold a piece of art and I never will. I'll give it to my children. But I can credit my father for all of my art.

Chapter 2
PJ Painter

PJ works as an attorney in Lexington, Kentucky. His coming out article in Outsports *was published in numerous languages and read around the world. PJ surprised his boyfriend by proposing to him outdoors during the height of the August 2017 solar eclipse. The two will marry late in 2018*

I was born in Spearfish, South Dakota on October 1, 1986, and have both a younger and an older sister. One of my very earliest memories is a fairly traumatic one. I was swimming in a pool at a hotel and I just remember being on an inner-tube and thinking to myself that I was bored with swimming and I wanted out of the pool. I remember looking over at my dad and seeing him talking to his friends. I didn't want to get anyone's attention while I was trying to jump to the side of the pool so I made sure no one was looking before I did it. I tried to jump from the inner-tube to the side of the pool and didn't make it and fell straight down in the water. I remember thinking to myself that my dad wouldn't have seen me fall in. I will never forget struggling at the bottom of the pool and looking up to the surface thinking to myself, "He never saw me. I'm gonna die… I was drowning, unable to swim, and the next thing I know I see my dad jump in on top of me and pull me out. He jumped in fully clothed and saved me. I've pretty much always been a good swimmer, so the fact that I wasn't able to swim tells me that it was at a very young age. It's one of the first memories I have.

I also have memories of my dad taking me to rodeos, even as a little kid. There are events for kids like boot races and stick horse barrels—things like that. He'd take all of us and my mom would come along as well. My mom played volleyball in college but she didn't rodeo. My dad was our primary coach when it came to rodeo.

We have a 35,000 acre ranch in northwest South Dakota with cattle, buffalo, sheep, and horses. It was a good environment to grow up in. I learned the value of a dollar and I learned to appreciate hard work even as a young kid, because on a ranch kids work right alongside their parents. When we were old enough to ride we'd be helping to trail cattle from one pasture to the next on our ponies. Then as we got older we got more active as far as driving tractors and helping give the cattle vaccinations instead of just helping trail them. Once I got into high school I was old enough to work on the fence line, pounding fence posts and putting up barbed wire and whatnot. So it's kind of a progressive line, where the older you get the more physically you're able to help out. But always we would help on our ponies and even before we were old enough to drive a tractor we still rode with our parents on a tractor to keep them awake. Sometimes in the hay fields you'll be out there for hours on end—twelve hours in a day or longer—trying to get it all finished, so it can be difficult to stay awake at times. Plus I guess that was a way for them to babysit us as well, so I shouldn't say it was just to keep them awake!

I would say I was always closest to my mom, but I also had a good relationship with my dad. My dad has always been very well-read. He spends evenings reading books or magazines or newspapers; anything and everything he can get his hands on he reads. So he's always been knowledgeable and aware of world events. Not only that, my dad is also very compassionate. Even though he's strict and conservative and runs a tight ship as the manager of the ranch, he's always been understanding and a good guy. For example, he took in one of my friends who didn't have any parents growing up; his grandparents owned a bar and kind of raised him. A bar is a tough atmosphere to raise a kid in, so my dad took him into our household, and he spent most of his time with us. My dad did it for the best interests of the neighbor kid. It just shows that he's really a compassionate person, which doesn't mean that he isn't also a stern father figure! He always pushed us as hard as we could be pushed in rodeo and basketball and football and all the sports we competed in because he just wanted us to be the best we could be. I think that, by nature, most kids don't push themselves as hard as they should, and that's where the father's guidance comes in. My mom was the opposite. She was always there when we needed someone to talk to and was super nice but she wasn't the type to push us, at least in the athletic department. She did push us academically, but that's pretty much how my parents differed.

I remember early on riding horseback with my dad and all the things he would teach me out on the ranch. He would always tell me that if you get lost in a blizzard you should always trust your horse and let the horse take you home, because the horse will always know where home is at. Even if you don't agree with the horse on the direction it is heading, the horse will find home before you ever will, and I'm talking about being in a whiteout blizzard where you can't see anything. People easily lose their sense of direction in a blizzard, but a horse never will. My dad taught me how to recognize when a cow is having trouble giving birth to their calf, what signs to look for, and how to assist in the birthing process. He taught me how to mechanic on tractors and pickups. I was always with my dad and always very interested to learn. My sisters were more often with my mom, and I was more often with my dad when it came to ranching activities.

I have lots of memories of riding with him, whether it be in the pickup out through the pasture, or on ATV or on horseback. My dad is a pilot so he has his own Super Cub airplane that he flies around the ranch to check on the cattle with. I'd always beg him to take me with him, and he'd only take me with him if the weather was nice because he didn't want to risk me flying with him if there was any wind at all or if there were any storms coming in. He just didn't want to put my life in danger, so it was always a highlight to get to go flying with him.

I wouldn't say my dad is especially affectionate. He's a weather-hardened ranch man. He will tell me he loves me these days when I talk to him on the phone. It hasn't always been that way, but it might be because he's getting older now. When I was six years old, his father—my grandfather—died of a heart attack, and my dad always told me that he and his dad didn't tell each other they loved each other very often. So I think for that reason as he gets older now he wants to tell his kids more often that he loves us.

Hugging is rare but I'll always shake his hand and give a slap on the back or whatever. Like I said, my dad is a ranch man so he isn't the type to be all affectionate, but it seems as he gets older maybe he tries a little harder. Especially now that I live several states away he doesn't see me as often, so when he does see me he makes a point to go out of his way and hug me.

Even from a very young age I was always aware that I was drawn to guys. That doesn't mean that I accepted it internally. It wasn't until college that I really admitted it to myself, and that probably made things more stressful with my dad, because I was always afraid of what he might think of it or how he might react. I tried very hard to be someone my dad wanted me to be. Not that everything I did was for my father, but I wanted to be respected by him and try to meet his high expectations, from football to basketball to rodeo to grades... I was always somewhat afraid of what he might think when he did find out someday. I never had that fear with my mom. I was always really close to her so I never did worry about what she might think when I finally had to tell her.

My mom talked with me about the birds and the bees once or twice when I was growing up, but I don't remember my dad ever saying anything about that. My dad's just not the type of person to talk about that stuff. My mom's always been the therapist in the family, so if there are any difficult issues, all the kids just address them through her. And not that my dad wouldn't address it; it's just that my mom is the type of person you just feel at ease telling anything and everything to, getting your concerns off your chest, talking and working through them.

With coming out, it definitely gets easier with the more people you tell, so I started with some of my coworkers and good friends here in Louisville and after that I started telling some of my friends in South Dakota, at least the friends I went to law school with. Then with the people back home on the western side of South Dakota where I grew up, my mom and my little sister were the first people I told. I simultaneously told them when I was more or less backed into a corner... Once I internally accepted being gay I always kind of wondered when I might come out to my parents. I was never really sure how they might take it plus I just needed time to figure things out for myself. Initially I thought I'd tell them once I had found a long term relationship but then I realized that would be somewhat unfair to my future boyfriend/husband to have to throw that burden on him to also have to deal with my family finding out simultaneously when he starts to date me. I decided the more proper course would probably be to get where I would be fine financially if they decided they no longer wanted to help support me, so I made the decision, for many reasons, that I would tell them after I took the bar exam. I was never really afraid of failing the bar exam so I didn't want to wait until I had my law results. I took a risk and decided, since I would be spending two months with them after the exam before I actually started full-time work as a lawyer, that that would be a good time to tell them. I hadn't spent a lot of time at home since I was an undergrad and used to go home for summers. So I took the bar exam and then drove the couple days to get back home.

I'd already made the decision I would tell them so I was really nervous. The whole drive just nauseated me and I dreaded every minute of it. When I got home we had talked about taking a family vacation, and it just seemed like a good time for one. My older sister is married and my younger sister had a fiancé at the time—she's now married—so we decided they would go with us on this family vacation. My mom and my little sister were both in the house with me and we were booking the trip, and they're like, "Do you have any significant other you'd like to take on the vacation with you?" I don't know if they were actually trying to get it out of me that I was gay, but the question did come up. And even though I didn't want to tell them in that moment—I wanted to tell them each individually—I decided that I wasn't going to lie to them anymore. So I just sat them down and told them. My little sister immediately took my side, one hundred percent. She cried but she just felt bad for what I had gone through. And then my mom, who I had always expected would take it well, just *struggled* with the news. I don't know whether she didn't see it coming or if she was just afraid of how Dad might take it. Over the course of the next couple days she told me, " Let's just keep this from your father for a while. Maybe you're confused. Maybe this is just a phase you're going through…" I told her, "No, Mom, it's not. It's who I am and it's never going to change and I have to tell Dad because I can't keep it from him any longer." So once I explained to her that it was something that I needed to do, she agreed, but she was just as afraid of telling him as I was.

We waited until we were down at our place in the Black Hills. My parents have a smaller ranch down there and my dad and I and my mom had worked outside all day alongside each other. At the end of the day I told Mom, "It's time to tell Dad..." She agreed, and so we just sat down at the table. I said, "Dad, there's no easy way to say it but I'm gay." I was terrified—you can about imagine—it was probably the scariest moment of my life. My dad took a second to absorb the news and his eyes got a bit glassy. I was just hanging on the edge of suspense, just terrified of what he might say... I think I quoted him exactly in my article, but he said, "I'll always love you no matter what. This doesn't change who you are at all. You'll always be the same old PJ that you've always been to me." He went on to say that his only regret is that I may not be able to have the traditional family that he had, that raising kids and having a family was the greatest joy of his life. His hope was for me to someday experience the same joy that he has, raising his family—including me—and at that point he offered to morally and financially support me if I ever decided to adopt my own kids or hire a surrogate mother. However I decided I might want to have a family and kids of my own, he was going to support me one hundred percent. He let me know without a doubt that he was supporting me, which meant more to me than anything he could have said.

Like I said earlier, my dad is very well read so he may have suspected before that I was gay and had probably done a lot of independent research on the topic. He's never once indicated that it's a choice or that I was doing this on purpose or being rebellious when I "decided" to be gay. Other family members have said something along those lines, but from the moment I told him, he was completely supportive. He knew right off the bat what I was going through and was very empathetic and sympathetic towards everything that I'd endured in the process of finding out who I was. The fact that he was well read and knew more about homosexuality and the struggles we face than anyone else in the family—and most of my friends for that matter, except for the ones who have gone through it themselves—was amazing. That and the fact that he is so compassionate made it such an easy process telling him ultimately. I've told everyone since that it's odd how the day I dreaded most in my life was coming out to my dad, and it actually turned out to be the happiest day of my life because he handled it so well and was just one hundred percent behind me. I'm not going to say it was easy for him, because like I said, he's a conservative rancher from South Dakota. So the fact that he put all his fears and insecurities about what the future might hold aside just to be there and support me and understand what I was going through, without taking into consideration anything else, really meant the world to me.

We had about a five or ten minute conversation. He didn't ask me a lot of questions or say, "Are you sure about this?" None of that. It was a really short coming out session with a parent in my opinion, especially after I talked to my friends, and I attribute that to him just being so knowledgeable on the subject. We didn't have to sit around and waste a lot of time. It was fine. It wasn't something we needed to explore further. He said, "This is all fine. Let's just be happy and let's change out of our work clothes and let's go to the casinos up in Deadwood and have some fun." So the fact that I had just come out to my dad, and he wasn't like, "OK, I need some time to process this…," was amazing. His first thought was, "Let's just go and have fun as a family." It didn't separate us at all. If anything it brought us closer together.

When we talk now he's not opposed to talking about my being gay but he doesn't necessarily ask a lot of questions. That's never been his personality anyways. Even when I dated girls in high school and college, he never, never asked anything about them. Same with my sisters; he just doesn't pry into stuff like that. He'll ask about volleyball, about rodeo, about how school's going, and will talk about things on the ranch. And we have talked about it, but it's not something we talk about every time we're on the phone. My mom is the opposite. She's always wanting to know if I'm dating anyone or if I'm going to bring anyone home for the holidays. But that's how she's always been. Even when I dated girls, she wanted to know everything about what was going on in my personal life. So the fact that my dad and I don't talk much about who I'm dating doesn't surprise me at all, nor do I think it has anything to do with my dad's thoughts about me being gay. The topics of our conversations have never been about significant others.

My dad is not often visibly emotional but he did have tears in his eyes the day I came out to him. The only other time I saw him tear up is when his father died, at my grandfather's funeral. Though my grandfather died when I was only six, I do have a lot of memories of him. My dad is very much his father's son, and not only that, but I am very much my father's son. All three of us share a lot of the same personality traits: hard-driven, understanding of people, genuinely a nice person. I also have to admit that I've developed my dad's same sense of stubbornness, and my grandpa had it too. Maybe it's just a sense of pride, but along with that comes being very stubborn!

My dad has mellowed as he ages. He's always been strict, and if we made a mistake on the ranch he would let us know he was disappointed in us. Like I said, you always want your dad to respect you and think highly of you, so if he's sitting there telling you, "I'm so disappointed that you wrecked this piece of equipment," or whatever the situation was, it was always really hard for me to have to hear that from him. It hurt my feelings. But as he gets older he's becoming more understanding. I think he realizes—as a father figure and as someone whom so many people respect—the impact of his words, so these days he's very, very careful in what he says and how he says it. He always makes sure that he doesn't offend anyone or step on anyone's toes. I'd like to think that I inherited that trait from him too. We always think before we speak, and as he gets older he just gets better and better about always saying the right thing at the right time.

In my own mind maybe I had insecure fears about the way he might react when I did come out to him someday which might have strained our relationship. So I think that—if anything—maybe it was me who was holding back our relationship beforehand. In a way we have gotten closer since then, but I can't necessarily say it's because of him. It's more likely because of me and the fact that I finally feel one hundred percent confident and comfortable around my dad. The last several times I've gone home to the ranch I went out and worked with him just like I always have, but now there's just a certain level of understanding and comfort that I'd never really felt around him before. Like I said, the day that I came out to my dad was the best day of my life. I just have a fondness for him now that I didn't have before.

I have my dad's height and his body build but I actually look more like my mom in terms of facial features. My sisters look more like my dad. As far as qualities I inherited from my parents I inherited many more of my mother's qualities than my fathers overall. I talk to my mom every day but I always talk to my dad once a week, if not more.

I definitely do want a family and I've often thought about adopting kids as a single father. But since I'm gone so much for volleyball and work I just couldn't do a kid justice right now, so I've decided to wait until I have a significant other. I do really want a family. I don't know that I'm the type to hold my dad to his word but I'm sure that if I had the discussion with my parents saying, "I'm thinking about adopting," or "I'm thinking about getting a surrogate mother," my dad would definitely remember what he said and would offer to pay for it. I don't know that I'd be willing to let him pay for it, but I know that he'd be more than willing to try.

After the Outsports article I wrote about my coming out experience was published I had so many people contacting me—thousands—but a large majority of them wanted to talk about my dad and how great he is. My publishers said, "You wrote a great piece, but your dad is the reason the article is catching fire. He's the nation's father figure right now. Everybody loves him. Everyone either wants to be him or have him as their father." And they're right. My dad did handle the situation so incredibly well that I just couldn't help but feel closer to him after that.

I had so many people tell me about poor coming out experiences. One guy told me that after his son came out to him he punched him in the face. He said he would give anything to go back in time to change the way he reacted to the way that my dad reacted. He said he'll never get that chance, and it will always be his single biggest regret.

Everyone who read that story was impressed with my dad, and it's hard for me to adequately put into words how much I agree with them. I am really proud of him. My parents received a lot of positive attention from that article too.

There are two things I would say to other gay men regarding dealing with their father. First, it's important to come out to your parents—especially your father—at the right time and to think in advance about how you want to do it. So many people either don't put any thought into the way they come out to their parents or it happens unexpectedly or, worst case scenario, they throw it in their parents face as a weapon or an argument or to spite their parents. I think that's just the worst possible way to do it, and it causes so many fights and so much misunderstanding. So my first piece of advice would be to really think about who your dad is as a person and to plan in advance how you want to tell him, because coming out to your parents is no easy task and it needs to be done the right way. So many of the stories I heard about which went poorly were due to poor planning, no planning, or just poor timing. Without being offensive to those people, some people also have ignorant fathers, I guess. But I think a lot of the trouble can be avoided by just putting thought into how you want to tell your father. That's my first point. My second point is not to underestimate how much your father loves you. I mean, your father is biologically programmed to love you, so you have that in your favor. And just remember that you maybe have insecure fears about the way he is going to react; I know I did. So I can't say that's true for everyone, but have faith in your dad. It will probably go better than you expect, especially if it is done right.

A few years before I came out a neighbor came out after he had moved away from South Dakota. I was able to see how my family reacted to him, and he was a very well-respected, very nice guy. I think that helped pave the way for me to come out, and that's part of the reason why I wrote the article. I personally believe that the more people discover that they already know a gay person or gay people, the more likely they are to be accepting. Once they realize they do know gays, then the whole subject is not as scary as they once thought. And because my neighbor made it easier for me to come out to my parents, I thought that maybe I could pave the way for other closeted kids in South Dakota and beyond too. My article ended up being published around the world, and someone pointed out to me that it had been translated into French and published in France. It was even translated into Asian languages and published in Asia, so I guess it reached a lot farther than just South Dakota, which was my intended target audience. The last time I checked on the article it had been shared almost fifteen thousand times. It really has been read by a lot of people. Since the article came out I haven't had any negative feedback. One or two people said they may not understand it but they fully support me and they think that I'm a good person. They may not be one hundred percent comfortable with the topic, but they're OK with it.

In 2007 I had a tumor which had to be removed, and a few days after the procedure I thought that I was strong enough to finally start walking on my own and to deal with things on my own. I remember being in the bathroom brushing my teeth. My dad wanted to help me, and I said, "No, I've got this. I can do it on my own." So I'm standing there brushing my teeth and all of a sudden I just started to blackout. I yelled, "Dad!" and then next thing I know I was falling and I was headed right for the floor. He caught me a few inches before I hit the floor. He's just so reactive and protective. I don't know if I would have died had my head hit the floor, but it was a hard tile floor. It definitely would have caused some trauma. So to my mind my dad has saved my life more than once.

Chapter 3
Mark Matousek

Mark is an acclaimed writer, teacher, and speaker whose work focuses on personal awakening through writing and self-inquiry. He lives in New York with his longtime partner.

I was born in Los Angeles in 1957. I have three sisters and I am the next to youngest. My mother was married to my father when I was born; my dad was a fix-it man, an electrician, sort of a jack-of-all-trades. My father left when I was four years old. He and my mother had split up a few weeks before and he actually came back to kidnap me before he left town. My mother luckily got a hold of me and they literally pulled me apart; he was holding me by the arms, and she was holding me by the seat. He wanted to take me with him. My mom kicked him in the right place and got me back and locked me in the house, and I never saw him again. I recall the experience deeply, profoundly. If you read *The Boy He Left Behind*, my memoir about my dad, that is the beginning of the book. I guess he wanted to take me along with him because I was his son and I was the only boy. That's all I know. I'm very lucky that he didn't get me because my life would have been very different. Unfortunately my father was a pathological liar and had trouble telling the truth.

Sometime prior to that, I remember taking a shower with him once and being fascinated by his body, feeling kind of attracted and repelled and fascinated all at the same time. There's a sort of erotic lens to it in my memory, but I think that I may have imposed that in retrospect. At the time I was a little three or four year old kid taking a shower with his dad. He started to tickle me. I just remember being in this secret world with him that was the only place we had to be alone together. I remember sitting on the toilet and watching him shave and seeing him cut himself and put toilet paper on his face where he had. Just small things. I remember the way his feet looked. But the memories are few and far between, and I have almost no memories of him other than those.

My mom never remarried. I grew up being told that my dad was a no-good, lying son-of-a-bitch, that he was a deadbeat dad, and that I was lucky that he left. She told me I wasn't the kind of son he would have wanted, which was a REALLY good thing to say to a little gay boy. But in general she never wanted to talk about him.

When I hired a detective to find my father several years before my mother died, she was very opposed to it. But in opening that door, information started to trickle out and I discovered that in fact my father had caught my mother in bed with her boyfriend at a motel, which is part of the reason he left and which is a piece of the story I had never been told before. My dad was apparently a very sensitive man; my mom said he was just too sensitive for her. So then I started to think that maybe he was gay but I don't think he was. I had kind of a fantasy that maybe he went off and lived happily ever after with a man, but that did not happen.

My two older sisters were from my mother's first marriage. They would have been around eight or nine when my dad married my mother. My oldest sister killed herself, and I think he may have molested her. There was a reference in her journal to something odd that happened, though she didn't get specific. The only picture I have of my father is with my mother and my two older sisters, and the way he's holding on to my older sister is somewhat strange. He had this peculiar expression on his face in the photo which has always bothered me. It's possible that he may have had some serious psychological issues to deal with.

I had a grandfather whom I didn't like very much. Not having a dad around was a big thing for me, because we were the first "broken family" in the neighborhood. That's what they used to call it: a broken home. So I grew up feeling broken in a broken home, and not having a father and growing up with a houseful of women was really, really hard for me. I was told that I was lucky that he was gone, but the truth is that I deeply missed having a father.

I knew nothing about my dad for over fifty years. I thought maybe he went off and had a wonderful life. But in fact he went off and had a double life and was a miserable man… About a year ago I got an email from someone who turns out to be my half-brother. When my father left us he went back to Illinois, which is where he's from, married someone, and told this new wife that he had a family but that we were all killed in a car accident, and went on and had a son with her.

This son contacted me out of the blue after his mother read my book, and we ended up meeting. I'm not sure how this woman came to read my book, but he went to my website and wrote to me through my agent. It was the weirdest thing. He lives in Tucson and is a retired police chief. He and my sister and I got together when I was visiting California, and it was surreal. He's a gun-toting, right-wing, church-going, golf-playing Republican. We have absolutely nothing in common, but now I have a half-brother. It's bizarre. We look a little alike. We have the same eyes, and you can see our father in our eyes.

Sometimes these early traumas are so severe that you block them out. And I didn't realize until I started to look for him—which I did on a dare in my late thirties—how much I had missed having him, because I had bought into the family myth that I was lucky that he was gone. I was having lunch with my editor friend at a magazine one day and we were talking about my family and I was saying all this stuff, that I was so lucky that my father wasn't there because I wasn't the kind of son who, blah, blah, blah… And he said, "Who told you that?" I said, "My mother." He said, "Well, do you believe it?" I said, "I don't know." He asked me if I'd looked for him, and I said, "No, I don't want to." He looked at me like I was lying and he dared me. He said, "I dare you to do it…" And I took him up on it. I feel like it was the right moment for me to do it. I didn't know that it was at the time but I'm really glad that I went ahead with it.

The detectives had sent me on several wild goose chases, and when I finally realized I wasn't going to find him I went through a real grieving time that I had never had when I was a child. There was the last person they thought might be him and I went to his door in Pasadena. I knocked on his door, and we had this really kind of pathetic scene together. I had a serious emotional explosion in response after I left this man's house and I realized it was over, and that all those years—in some weird way—I had thought maybe he would show up or maybe he was thinking about me… I realized that was over and I had to put that dream to bed. It was at that moment that I felt like I stepped into my own manhood in a different way. There was a part of me that never felt quite grown up. In certain ways I felt like a boy still. Although I was masculine I never felt like it was real. It was sort of a papier mache version of a man; it all looked good on the outside but inside there was something really deeply missing, and what was missing was the father. I didn't know it, because you don't miss what you never had. That's a cliché, but it's really true. But I became a man when I realized that he wasn't coming back.

I think there are esoteric reasons why we do things. There are outer reasons and inner ones. I think my inner reason was that I needed to become a man, and it didn't matter if I found the physical father or not. It was about looking. I needed to make the search. When I hired the detective, my mother told me about the motel and her boyfriend, which I hadn't known about before. She told me that my dad had good qualities, which she had never mentioned before. And paradoxically, looking for my father became a healing experience for me and my mother in a completely unexpected way. I was grateful for that as well.

I was super-precocious. I don't remember a time when I wasn't having sex when I was a kid. I was messing around with other kids from a very young age, so by the time my mother wanted to have the birds and the bees talk with me, it was a little late! On the night of my bar mitzvah my mother and I were out to dinner and she asked me how I compared to other boys in the locker room. It was the weirdest thing. I said, "What do you mean?" She said, "You know…" I felt like she had stuck her hand down my pants. I said, "I'm fine." She said, "Because your father was ENORMOUS. To the last time we did it, it hurt me." I'm sure that imprinted itself somewhere in my psyche too. That was bizarre. I mean, that was her most vivid memory of him.

I believe they hooked up the day they met. He was a good-looking guy and was quite hot and so was she, so I believe it was lust that brought them together. It definitely wasn't love because she was in love with another man all through both of her marriages, but it was definitely lust. Sexually it was really hot between them.

My mother never should have been a mom. She was not at all maternal. I'm one of those kids who was more or less "raised by wolves." There was love. But she did not know what to do with me and she was not the world's greatest mom. My mom was out of her depth as a parent and just didn't know how to handle being a parent in general and had a lot of her own issues. So we kids raised ourselves mostly, and one of my two older sisters was very loving, so there was love. And you take love where you can find it. That's what survivors do.

I always say my mom didn't like homosexuality but she loved my friends. My mom was a *broad*. She wasn't a great mom but she was a wonderful person. My friends loved her. She liked all of my partners and she was great with them. She didn't like it ideologically, and there was the issue of feeling like it reflected on her; she felt guilty that she had made me gay. I used to say, "Mother, trust me. You did *not* make me gay."

When I was a kid my mom tried to get me a Jewish big brother, which turned out to be a disaster. She had been told that if she didn't get me a male role model that I was "going to turn out to be a faggot," which I was already. When I was eighteen I was really a lost kid. I was a delinquent. I was in jail three times before I turned eighteen. I was a mess. One night I was at a gay bar and I got picked up by this guy who became my first partner. He was twenty years older, and meeting him completely changed my life. He was my first real male role model. He was successful. He taught me how to be in the world. He told me I was a diamond in the rough and he educated me and gave me confidence in myself. I saw what a successful man looked like and how he did it and it gave me a major leg up in the world. Meeting him literally saved my life. He got me to go away for college and he was a great gift in my life.

We were together about four years, and I outgrew the relationship. We kept in touch. He died of AIDS in the late '80s. He might have infected me, but I don't know for sure. That was the story I told myself because we had one illicit moment after we broke up. I'll never forget.... We were broken up. I still found him really attractive and he was single and I was single. I can remember leaving his house and thinking, "I shouldn't do this...," but I went back and we had this wild unprotected sex. He got sick a few years after that. I found out I was HIV+ but thank God I never progressed. I never got sick but I'm HIV+ and I may have gotten it from Bob. I had ten years of being positive—before the good newer medications became available—when I thought I was going to die. That's when I wrote *Sex, Death & Enlightenment*. I never thought I would make it, and then the medications showed up in the mid 1990s and, thank God, here we all are.

There was a lot of pain and confusion in my house growing up. I often felt displaced, fragmented, lost, and confused. My dad's absence was like the elephant in the room. I didn't know how huge it had been because I had been told that he was not a good person and I should be glad he wasn't there. But it really did throw everything off in ways that it took me a long, long time to understand. Did I grow from it? Absolutely. Is it integral to who I became? Of course. I do think though that it's better to have no father than to have a father who's a shitty role model.

My boyfriend had a good relationship with his dad, though his dad wasn't the way some of these nurturing attentive fathers you sometimes see around are. I cannot imagine what it would have been like to have had a dad like that in the same way I cannot imagine what it would have been like to have had a doting mom. To have a father like that? It's so beautiful when you see these little boys and their loving fathers. It's just stunning to me.

Chapter 4
Sean Smedley

<hr />

Sean lives in Connecticut where he works in the healthcare field.
His overcoming an especially traumatic childhood is inspiring.

I was born in 1968 and grew up in New Haven, Connecticut. My father originally worked at a factory called Pond Lily in Westville, Connecticut, which is right next to New Haven. After that factory closed down he worked as a full-time truck driver for Shuckey's Express. My father was married before he married my mom so he had two children with his first wife and then two children with my mom. I have an older sister, and she and I have a pretty good relationship.

I have mixed recollections of my dad. He was an alcoholic, and I have recollections of him being a good father, like sitting on the floor with us making tapes for my mother for Christmas or her birthday, and then I have recollections of my father when he was drunk coming home and terrorizing the house. So I have some bittersweet memories of my dad. I think he tried to be a good father, but his own father got shot to death when my dad was a young boy, younger than age six. My dad was always on a quest to find out who shot his father and why they did, and he never found that out. So I think he was the best father he could be, based upon what he knew of a father.

I saw him cry a couple of times. He'd cry when my mother was about to leave him. My mother separated from my father several times, and when she separated from him, he became a saint. Until she was back home for a couple weeks, and then he reverted right back to his old ways again.

None of my friends had fathers. In my neighborhood my father and mother were probably one of only a few married couples. The majority of my friends didn't have fathers, and I didn't want my father around because it just seemed easier for my friends who were without one. And because my father was often volatile—he was abusive mentally and physically—I really didn't want him around. So I definitely had a closer relationship with my mom, because she was sort of my safe haven, I guess I'd say.

My dad was definitely more affectionate with my sister because I think he expected a boy to be "a man." I don't recall us having any Hallmark moments. There was a hobby shop in town, and I loved model cars, so he would take me there as a treat to get cars. He did do that stuff with me, but that was more of a father/son type activity rather than him saying, "You're my son and I'm glad that I have a son and I love you." That's, I guess, what he thought his role as a father was supposed to be.

I think my father knew early on that I was not a regular boy. He probably sensed that I was gay, and I think he always had some resentment for me being gay. He was abusive to everyone in our family—my mother, my sister, and myself—but he was more abusive towards me in certain ways. There were times where he punched me right dead in my face for something that I did when he and my mother were separated, and he was just very hard on me. The general way I felt about him was that I never really liked him. He knew I wasn't the son he wanted or had bargained for or hoped he would get, but he got what he got.

I was always afraid of my father and, quite honestly, I liked it more when he wasn't around than when he was. He always caused turmoil. That was one of the reasons why I turned to drugs and alcohol, because as I grew up I realized that, "OK, I really did have this person who created me who didn't want me." And then my father committed suicide when I was a sophomore in college, and he completely abandoned me. So he went from abusive and not wanting me around to a permanent abandonment of never giving me the option to have him around.

When my mother and father would separate—she left him multiple times—and we would run into him somewhere, he would be like, "Why don't you people just leave me alone?" He didn't want to be bothered with us. I don't think I realized it at the time but my reaction was to put up a protective barrier for myself of "Well I don't want to be around him so I won't give him the option of not wanting me around." Later I turned to drugs and alcohol.

My mother and sister and I wouldn't discuss him. From what I've seen, I think it's a cultural thing—especially in the African-American community I grew up in—that you just sweep it under the rug. You don't talk about it. It's only in the last three to five years that my sister and I have started to acknowledge that my father had a mental illness. Nowadays they'd have a treatment for it; they'd have him on some kind of medication. He had an alcohol problem, and now it's more acceptable to say, "I have a problem and I'm getting help for it." Back then, in my opinion, as a man you never admitted you had a problem, and you're never going to deal with it if you're not going to recognize that you have a problem.

I think the hobby shop moments were the best moments for my father and me. It was probably his way of being able to connect with me, because my uncle—his brother—had gotten me a Lionel train set for Christmas one year. And every year that he and my mother were together he took me faithfully to that hobby shop and bought me a new car or a new something for my train set. And we didn't grow up with the best of means; my parents definitely lived hand to mouth and paycheck to paycheck. But every year they were together, he would buy me something for that train set. I specifically remember him having my sister and me tape a message for my mother—this was back when tape recorders were popular—about how much she means to us. So there were some bright moments.

My dad did have the birds and the bees talk with me, and I'll never forget where we had it. My sister had to go to Planned Parenthood for something, and we had the talk in the Planned Parenthood parking lot. I forget how he framed the conversation, but I remember sitting in his Ford LTD in the parking lot.

My father had some addiction issues. He had an alcohol addiction and apparently he had a bit of a sexual addiction too because he sexually abused both my sister and me for some years. Apparently he had started to date the woman who lived downstairs in the house that we lived in. We think that he was seeing her while my mother and he were still together. But I remember it was a bad Friday night, and my mother had already made the commitment that "If your father goes to this one bar—called the Dunbar—we're leaving for good." I prayed all day that he'd go to the bar that night because I was just ready for it to be over. So we left that night and we never went back again, and I never really had any relationship with him after that, until around the year before he died.

He had started dating the woman downstairs, and the rumor is that he had physically molested one of her children and she pressed charges, and he was going to do some jail time. So before he went to jail, he hung himself, on the day before his birthday. I think my father was just so messed up from his childhood that he didn't know what was right or what was wrong. He was so traumatized over the death of his own father and not knowing what happened to him that he was just never able to really function. Then you mix that with alcohol, and that was his way of medicating or not dealing with whatever he needed to deal with.

My sister has been married four times, and for her second marriage she had a wedding, and he was in the wedding. My sister and father had reconnected and had started to develop a relationship, and he walked her down the aisle. He had taken me to get shoes for the wedding and had talked a little bit, and then I was off to school the next year.

I was attending college at Norfolk State in Virginia. One day when I got back to my room, there was a note on the door to go see the Dean. So I walked over, and the Dean sat me down and said, "I have some bad news for you." I was thinking it was something with my mother or my sister; my father quite honestly didn't even pop into my mind. He said, "Your father has passed away, and your family is going to make arrangements to get you home as quickly as possible." I called my mother, but no one said why or how—none of that. Nobody really wanted to tell me. It was a while before they actually came clean with how it happened. I was pretty shocked. I'd perceived him as more selfish and would never have imagined him as the type of person who would end his own life. I was definitely sad and I cried and probably had some remorse that I carried around for a couple of years.

I got into drugs and alcohol to self-medicate, just to cope with some of the pain from my childhood. I always looked for the love that I never got from my father in another man and have had dysfunctional relationships because of it, because I wasn't looking for them for *them*. I was looking for somebody to rescue me. I carried an abandoned kid around with me for years, and that kid drove the bus all over town recklessly. And when I couldn't find that missing love from my father in somebody else, I turned to drugs and alcohol where you can feel whatever you want to feel or not feel whatever you don't want to feel. At the point I started getting high, everything was going pretty well in my life. I had gotten a great job and was making excellent money and traveling across the country, but I didn't want to deal with any of the stuff that I really needed to deal with from my childhood to be able to live a productive and healthy life.

In 2008 when I turned forty I decided that I wasn't going to do drugs anymore. I was going to find a boyfriend, buy a house, and get a new job. So I did all of the above—check, check, check—plus I got a new car. The mortgage process didn't work out, but I ended up renting the place. The job I ended up not liking, and the car I bought was a gas-guzzler, and in 2008 gas prices shot through the roof. The guy I was dating decided the week after my fortieth birthday to take me to the place we went on our first date and break up with me. It was just like my father abandoning me all over again, but it hit me even harder this time. That led to almost a full breakdown. I couldn't take it anymore. I was done and I ended up trying to kill myself by taking an overdose of Xanax. But for grace or mercy up above I did not die, and it's still a mystery to the medical people how I didn't die after taking sixty Xanax. I woke up after sleeping for a couple of days. My job had been calling and trying to reach me....

I knew I could either live or I could die. One of my friends had met this really great life coach that she talked about and recommended I see. I knew the life coach was going to tell me to remove all mood-altering substances from my life. And that's exactly what she did when I first sat on her couch. That's when I made the commitment that I was going to get my life in order. When I started to tell her my story, she really honed in on the abandonment piece and gave me a book called *Until Enlightenment* by Stuart Alpert. It talks about how the inner kid in you drives everything that you do, all your actions. For me that was spot on, and once I talked to the inner kid in me and let the kid know that I'm the adult now and I can handle my life and I'm definitely going to protect him and carry him through the rest of our life together. That's when everything started to fall into place and that's when I was able to forgive my father. I actually wrote a letter to him that he'll never get because he's no longer here. I wrote it to him to release everything that I was feeling and I forgave him for everything that he had ever done and I thanked him for who he was and for who he did try to be. But I had to free myself and I had to free him, and today I really don't hold any grudges against him. He had an illness, and that was his way of dealing with it. I'm thankful that he produced me, because but for him I am. I have forgiven him and I've been able to move on pretty peacefully in my life, and my life is better than it's ever been. I'm sober. A year ago I took a great new job in May. I closed on my condo. I had to buy a new car—didn't plan to—and I love it. I don't have a boyfriend yet but I don't actually need one because I don't need anyone to validate me from that perspective. Would it be nice? Yes.

When I reflect back on my father I can appreciate everything he was, but he's also shown me, in a lot of ways, who I *don't* want to be. I don't want to be an alcoholic who ends up doing harm to myself because I never dealt with my stuff. I know that when I hit my rock-bottom and wanted to check out permanently, my life flashed before my eyes, like when a person in a movie is falling off a cliff. So I have no doubt that as my father was taking his own life, he was regretful for probably many things. I forget what Bible verse it is, but they did find his little orange Bible open to a certain scripture when they found his body. I carried that Bible with me for some fifteen years everywhere I went.

He does have a gravesite, but I don't visit very often. I grew up Baptist so I believe that the grave is just where they put your body. Their spirit is free, and you carry their spirit around with you. I'll tell you an ironic story… In 2003 I broke up with a boyfriend of five years on Friday the thirteenth. I was deciding if I wanted to take the day off work or not and I said, "Nope, I'll go to work." During the course of the day a client had said they needed something, so I ran out to deliver it. I'll never forget it… The song *Dance With My Father* by Luther Vandross was playing, and I got hit head on. My car spun around multiple times—I got hit by a couple of other cars—and that song was still playing. It was a very bad accident, and when my car stopped I had to crawl through the driver's side window to get out of the car. So when the fireman came over he said, "What's your name? What's today's date? What car were you driving?" I said, "Sean Smedley, Friday the thirteenth; I was driving that silver car." He again said, "What's your name? What's today's date? What car were you driving?" I repeated my answers, and he said, "There's no way you could be driving that silver car and be sitting on this side of the curb." He goes, " 'Cause nobody who was in that car should have made it out of it." So I believe my father was watching over me in that case, because the song *Dance With My Father* was playing, and he was like my guardian angel protecting me. I always think of my father when I hear that song. I thank him and my higher power for watching over me.

I've thought about being a father. As I look back on my life, if there's one thing I wish I would have done differently, I probably would have had a child or adopted one at some point. But I'm now forty-seven, and unless I meet someone and we develop a dynamic relationship and that just happens to happen, I don't think I'll have kids. But I would love to have been a father. I'm a pretty great uncle to my sister's children and I was like a father to all of them growing up because their fathers were often absent. Most of her husbands have been just like my father in many ways. I adore those kids, because they're innocent and they didn't ask to come here and they should be given as much love as possible. That's what I wish I would have had.

October sixth and seventh are always hard days because his birthday's on the seventh and he killed himself on the sixth. I do change my Facebook profile a lot during that time of the year, and people will say, "Oh my God, that's a great picture of you," and it's not me; it's my father. I didn't really realize before how much I look like him. I hold him close in my heart now for a different reason. I would like to have a relationship with him now because I'm very comfortable with who I am, and I wonder what our relationship today would be like. In some ways for many years I think I felt inadequate being a man. But now I'm really comfortable with who I am, and I'm appreciative for everything he showed me, the good and the bad. The hobby shop trips showed me what a father-son relationship could potentially look like, and the abusive piece showed me what a father and son relationship should never look like. It helped me be a better man, because a lot of the things I've gone through, he was a part of—right, wrong, or indifferent. I'm a pretty happy, functioning man today, even as I reflect on the past and the many bittersweet pieces of it.

A lot of gay men's relationships with their dads are different just because they're gay. My advice is to try and find that happy place in the relationship. Try to find the thing that connects the two of you, whether it's the hobby shop or the cars—whatever it is—and be happy with that. You don't have to have a full 360 degree relationship. If all you have with your dad is that one piece of connection, that's good enough. At the end of the day, even if you don't have a relationship with your father, forgive him and love him. That's huge in a father-son relationship. Some fathers just don't know how to deal with a gay son. I don't want to live my life with any regrets and I believe that being unwilling to forgive him was holding me back as a person. Forgiving my father opened the door to freedom for me. I had to learn to love my father, even if he wasn't sorry.

Chapter 5
Stuart Gaffney

Stuart is the cofounder of Marriage Equality, where he is employed as Communications Director. His superb interview about his longtime relationship with his husband John can be found in my first book, Love Together. *Stuart makes his home in San Francisco.*

I was born in Milwaukee, Wisconsin on November 1, 1962. My family moved a lot because my father was an aspiring academic, and by the time I was born, he was teaching at the University of Milwaukee. I'm very clear on my earliest recollections of my father because my parents divorced when I was quite young. The few memories I have of my father living at home are some of my very first memories. What is probably the first memory of my life is a sleepless night, and my father picking me up and carrying me back and forth in front of the windows in our home in Whitefish Bay and singing me a lullaby until I went back to sleep.

Since my parents divorced when I was quite young, most of my memories after that involve visiting him on the weekends, first in his apartment near the university, and then later as he moved around the country, I would fly at a very young age to Washington DC and later to British Columbia, and finally to California. He would fly to Milwaukee to see us kids too. So it quickly went from this very intimate memory of him singing me a lullaby at home and putting me back to sleep to much more of a long distance relationship. But we have always been in each other's lives, and even though I wasn't living with him from an early age, he has always exerted a strong influence on me, even from afar.

From very early, I realized that I was different, though I didn't have the word gay to attach it to until I was older. During a family move I discovered a letter that was written by a school counselor to my dad, actually back when I was in kindergarten. The letter said that my dad needed to spend more time with me doing typical male activities, because the counselor was worried about my sense of masculinity. I think my father was quite horrified, and he wrote back and he made a copy of that letter. Here he is being taken to task by a school counselor for not raising a son who is sufficiently masculine. This was in the early 1960s but it feels like the typical 1950s regimented gender roles where every family must look like this and be like that... Our family was already breaking the mold: My parents were an interracial couple and then they were a divorced couple, and now they're raising a son who isn't masculine enough, to the point where the school counselor was even writing my dad letters about it.

I think my dad was really mortified. He wrote back something like, "Yes, I will do more manly activities with Stuart. I will take him to more ball games. I will play catch with him more." As kids we don't think of our parents as being insecure, but I think that my parents were very insecure, especially in not having a guidebook for how to raise kids now that they were divorced. And the idea that any of this might relate to deficiencies in their parenting or that the divorce itself might be to blame for any of this—I think—immediately set off a lot of guilt in my dad. So his response was like, "Yes! I will take corrective measures immediately! I will make Stuart hyper-masculine; don't you worry!" I think now with hindsight we can say that that didn't work, but it may have alerted my dad to the idea that there was something different about me, if he hadn't already perceived that himself.

My dad loved the outdoors so he always wanted to take us on hikes and wanted to take us camping. I actually love hiking now but I hated it as a kid. If he thought he could make me more butch by taking me on more hikes, I would say it didn't work because I probably started crying. But we did bond over different things.

I was fascinated by trains and planes, which I guess could be seen as a stereotypical boy thing, so my dad took me to airports and train stations a lot. I loved to collect airline timetables and see the planes come and go.

When he no longer lived in Milwaukee and would fly back for the weekend, I would often just want to stay at the airport all day, which I'm sure he found a little curious at first. But I think he realized over time that it was a great way for us to spend the day together. I was engaged and fascinated and having fun, and also we were just hanging out and there was a lot of down time where we could talk or not talk. So that worked out very well.

My dad remarried when I was still fairly young. He was living in DC at the time, and I was on vacation and spending like a week there. It was interesting to me that he had become serious with the woman who would become his wife, and a few days into my visit he told me, "Tonight at dinnertime, there is a new woman who's going to come over for dinner. I like her very much and I think you may like her a lot too. But if you don't or you don't feel comfortable, we could ask her to leave." In hindsight now I'm actually kind of shocked that he would say that. What if I had asked her to go? How embarrassing would that have been? But it was his way of saying, "Hey, your opinion here matters to me too. I know this could be a big shock to you and I want you to feel comfortable and I want you to feel like you have a voice as we create a new family together." In retrospect it was a pretty perfect way that he handled it. I didn't ask her to leave, and she is now his wife of almost forty years, and they have three more lovely children. I consider my mother and my brother and sister and me and my dad and wife and their three kids as our extended nuclear family; we're all one family but in an extended way, and we actually all get along quite well.

I grew up at a time when schools were allowed and encouraged to have sex-ed classes. I think that was an easy way out for both of my parents to say, "Here, take this class," instead of having to have "the talk" with me. I did ask my dad some questions which were a little more intellectual. He sometimes gave me books to read that were not about sex but had sexual references in them. I was reading beyond my age level, and he would give me more adult books, and sometimes I would just be confused, like "What is this word?" I do remember in about fourth grade asking him what fellatio was, because I had never heard that word before. I think he felt pretty awkward about explaining that to me.

I respect my father a lot but what was disappointing to me was that he would thoughtlessly make disparaging references to people he perceived to be gay. One time many years ago we were having dinner in a restaurant, and there were two men at another table. I couldn't say if they actually were gay or if they were a couple, but my dad thought that may be the case because he said to me in this very offhand way, something like, "What a strange and lonely life those two must lead..." Well I hadn't been interested in the two men at that table before but now I was very interested! *Who are they? What does this mean?* But certainly it was a very negative way of talking about them, like they were completely different and other, and nobody we knew—especially not me—would ever be like them. In reflecting back upon remarks like that it just makes me sad, because my dad is very open-minded, very progressive, and fashions himself quite the free-thinker. So I'm not sure why he would have been more closed off to the two men at that table or the fact that he might be sitting at the table with his gay son.

I was always basically out to myself but there was a long process of coming out to others. I started that process when I went to college and it felt to me like a chance to start over with a completely new life with new people and I could now be who I truly was. I had my first boyfriend, started telling friends in college, and when I came home in the summer to stay with my mother I started telling my high school friends and then I told my mother. I waited until the very last minute to tell my dad, and what I mean by last minute is I actually let several more years pass. It wasn't until graduation that I told my dad and I kind of forced the situation because I had decided upon graduation that I was going to take an internship with what is now called the Lesbian and Gay Task Force. Of course everyone asks you what you're going to do when you graduate from college, but I kind of put off answering that question as long as possible with my dad.

I came out to him when he and the family were there at graduation. I didn't want to do it one-on-one with him; I wanted it to be within the family container. When I told him, he was very sad. I have only seen or heard my dad on the verge of tears a couple times in my life, and that was one of those times. He didn't articulate what he was feeling. What I got from him, more than any words he said, was that it made him really sad and confused. He really didn't know what to do with this information, and

I'm sure part of him wished we could just rewind the tape and pretend that it never happened.

But I'm putting words in his mouth because my dad didn't say any of those things. My dad's a brilliant intellectual/academic. He had a lot of questions. He wanted to talk about this a LOT but he wanted to talk about it from a very intellectual perspective. He wanted to know why I thought I was gay. He wanted to know why I thought people were gay. He wanted to know what it meant, what gay people were like… He just asked so many questions, and sometimes they were very personal. He asked if I had dated women, and what was that like? Sometimes the questions were so abstract, like he asked me if I thought there was a homosexual underground that was secretly running the State Department… It was like, *OK, what does this have to do with your son coming out to you?* But I made a decision early on that I would kind of walk him through this and be really patient with him. I had so many conversations with him where it was like, "OK. What do you want to know today?" He'd say, "Oh good. I'm glad you called. I have like twenty questions to ask you about what it means that there are gay people in this world…" I'd think, *Oh my God…* But we would talk about it, and at some point I said, "Dad, I wonder if all these questions are beside the point, and maybe what you need to tell me is that the thought of me with another man makes you want to throw up," and he said, "No, it's not that at all. I'm just worried that homosexuality may have caused the downfall of the Roman Empire…"

There were a lot of "I can't believe this is happening" moments as we had these conversations over a period of years. One time he said to me, realizing—I think—how exasperating his questions must be, "You know, Stuart, maybe what you need to do is to tell me to fuck off…" I thought, "Wow… That's really a Catch-22 sort of conundrum, because now that you've told me to tell you to fuck off, if I tell you to fuck off I'm just doing what you told me to do." I didn't say it. It would be so unlike me to say that to him, which is probably what my school counselor was referring to: "You need to tell your dad to fuck off!"

But over time though, the idea that we would just talk this out and I would answer every question until there were no more questions worked.

It took years and it worked in part because he really found that I remained an open book and that no matter how silly his questions were or how contradictory, that I would take the time to take him seriously. The questions were sometimes ridiculous to the point where he would say things like, "I think the problem is that women have always been distant and mysterious to you. You have no idea how to talk to a woman much less how to date a woman, so you're scared of women and it's much easier to be gay." Which is absurd because you think, "Well if this is easy to be gay, having this endless series of conversations with your father who won't understand you…" But I said, "No, that's far from the truth. I'm very comfortable with women. I have lots of friends who are women and lots of women who've been interested in dating me. In high school I went to dances with women. Dating women just never interested me." He said, "Now I see the problem is that women have been too aggressive with you. You're too familiar with them. They're not mysterious…"

I think over time he realized he was being ridiculous. One thing he said to me was, "I need you to be patient with me because I have never met another gay person before in my life. So we have to start from scratch." But over time I realized that he thinks a number of people in our family were gay and also suspects a number of his colleagues may be gay. He just never had someone to talk about it with before, and he has lots of thoughts about it, some of them pretty advanced and some of them pretty absurd.

The thing that really ultimately turned the corner though was when I met John, my husband, and when I introduced him to my dad. That made it real in a different way, like, "OK. You're not just telling me you're gay but you're in love with somebody, and here he is. He's a real person, and you're a real couple." That, once and for all, took the subject out of an intellectual realm. He liked John too, which was helpful. Meeting people who are good with parents can certainly have its benefits!

The other big thing that made it come full-circle with my dad was when John and I became marriage equality activists. My dad is an economist, an activist, and has always seen himself as a free-thinker and very much an activist in his profession. And so when John and I became plaintiffs in the California marriage equality case and became very outspoken and visible and active in the marriage equality movement, that actually is the first time I experienced my father saying, "Oh, you're a chip off the old block! You're my son." I couldn't have predicted that, and it was unexpected to receive that affirmation, but that was this moment of recognition where he saw a big piece of himself in me, like, "You're actually out to change the world and you want to make the world a better place for yourself and others, just like me..." That was decades after I came out to him, but I would say that sort of completed the process. He was *with* us in the biggest way from that moment on. And because he saw himself as an activist he was much more outspoken than I ever would have thought during the Prop 8 campaign. He came to our legal wedding and celebrated with us and then later emailed his friends and colleagues and he said, "I just went to the legal wedding of my son and son-in-law, and their marriage and marriages like theirs are on the ballot in California this November. Please don't vote against my son and son-in-law and don't vote against me and my family." So he took a very public and personal stand for us and with us. That was unexpected and beautiful.

My dad is an amazing person. He's ninety-two and just retired at eighty-nine and he's working on another book. He's announced his intention to live to be one hundred, which sounds like a great goal, but I'm wondering if he's selling himself short. Maybe he should be planning to live well beyond one hundred. That's not to say that he isn't feeling his age, but he's an inspiration to me in many ways. He's a land economist and a student of the economist and political-historical figure Henry George and the single tax movement. That is his life-work.

My father and his wife recently moved to a retirement community after living almost forty years in a fantastic family house that they never wanted to leave, but the time had come. So when John and I visited them for Thanksgiving that was our first time visiting the retirement community. The day after Thanksgiving we had dinner in the communal dining hall there, and they have a tradition in this community where—if you wish—if you have a new guest at your table, they pass a microphone and you can stand up and introduce them. This is a Baptist retirement community where the meal started with a prayer, and right after the prayer my dad takes the microphone and says, "Tonight we are giving thanks because we are joined by our son Stuart and his husband John, who is our son-in-law, and they are legally married." There was silence in the room and then the room applauded. I don't know exactly what that might have meant to the other folks in the room, and with hearing loss I'm not sure what everybody heard, but I know that it meant a lot to John and me, and I think it was very meaningful to my dad to do that. He thought a lot about how he wanted to do it and what he was going to say, and that it was important that the world see that we are a family, in all of its possibilities. To me that's the best possible Thanksgiving.

In other ways it was a very bittersweet Thanksgiving. My dad's wife was just diagnosed with ALS. There are many horrible diseases, but ALS is such a sad thing to be a part of because it slowly subtracts, one by one, all your abilities until there's nothing left. At this point my stepmom is doing really well but it's getting harder and harder for her to talk clearly, and we have to realistically think about the time—hopefully a while from now—when she will no longer be able to speak or feed herself or put on her own clothes by herself. We often talk about how aging is kind of the reverse of childhood, a return to dependency, but with a disease like ALS it just makes the process so explicit and lays bare the way your loved one suddenly becomes vulnerable and needy and needs your help just like a little kid again.

It seems to take a long time for my dad to become emotionally available about topics that would seem to be just immediately emotionally raw for many people. We've been through a number of family health crises, and this summer my dad's brother had a protracted illness and then died. At first as my uncle was getting sicker and sicker, it was kind of abstract for my dad, almost like it was something he was reading in the news. It took a few months before my dad really engaged with it emotionally. I'm so glad that my uncle lived for my dad to be able to take a trip across the country to see him, and I think that those days that he and my uncle had together were extremely meaningful for them both. It's probably going to be a similar process with his wife, that at first he's receiving this information in sort of an abstract, medical way, and as time goes on he will likely connect with it emotionally in a more profound way. And when he does, we'll be here to support him and be a part of that journey together.

Another thing for my dad, with his amazing longevity, is that one of the hard things about living well into your nineties is that many of your contemporaries are no longer with you. I'm sure that there's an increasing feeling of alone-ness for my dad, and the prospect of losing his life partner is probably too much for him to contemplate right now. But this is a time, more than ever, for us to be there for him.

When I was little, we were not a hugging family. That has changed over time, and like a number of kids, I learned to love to hug all my friends. So it became much more natural then to hug family members, and now we're a hugging family, even though we didn't start out that way. I don't think my dad literally says, "I love you," but he has taken to signing off on every single email he sends with "Love, Dad." I don't think that's an afterthought either; he affirmatively took that step, because he didn't used to do that. That's his way of saying, "Every time I email you I am telling you I love you, even if I don't call you up and literally say so." But I do feel loved.

I've noticed with family and friends that often when someone you come out to is not immediately understanding or accepting and then later they do come around, they never acknowledge that journey or say, "Oh, what an idiot I was," or "I'm sorry for all the pain I caused you…" Often, I think, people just say, "OK, I'm with you now. Let's move on and let's pretend that other stuff never happened." I can understand why people do that. It may be easier, and there may also be a sense of embarrassment, like, "Oh my God, I can't believe I said those things…" But it's always felt somewhat hollow that people don't apologize for that, especially to their own child. Like "Oh my God, I gave you hell. But I'm not going to say anything." So it was meaningful to me that at our wedding reception, as part of his toast, my dad apologized to us. He said, "I wasn't there for you and I let you down. But now I am here for you." That's not easy to do. But it meant a lot to me because in many ways, big and small, I had and maybe still do live with a sense of not living up to my father's expectations, and that moment was a big step towards lifting that burden. I think more than anything, you just want to feel that you're OK, that your dad thinks you're OK. And I don't mean OK in a flippant manner; I mean in a profound manner. It might be the most basic thing you want from a parent, like "Tell me everything's going to be OK. Tell me that you love me no matter what, and that I'm OK, no matter what I do or who I am. And you are OK with me." For a long time I was cut off from that feeling, but I think that at that moment I got it back.

Like my dad, I wake up very early in the morning and I go to bed very early at night. I would love to sleep in but I can't seem to change the pattern. Sometimes if I wake up at four in the morning I might happen to check email, and if there's an email from my dad, my first thought is like, "What the fuck are you doing up at four a.m.?" Then I realize. "Oh, I'm up at four a.m…" Is there a pattern here? When John met my dad for the first time he said, "Now that I've met your dad, it explains so much…" From the way we both carry ourselves to things that are more subtle, there was that instant recognition for him of, "Oh, you are this man's son. I can see that in an instant…" Things like believing that I *can* make the world a better place, and that that is one of the highest and best things anyone can do in life. I got that from both my parents but most certainly from my dad. As well as some less admirable traits, like my dad likes to be waited on, and I like that too. I certainly don't want to blame my dad for any of my shortcomings but I do see some similarities, like sometimes I'm emotionally clumsy in ways that my dad is. When I have seen him in a family fight with someone else I recognize the way he reacts. He goes to kind of a hurt little boy place and quietly pouts and shuts down and goes off and sulks, and goddamn it, that's exactly what I do. I see it in him and I think, "I don't like that!" But somehow I still do it.

There are definitely no one-size-fits-all rules, but I think that for me and my father it actually worked for me to be very patient with him. It required almost stepping into the parental role, like "OK, now that I'm gay I can see that you can't be what I would expect a parent to be like, so I'm going to do this journey with you and partner with you in it." I had hoped my dad was going to be able to be helpful, but when I saw that that wasn't what was going to happen and, in fact, he needed me to help him figure it out, I stepped into that role and I did that with him.

One of the things that certainly was not ideal during my upbringing, with both my parents, was that I was expected to be very adult from a very young age. There are some real drawbacks to that and there are advantages too, and so I thought, "OK, you need help dealing with the fact that you have a gay son and you actually don't really have anyone else to talk about this with either because right now you are kind of closeted about the fact that you have a gay son. So who's going to help you with this? Your gay son! We're going to do this together, and although in the ideal world YOU would be taking the lead on this, I'm going to take the lead on this, and we're going to walk together until it's OK between us."

It took years. I would love to have those years back and instead just have had a fun and loving father-and-son relationship without ever talking about whether homosexuality caused the fall of the Roman Empire. But it was all worth it. That approach may not be right for another person and someone else might just want to tell their dad to fuck off. Who knows? Maybe I should have, too. But thank goodness my dad is still alive at age ninety-two and we now do have the relationship we always wanted and deserved to have. Although I said I shouldn't have had to take the lead on that part obviously I'm an adult too, and it is a partnership, so it takes both of us to make it work. And certainly now as he's aging and his wife is dealing with a debilitating illness, I really need to be there for him now more than ever. I'm glad that we've done the work on our relationship so that now we can truly be there for each other without distractions.

The other thing I'd say, which probably applies to everybody, is that even though I made a choice to be relentlessly patient with my dad I also never, ever stopped being anyone other than who I was, and I think that that—more than anything else—is what convinced him. He was like, "You are so clear in your knowledge of who you are, that even if I don't fully understand why you are this way, I get that this is who you are because you are so consistent and earnest in telling me about yourself." I think that that kind of clarity and being true to yourself is really important in so many areas in life, and it was the key to making my relationship with my father better and more honest.

Some time ago John and I went and saw *The Laramie Project*, about Matthew Shepard. It's a wonderful play where people bring to life the voices of real people involved in Matthew Shepard's life, and there's a moment where Shepard's father is speaking publicly about the memory of his son and he starts by saying, "My son, my hero, Matthew Shepard." Those are beautiful words for any father to say or for anyone to say about anyone else, but when I was sitting in the theater and heard those words I thought—and this was when my dad and I were going through some of our more difficult times—"I cannot imagine my father saying that about me." I felt a very profound sense of sadness and loss about that. It doesn't seem like too much to ask that your own parent would think of you that way. So it was kind of a way to name something that was not right, the difficult experience of my dad not being there for me when I told him who I really was. It made me realize that in many ways I felt like he was holding it against me: "You're not the son I thought you were." Or even worse: "I used to think of you as my hero and now I don't anymore." I mean, he never said those words, but that's really the way it felt to me.

But the bookend to that story was that very simple moment I told you about just last week in the Baptist retirement community where my dad stood up and said, "This is my son and this is my son-in-law. They're married, and we're here celebrating Thanksgiving as a family." That's the antidote to what I felt in that theater watching *The Laramie Project*. I now feel like my dad is proud of me. I'm really glad that we've taken the journey together to get back to the point where—as any father should be—he is proud of his son. That just means the world to me.

Chapter 6
Danny

Danny works as a policeman in a small town near Birmingham, Alabama. He lives with his husband and their teenage son.

I was born in September 1977 in Decatur, Alabama, which is just south of Athens, the city that I was raised in. No one was really born in Athens at the time because the hospital had a high infant mortality rate. There was a drawbridge between Athens and Decatur, and all the pregnant women in Athens were given the phone number to the operator of the drawbridge so he could stop the barges. Back then Athens had maybe fourteen thousand people; it has around twenty-five thousand now. My family had been there since before the Civil War. My parents were teenagers when they had me. They got married before I was born, though they told me they would have married anyway. Dad started as a minimum wage helper with a sheet metal company during the day and put himself through night school. He became a certified mechanic for sheet metal and eventually a journeyman, then a foreman, and a superintendent.... He started with that company as a minimum wage helper and left it as the president with a six-figure income. He's a good guy.

I always remember my dad working quite a bit, but he always made time for his family. When he wasn't working he was home; that was very important to him. On Fridays he would come pick me up and he'd take me to go get a toy at Itasco—we didn't have a Wal-Mart back then—and then we'd go eat at a restaurant. That continued until my brother came along. Of course my parents didn't have a lot of money back then, and we were very poor growing up. But those trips were always a treat for me.

Danny

My dad was not affectionate when I was growing up. He got that from his dad. He's since changed and is not the same as he used to be. I remember there were probably five times that he hugged me and told me he loved me, up until I came out to him. I was closer to my dad up until a certain point and then I was probably closer to my mom. My dad was real big into discipline, and I probably feared him more than I should have. I guess we would use Mom as a crutch against Dad. Mom was Southern Baptist, and she put us in church every Tuesday, Wednesday, and Sunday.

Dad was into sports, especially baseball. My brother played baseball and Dad was a coach. I became a Civil War re-enactor when I was twelve, and that became my thing. My dad wouldn't participate but he would come watch it occasionally. Since he was a teenager when he had me, he likes to joke and say that we grew up together. He liked to say to me, "It's a pleasure growing up with you." He liked to work on old Mopars; the Plymouth Barracuda was his favorite. He would basically pull apart engines and rebuild them. My first car was a 1969 Barracuda that he had refurbished.

When I was a kid, there was no one in our family who was a cop except for my mom's dad, who died ten years before I was born, so I really didn't know any cops. I just knew I wanted to be one.

My parents stayed together for twenty-eight years, but after both my brother and I moved out of the house, my dad filed for divorce. He was miserable in the marriage but he stayed there for us because he didn't want anyone else raising his sons.

I was aware as a kid that I liked guys but I fought it pretty hard. Like I said, I was raised Southern Baptist, and there was a time I thought I was possessed by a demon because that's what they told us to believe in church. I spent a lot of time praying and praying and praying until I finally realized that that was just horseshit.

During my adolescent years I stayed to myself quite a bit, because I always thought something was really wrong with me and I was always embarrassed about it. I dated girls in high school and ended up marrying one of my high school girlfriends. When I met my wife I didn't have a physical love for her but it was emotional, and I thought, "Well this is a start…" When I actually felt something for her I thought, "Maybe this is what it's supposed to be." My parents were very supportive because we were dating for a long time, and we got married when we were twenty-one. I don't think Dad ever really liked her much, because even back then she was just real controlling and liked a lot of drama. I stayed with her until I was about twenty-three or twenty-four, and the first time I ever said "I think I'm gay" out loud was to her. I had never acted on it either. We talked about it for a good six months. She asked, "Are you about to leave me?" And I said, "Well I don't want to cheat on you." She said, "Well why don't you go try it?" Of course I did, and I told her, "There's no question…" We'd had my son by then, and she said, "Well I don't divorce," and I said, "I don't either." Then she said, "Well why don't you get it on the side and come back home…" So we tried that for a bit, and that just didn't work either. She and I stayed together for three years, and I finally asked her for a divorce before we killed each other. She agreed. We stayed friends for a good long time until she married somebody with a cocaine problem who was also abusive. I have full custody of my son now.

Over the years my dad would make jokes about gay people, and he was pretty racist and bigoted too. We've talked about it many times since, and he's said, "It's just the way I was raised." Ever since I came out, his mind has done a complete turn-around on a number of things. There is still a lot that needs work, but he has make progress for sure. I remember back in high school we were going through my yearbook, and there was an interracial couple there. He said, "What the hell is this?" I said, "Well that's so-and-so and so-and-so. They've been a couple for about two years." He said, "Do you and your friends approve of this?" I said, "It doesn't matter if we do or not." He's like, "Well I guess you need to move up north and live with some damn Yankees that think that way." I thought, "I can never talk to you about anything…" The whole family—a good bit of them—were that way; they grew up in Alabama during the sixties and had a different mindset from my generation of Alabamians. The people my age are just not that way, the majority of us anyway.

I came out to my mom before my dad. She didn't know and didn't have a clue. I went in late to work and asked her to come to the house. Me and my wife had had a pretty big fight, and it was probably the most depressed

I had ever been, ever. I thought, "I'm fixin' to lose my family. I'm fixin' to lose my son. I'm fixin' to lose my job..." I thought for sure my police department would fire me because they treated gay people like shit, and it was a small town. There were only forty of us in the PD. Of course when I came out to my mom, she did the whole, "You're going to hell..." Her exact words were, "You need to lie to your wife and pretend to be happy for her, for the sake of your son..."

I almost killed myself that night. She had told me never to tell my dad, that he would disown me and kill himself, and blame her. Shit like that. So I was very depressed when I left for work. I thought, "You know, if I wreck my car to the point where I can die from it, then my son can go to college for free, and none of this ever has to happen. It'll go no further than this..." I went so far as to drive my car up to 110-115 miles per hour and got on the radio and said on the speaker that I was turning around and gave my location. I'd picked out a metal telephone pole that I knew I wouldn't win against and had my seat belt off. But there was a picture of my son on the dashboard, and I looked at it and thought, "I can't do this. I have to be around for him." So I didn't do it and I thought, "I'll just take whatever comes to me. If I have to live in a damn cardboard box, then so be it."

Of course my mom had made me promise not to tell dad, and the way he talked and joked and said things, I thought not telling him was probably for the best. Well about a year later folks in town started finding out about me, because it's a small town. One of my friends who was a police officer got in a fight in line at the grocery store, because there was somebody in front of him in line talking about me. I didn't even know these people and I thought, "I'd better go tell Dad before this same thing happens..."

When I went to my dad's place I thought, "This will probably be the last time that we speak..." I was prepared for that actually. When I sat down on the hearth to tell him, it was small talk at first. He asked me how my son was, and I said, "He's good. But things are about to change drastically," and he looked at me. He was sitting on the couch eating a bowl of chili off a TV tray. I said, "You know how I used to stay up in my room all the time and didn't come out much?" He said, "Yeah." I said, "It was because I was always fighting something, and I just can't fight it any more. I'm gay." I started trembling a little bit when I said it and I couldn't tell what was going on in his head when I said it. So when he stood up, I was bracing myself for a punch. And I told myself, "Alright, you take one punch but that's it. Then you walk out…" But he didn't do that. He came over and hugged me, and as I said before, I can think of five times in my life he'd ever done that. He had never kissed me and he kissed my cheek. First time ever in my life. He was just super supportive. The first words out of his mouth were, "I love you." He told me he was shocked. He said, "And I'm terribly sorry about everything I've ever said, because I promise you I had no idea you were gay, and if I had ever known I never would have said those things." We spent about an hour and a half, two hours talking. He even asked me, "Are you dating anybody?" I said, "Yeah," and he said, "Well I'd like to meet this person. I want to be part of your life and I don't want anything at all to change. I want you to be happy." He was awesome about it. One hundred percent. He considers my now-husband his other son.

Then he said something that stuck with me for a long time; he said, "Do your friends at work know?" I said, "No, they don't. I'm not going to lie. If they ask me, I'm going to tell them." He said, "Well you'd better go tell them because I didn't raise a liar." I was like, "Damn it!" So I went and told my six best friends, and of course the entire department knew after that. There were a few people who were standoffish at first. It took maybe six months and then it was just not even an issue. They started treating gay people much, much better, and I was told later it was because gays were an unknown to them. Once I came out it put a face on it, and it was a face they liked, so then they were like, "I could never mistreat a gay person now, because Danny is gay."

After I came out to my dad, it made me feel horrible about the way I had thought of him: I had basically misread him my entire life. He was not somebody who ever talked about his feelings or emotions. He's much different now. He'll talk freely about things, and he's a hugger now too. He'll hug you goodbye. My brother is great too. He loves my husband. I think he likes him more than he likes me!

I'd always wanted to be a father. There was a time when me and Tammy were eighteen, and she missed her period and she was scared to death that she was pregnant. I wasn't scared; I was happy as hell. I thought, "Good!" But she wasn't, and it wasn't until we were twenty-three that our son was born.

Everyone wants to be a better parent than their parents were. I think that where I'm weak as a parent, my dad was very strong and vice versa. I don't think my son is afraid to tell me anything, which was my problem as a kid. I learned well from my dad to be at home when I'm not at work. There are a lot of guys out there who want to attend all these parties and whatnot; I care nothing about that. I've always been a parent, ever since I came out. My husband asked me, "What are you going to do when Tanner leaves the house?" I said, "I don't know. I guess whatever we want to do." I don't know because I've never had that freedom before. At the same time I'm happy that I don't because I wouldn't trade it for the world.

When I was growing up, my dad was very into discipline. When I got too old for whippin's, my dad went and got boxing gloves. That's how he'd punish us, and my brother and I actually learned to fight that way. But he knocked me out twice prior to my turning sixteen. A lot of people look at that like that's extreme, but it really wasn't. Growing up here... You think about bullies, and I became a cop. You go up against people all the time and you can't be scared of them. So after the first time you get punched in the face, you're not going to be scared of it anymore. And when me and my brother would start fighting, Dad would make us stop and put on the gloves and fight that way, and of course the winner had to fight him! But you learn, and he didn't go full throttle on us. It was nothing like that, and actually you had a chance. It wasn't like a whipping, where you sit there and take the pain; you had a chance to dish some pain back out. You learn to fight and defend yourself and protect yourself. Most people wouldn't appreciate that, but I did. Still, I'm not going to do that to my son.

My dad's work ethic is amazing. He can start from the bottom and work his way to the top and he's done that actually a couple of times. Because when he left that secure job as president with a six-figure income to start his own business, it didn't work out, and he had to start all over again and he did. He always does amazingly because he has this drive to do well. He has very good morals, though they're not the same as mine. I don't fault him for any of his. He always tries to do right by people. He's always had little words of wisdom, just good things to say to people. He always seems to say the right thing at the right moment, and has done that throughout my entire life actually.

I would like to be my own boss, which is why my husband and I started our own business. I'm very much into law and order obviously. I love my family. I had a really good family life as a kid, which I guess is why I wanted a child of my own. My dad owns a business, and my husband and I own a business, and we constantly discuss that. He talks about his trial and error, and I talk about my trial and error…

Early in the year one time he asked me what my favorite pistol was. 'Course I had this old cheap thing I carried when I was with the sheriff's office, and for Christmas one year we were all at the house and opened our Christmas presents. Stockings usually just had candy in 'em, but he had put a new Glock in it, and that was a total surprise. We're a typical Southern family, where you're taught to shoot at an early age.

My definition of a man is probably not what a lot of other people's definitions are. You should help out with your partner's chores. There is no "this is a woman's duty…" and "this is a man's duty…" I never had that in my mind, and I think me and my dad are a lot different there.

I wish I had been honest with my dad sooner, but who knows what the outcome would have been? Still, the way it worked out, it worked out good for both of us. I've always been honest with him since.

Chapter 7
Luke McAvoy

Luke lives in southeastern Wisconsin, where he was recently promoted to Dean of Students at the high school where he works.

I was born in Lake Forest, Illinois in 1992 but grew up for most of my childhood in Bloomington, Illinois, which I call home. I have an oldest sister, an older brother, and I have a fraternal twin brother named Kyle. My dad has been a salesman for most of his adult life for either Koops Mustard—it's fantastic stuff—and then he had a brief stint with Cisco Systems, which brought us down to Bloomington. But he's since gone back to Koops.

My dad loves turtles. There's this one road near Bloomington he always calls Turtle Alley. It's between two swamps, so a lot of turtles would get up and try to walk across the road to the other swamp and some would make it and some would not. I always remember that whenever he saw one, we would stop and he'd always pick it up and let us pet it or whatever and then he'd walk it across the street. So one of my earliest memories is doing that. My dad had four pet turtles he kept in his office. I forget the variety, but they were just little things and he had those for a long time. They were more of a nuisance for me and my brother because we would always end up having to clean out the tank. Those were our only pets while growing up actually. They didn't have names and we honestly couldn't tell them apart. They were these four Louisiana Red Striped Turtles or something like that and they were all probably no bigger that three inches in diameter and they all looked the same. If you go into my dad's office these days, there are probably thirty or forty different figurines of turtles. I actually don't know why he likes them. I don't think I've ever asked so maybe there's a story I need to unearth!

We're a big football family. My dad was a quarterback at U of I. My older brother was a lineman at Michigan, and both Kyle and I were linemen at Minnesota. So we were the quintessential father and son playing catch in the front yard with him teaching us how to throw a football and things like that. We did a lot of outdoor things and the family would go camping every now and then. So I definitely had the traditional American upbringing.

My dad is a compassionate person. He's affectionate. He has the hard-line father aspect too, but there's never been an issue I couldn't go to him with. He's always just been there. My dad worked a lot in my early childhood, and we probably didn't get really close until I was in high school, with football recruiting when he'd go on trips with us. These would be long road trips, and we got really close through that. But before that, during the week he was just mostly working while we were doing school stuff and sports, so there wasn't too much daily interaction. We'd all sit down for dinner for that half hour and talk, but that was about it. My dad treated all us boys the same. I think he had a special spot for my older sister, she being the only girl. Both parents play the "You're all my favorites" card, but I think she's probably his favorite, though he doesn't treat any of us any differently.

I do think I'm my mom's favorite son. That's a claim we all battle for, but I think I actually am. I'm the biggest mama's boy in the family, so I think that rubbed off on her. I was attached to her hip until probably eighth grade and even today I'm not ashamed of being a mama's boy. I talk to my mom just about every day. My father and I might miss a day here and there but basically I talk to each of them every day.

It was most always the three of us—me, Kyle and my dad—doing things together. It was rarely just Kyle or I. Probably the thing that we did the most was that we started a garden when we moved to Bloomington, and that was kind of me and my dad's thing for many a year. Every Saturday we were out there picking weeds and doing whatever was needed. It was a pretty decent size garden, probably twenty feet by fifteen feet, and was a vegetable garden mostly. We lived in an older Victorian house so we were always working on something and fixing this or that. We had a few rental houses which my dad owned that we were always working on too, so a lot of our father-son bonding was work related, which has really benefited me as an adult. It's funny that fixing things these days is getting things done that I need to get done but it's also recreation for me. I definitely learned a lot of work ethic from those experiences, that before you get to do what you want to do you often have to do what you need to do. There were a lot of weekends my brother and I spent working with him on different things, but there was always fun mixed in. My dad taught me a lot about how to be handy, and if I didn't know how to fix something, he taught me how to figure out how to. At the time I didn't realize he was teaching me self-reliance but, looking back, I think that's what it was.

My dad is a storyteller. He has probably seven great stories that he tells whenever he gets a chance. And because he tells them so often, me and Kyle especially can tell him his stories. We spend a lot of time teasing each other and poking fun.

The birds and the bees talk was left to my mother. That one shifted to her, and she told me and Kyle together. It was never like one sit-down talk. I do have an older brother—five years older—and so I got a lot of second hand knowledge from him too. But Mom's birds and the bees talk was, "I don't really care what you do as long as you do two things: You wrap it up and you know where your shit goes. If that's what you guys choose to do, I just want you to do it safe, and if you're embarrassed to buy any of the stuff you need to buy, ask me and I will do it for you." That talk I think we got in the car on the way to football practice. It was an impromptu thing. We have a pretty open family. I don't know how many other people have that kind of relationship with their mom, but I did. Overall I was a lot closer to her.

I felt different as a kid but I didn't know what it was. In sixth grade I was aware that my friends who were boys were kind of good-looking and I started figuring it out then. But I still don't know where I got the idea that I couldn't talk about that—where that came from exactly—because we were a family that talked about *everything*. I'm not sure why this was the one thing that was off-limits for me. As I've thought about it more I think a lot of it was being around the friends I was around—that middle school joking around about gay anything—but also shaming it at the same time. And then football with its hyper-masculinity and coaches always referring to our girlfriends… Just internalizing all of that I guess is what made it off-limits to me. I'm still not exactly sure why it took me so long to really bring it up, since our family talked pretty openly about everything. With my dad, I don't think it was until gay marriage was up for a vote in Minnesota and I was talking with him that we ever talked about anything gay-related. I was in college then, and his basic attitude about it was, "If it makes people happy, why stop them from being happy?"

About a week before starting my senior year of high school I came out to my mom. I had finally figured out in the middle of freshman year, "OK, I'm gay. This is what this is…" Since that year I had always been playing this "OK, I have to tell someone, so who am I going to tell" game. Finally going into my senior year I just couldn't put it off any longer. She and I were in the car going to Los Trios for lunch, and I said it. We talked briefly, and it kind of put the kabosh on the lunch plans because I was in no state after our talk to be seen in public. She had no inkling. What she said to me was one of the best and worst pieces of advice I've ever received: "Hide it. Whatever you do, hide it." I was crushed. I don't think I've ever cried as hard as I did that week.

Five days after I told her, my mom had the first of seven strokes she had over the next three months. After that my focus wasn't so much on that part of my life anymore; I thought if I ignored it long enough my being gay would go away. My focus was more on family and on taking care of what needed to be taken care of. My mom is in an assisted living place today. The right size of her body is paralyzed and her memory comes and goes. I go and see her most every Saturday. She's doing well though.

If you can call dating a few girls for a month in high school dating, I dated. I was Prom King my senior year. In college I dated a few times. After that I realized that while I wasn't getting attached, the girls were getting attached to me and then when we'd break up they were brokenhearted about it. So I thought, "Why am I doing this to somebody? Just so I can hide this?"

I keep a journal on and off and every year around New Years I'd have this same old journal entry: "This is the year I'm going to tell somebody. I'm finally going to do it," and I'd always break that promise to myself. In my junior year of college Michael Sam came out and gay marriage passed in Minnesota, and I just finally couldn't keep it a secret anymore. Football has been such an incredible part of my life since the beginning, and I considered, "OK. It's either I tell someone or I'm going to quit college football because obviously I can't do both." How wrong I was about that.

I'd gotten really close with two of my football teammates that year, and we hung out whenever we were free. I would also hang out with my twin brother. It maybe sounds cold or callous, but I knew that if they rejected me they respected me enough not to tell somebody else, and it wouldn't be like I was losing my brother or a family member. It would just be two friends of mine, who are now two of my best friends. My coming out to them was a very planned thing. The night Michael Sam came out I texted them saying, "Hey, can we talk?" This was right around the time between the end of the season and the beginning of winter workouts, so they kind of thought it was about that. It turned out to be two days before the three of us could finally sit down and talk. We got in my car and drove down to the River Flats, and I had this whole spiel prepared in my head but I didn't end up sticking to the script at all. I just panicked—God, did I panic—and said, "However this goes, I trust you guys to keep this between you..." I don't think I've ever struggled to say words as much as I did those, where you're trying to say it but you just can't... I just sat there dumbfounded, and they were both looking at me. Finally my one buddy who's very blunt says, "Just spit it out already!" That's why I finally said it. My other buddy said, "I'm proud of you. That takes balls." I started bawling like a little baby. The three of us talked until probably midnight, and then me and my one buddy talked until two a.m. About *everything*.

When you tell somebody a secret like that—something they know is a secret—they want to tell you something private and equally important to them. So I learned a lot about both of them, about things that they had been struggling with. I mean, we were best friends—we talked about pretty much everything—and these were things I had no idea about them. So I learned a lot about them and a lot about myself that night. The three of us are still very close.

It's amazing. I don't know if I'm still not one hundred percent comfortable with being gay yet, because it's only been two years since then, but it's still nerve-wracking to me whenever I have to come out and say it. And I don't know why that is. I think it's all the "what if's." I don't know if I just have a negative bias in my brain but I always imagine bad things happening. I rarely imagine things going well.

I told my whole family, at once, in person, although I had told Kyle the Friday before Spring Break. We were home for Spring Break, and close to the end of the break we all got together for a family dinner. I was telling myself, "OK, do it before dinner…" "OK well, do it during dinner…" "Nope, after dinner…" So after dinner I told them all to sit down and that I had something to tell them. I was still struggling with it; it took me a while to build up the courage to say it. My older brother Tim, being Tim, goes, "What did you do, knock some girl up?" Me and Kyle both almost died laughing. I was really happy he said that because it kind of broke the ice and allowed me to joke around with it: "Oh how wrong you are!" and then I just blurted it out. It went well. My sister said, "Great. Now I have someone to go shopping with…" How wrong she was; I have no fashion sense. My dad said, "It doesn't matter. We still love you." He was crying a little bit when I came out, and my mom was too. It's a weird thing with my mom because her memory comes and goes. If something is not there in front of her every day, she loses it, so I actually have to come out to her all the time, and it goes well every time.

But that was kind of that for the night. Everyone went their separate ways. My dad and I had lunch two days later and we sat down and talked a lot about it. He asked me what I call the classic questions: "When did you know? Why did you take so long to tell us?" We went through that conversation, and he just kept saying, "It doesn't matter. We love you either way. I'm excited for who you bring home." Things like that. I mean he's incredibly supportive. I don't think I could have asked for a better dad or family with all of this. I'm really lucky about that. Since then I think the topic comes up just as much as it would for anyone else talking about their significant others with their father. I haven't dated anyone really significant yet so I haven't brought anyone home for Christmas yet either. We still have to cross that bridge, but I have a feeling it's going to go just as well as everything else has.

I'd like to have kids someday. I've always wanted to be like my dad and I've always wanted to be a dad. I'd like to have four kids. I like our family size and I think six people—two parents with four kids—is a good size. With a big family like that, there's always something going on, and I like being busy.

Every once in a while over the years my dad would surprise us with little things, like showing up at a wrestling meet he'd said he wasn't going to be at. Or "OK, I took the next three days off from work. You guys aren't going to school for a few days, so we're going to do this or that as a family…" We went to Rend Lake one time like that. One day when I came home from school there was an RV trailer in our back yard. My dad went and bought an RV trailer. That was the summer of my freshman year, and we took it out a few times as a family. It was kind of a way for all of us to be together and doing something. The RV was a really good surprise but it became this giant hassle. Our driveway pitched down in a V, so we could never get the RV up the driveway. We had to create these giant six hundred pound ramps to bridge the gap so we could drive it up out of the driveway. Most of the bonding with my dad and me was through doing projects together, and this RV became a big project because we had to make the ramps and then we had to do different things to winterize the RV and all that. It became another one of those projects that we worked on together. But most of my dad's surprises were things like waking up on a Saturday morning—and it doesn't sound like much of a surprise, but I really enjoyed it as a kid and it's one of the things I really miss—and hearing him say, "Hey, we're building a patio this weekend. Get dressed." Doing things like that. I enjoyed those projects a lot.

I have a really ridiculous laugh. Kyle describes it as the sound of a dying whale. I got this laugh from making fun of my dad's laugh, so it's kind of my curse. But it's one of the things that binds us; we both have this really stupid laugh. To me, it's one of the things that is a key part of our relationship. I make fun of a lot of the things my dad does, but I also find myself doing more and more of them! Especially in the last year or so, having graduated college and become more of an adult, it's like every day I see myself taking on mannerisms of his which used to drive me nuts or that I would give him crap about. As a kid, whenever we'd fly anywhere he would talk to everybody on the plane. Being a teenager at the time, it was like, "Dad, just stop it. You're embarrassing me…" Now whenever I'm on a plane I talk to everybody and I've met some really cool people that way. My dad has met some really cool people that way too; he met a captain of a nuclear submarine one time who sent us water from the North Pole. Just the other day I tweeted that I'm becoming more and more like my dad, and my followup tweet was, "And I don't know if that's a good or a bad thing." My dad has Twitter too and he actually re-tweeted the second one. So we had a good laugh about that.

The thing I've learned through various family members who haven't taken my coming out well is that it's better to actually come out and have a genuine negative reaction from people than not to come out and just imagine all the horrible things that might happen if you did. For so long when I thought about coming out to my dad I was sure that, "Oh, he's going to be pissed. He's going to disown me," and all this stuff. And just by having those thoughts it changed how I interacted with him, and those assumptions were totally wrong. If anything, we've become so much closer since I came out. We're able to talk so much more now. So my advice is to just do it because things can get a whole lot better when you do.

And if you want to talk about it YOU have to bring it up. As I've talked about it more with my dad, he told me he'd had his questions about it as I was growing up but he never asked them because he didn't want to put me in an uncomfortable spot. He didn't want to feel like he was forcing me to tell him something that I wasn't ready to admit myself, whatever it was. It wasn't until I brought it up that he finally felt comfortable talking about it with me.

I admire my dad's sense of humor and I wish I could tell stories like he does. I admire his consistency in what he does. Who he is on Monday is who he's going to be every day of the week. I admire how caring he is. I don't think he missed a single football game of mine until I went to college, and that included senior year when he was up in Chicago with my mom when she was in the hospital, and he'd always drive home every Friday to make it to the game on time.

Chapter 8
Jay Larson

Jay lives in Dallas, Texas where he works in real estate. He devotes much of his free time and energy to community events serving the city's diverse LGBT community.

I was born in Sepulpa, Oklahoma in December of 1977. My parents were high school sweethearts, and I was born the year after they graduated. Two years later they had my sister. My mom and dad divorced when my sister was six months old, and my dad left and moved to Dallas. He was and is a very good guitar player. I think he had big aspirations to be a musician, and since the family just tied him down he basically took off. I vaguely remember that he would come to visit, and I'd see him a couple of times a year. These were rare, quick weekend trips. It was dinner and a movie and then I'd go home. It was never really anything substantial. Sometimes it would be long periods of time before I would see him, so the memories are few and far between. He would hug and kiss us when he'd see us and he was affectionate with my sister and me but beyond that it was a call on my birthday or the one or two times a year I'd see him.

When I was a kid, it was just my mom, my sister, and me, so when I was around him I was just so happy to be with him. I worshiped him and I knew he was this good guitar player. He played in a band, and we would sometimes come to Dallas and we'd go listen to him. I just was like, "That's my DAD!" Just this little kid idolizing this guy up on stage playing the guitar. I felt so proud. But then the next day I'd come home and he wasn't there for the everyday stuff, the school, the homework… That was all my mom. So as a kid I had a glamorized version for a while of my dad, not fully comprehending that he was also a deadbeat dad.

My mom's sister is a few years older than my mom. Her husband attempted a few times to take me camping and fishing, but I was miserable. I hated it! I don't know when I knew I was gay but I knew even then as a kid that I hated the outdoorsy stuff. But he did make an effort.

My mom dated a little bit and she did date one guy I remember fairly well. His name was Mike and there for a little while he was part of my life, when I was maybe about seven or eight or nine. He had a huge house. I remember going there and being overwhelmed with how big the place was because we lived in a tiny, little house. He got me all these Legos and Lincoln Logs, and I would spend hours in his living room just building things. So between Mike and my uncle, that was pretty much it in the way of father figures for a while in my life, until my mom remarried.

When I was eleven, my mom went to her ten-year high school reunion and she took my sister and me to it. She grew up and went to high school in Kellysville, an even smaller town outside of Sepulpa, and the reunion was an outdoor picnic. There was this man there and he was talking to my mom a lot, and we all kind of hung out and were walking around. He was just there for the whole afternoon, and I'm thinking, "Who is this guy and why is he talking to my mom all day?" I guess they were reconnecting and then they started dating and he came around a lot. He had been single all his life; he'd never been married or had kids. I remember liking him. My sister and I had been used to the other guy that she had dated, and so here was this new person, but he was very nice to my sister and me. Even when we met his parents and the rest of the family, they were all very sweet and accepting. I remember thinking he was a nice guy though I didn't know at the time that he and my mom were going to be getting married. But we got along. He was great. It didn't seem like they dated very long and then they got married.

Because we really didn't have a dad in our lives, I remember that my sister and I both immediately wanted to start calling him Dad. We wanted someone to call Dad in our lives, and so we pretty much did from the beginning. Step-families can be scary; you just never know. But his parents, his siblings and their kids, who would become our cousins—everyone—

just accepted us. It was never like we were an outsider or were the step-kids. The whole family just took us in.

We moved into a bigger house and we had more space. The day we went to look at the house my sister and I were running and playing in the backyard, and there was this little brick ledge and I tripped and fell and hit my head on the brick and knocked myself out. I remember him carrying me very lovingly inside. He really cared for my sister and me.

When I was growing up, my mom taught me how to ride a bike. She took me to Cub Scout meetings and was struggling as a single mom, and all of a sudden she didn't have to struggle any more. There was someone else to help with the load, and I remember even as a kid being glad to see someone love my mom and want to take care of her and my sister and me. Even as a teenager, at twelve and thirteen I remember being thankful for him.

About the birds and the bees talk, my parents hadn't been married very long then and we had moved to our new home, and I remember my mom coming into my room and handing me a book—basically a cartoon book—and closing the door. I read it and then we never discussed it again. I don't know if my dad was embarrassed and thought it should be my mom's job, but he never talked about it. I also knew at twelve or thirteen that I was different, though I didn't know how exactly. I think gay people always know they're different and maybe struggle with it and fight it—and believe me, I did—but I knew I was different. So that book meant nothing to me.

Once my mom and dad got married, we started going to the Nazarene church in Sepulpa, Sunday morning, Sunday night, Bible study Wednesday night; in our teenage years especially my sister and I were always in church. We were very involved in church activities, retreats, and camps. Interestingly enough though, my dad didn't go to church with us very often, especially when I was a teenager. It wasn't really until I was a little older that he finally started coming to church more often. My dad was always very scientific. He's an engineer and so he's strong in math and science. I think it took a while for him to believe like my mom did, as he's always been very black and white and "I've got to prove it scientifically…"

In my middle teenage years I was kind of nerdy. I had glasses and braces and curly hair and acne so I felt awkward. The kids at church were pretty nice for the most part, and we had a little group of friends. When I was sixteen or seventeen the braces came off, I got contacts, cut my hair back, the acne cleared, so by sophomore year I felt more sure of myself. But junior high sucked, and I was very insecure about myself during that time. I also was insecure because I wasn't into sports and didn't like any of that kind of stuff. I do think that even though my dad was good to me I missed out on that connection because I didn't want to go outside and play sports with him or go hunting or camping or all those classic guy things. I wanted to go to the mall with my mom.

My parents have some acreage and for a while they thought about building a house. On a couple of weekends my dad and I went out to clear some of the land. I'd help him clear the brush, but again, I hated it. I was miserable. I didn't want to be outside clearing brush. Are you kidding me? It was torture!

After all these years of seeing my deadbeat dad, Steve, my stepdad, wanted to adopt my sister and me. I was in between my ninth and tenth grades and I struggled with that because I thought I'd be betraying my real dad. It took me some time but I finally came around. I realized that I have this loving father that I maybe didn't connect with on the traditional guy level, but he loved my sister and me so much that he wanted us to take his name. I finally woke up one day and said, "OK, let's do it," and we did. We went to court and changed our name, and the one thing I'll never forget is that as we finished up at the courthouse—the whole family was there— my Uncle Kent, my dad's younger brother, said, "You know this is just a formality. You guys have always been family." That was just so cool that our dad loved us so much that he wanted us to take his name.

I remember one time my birth dad was in town and wanted to come by and see us but he had his girlfriend of the moment with him. I told him, "I just want to see you. I just want to visit you," but he brought her anyway. I just remember feeling so hurt, and both my mom and my dad were upset because the one thing I asked for—some quality time with my dad—he just ignored and had to bring his new girlfriend along. He had a number of girlfriends; I can't even remember all of their names. I was about twelve or thirteen at the time and I was like, "I just want to spend some time with you, but you have to bring this girl along who I'm never going to see again..." It was those kinds of things which factored into me finally realizing I had no relationship with him, and that it was always all about him.

He signed away his rights because he had to in order for us to be adopted, and he did it without hesitation. He tried to lay a guilt trip on me about, "Well, there's not going to be any more Joneses to carry on the family name now...," yet he still signed away his rights without hesitation. He just didn't really care, and it's his loss.

As a kid I looked more like my birth father. As I've gotten older I hear more and more that I actually look like my mother's father, my grandfather. I have a picture of him in my apartment, and he has the dark eyebrows like I do and the same strong jaw. We have similar features, and people say, "God, you look just like your grandfather!" My mom's even said, "I'm so glad you don't look like your dad anymore," and I'm like, "Yeah, me too!"

I didn't appreciate it at the time but when I was in high school my dad always pushed my sister and me to do better and be more. I struggled with math and science and, being an engineer, sometimes he'd get flustered because he couldn't understand why I couldn't understand those subjects. He'd make me do math flash cards and he'd look at my homework every night: "You didn't do this right. Go back and do it until you get it right." I remember as a kid thinking he was just being mean but when I look back now he really was just pushing me to do well because he wanted me to succeed. He wanted me to go to college and he wanted the best for me.

My stepdad—and I don't even like calling him my stepdad because he's my dad—had gone to college in Stillwater, Oklahoma so I felt I should go there. My uncle had too, and it was like a family thing. I got there and it was at Stillwater that I really started to realize I was gay. I was alone and had my own apartment. Dad had moved me up there with his pickup truck and what little bit of furniture I had. That was the first year OSU had the first gay and lesbian club. I remember walking down the hall and I was going to go to it, thinking, "I need to meet people who are like me..." I heard people inside and I almost opened the door but I got so terrified that I ran off and never went.

When school was over that year I moved back to Sepulpa and decided I didn't want to go back to Stillwater. I hated it. I was miserable and homesick. My mom and dad had at that point adopted my baby brother, literally taking him home from the hospital right after he was born. Regardless of our age difference it was cool to have a brother, and Andrew and I just have this bond. I'd come home most every weekend because I'd want to see him and play with him, and he'd cry when I'd leave on Sundays. Even as a two or three year old my brother knew that if I put on my shoes it meant that I was leaving and he knew I'd be gone for a week or two at a time. We'd have to hide him in another room so I could sneak out the back door. But when I came home that summer from OSU I was really struggling because I was coming to terms with being gay and still feeling that it was wrong due to my religious upbringing. I got a part time job and started working retail.

There were a couple little gay bars in Tulsa, and one night I closed at work and got off around 9:30 and I remember pulling into the parking lot of this bar called The Storm, and there were like two cars in the lot. I had never been in a gay bar and was terrified and I sat in my car for about thirty minutes. I'd see a couple guys going in at a time and I thought, "OK, it's starting to fill up." I got up the courage and walked in. I'd just turned twenty-one so I ordered a drink and I'm shaking in the corner. They're playing dance music and I'm secretly loving it but also scared and I don't know a soul. A few minutes later I heard my name and I turn around and see this guy I was at OSU with. Marc comes up and says, "Jay, what are you doing here?" I said, "Uh, I'm just waiting for a friend. I'm not gay…" He goes, "Yeah you are." I'm like, "Really. I'm waiting for a friend," and he goes, "Dude, it's OK. I'm here too." I go, "Yeah. OK." It was like, "Fine, I'm busted." But I was so scared because it was the first time I had recognized someone there. Later I met this guy Dylan and at the time I thought he was super cute, blond, and tan. I was smitten, and he started to hit on me and asked me out, so we started hanging out.

This was in the late 90's, and there weren't these unlimited cell phone plans then, and my parents paid my cell phone bill. So I started calling this guy all the time, not thinking that his number is going to show up every single time on the bill. I was hanging out less and less with the Bible study group and the church group and all of a sudden I had these friends that my parents didn't know about. I had this girlfriend Sheri I worked with and I was friends with and I'd always say, "I'm going out with Sheri." "I'm going to dinner with Sheri." Going to the movies with Sheri…" I never went out with Sheri but she was a friend and she was my excuse.

What really did it was one night I was out with Dylan dancing at The Storm, and my mom calls my cell phone at around eleven p.m. and says, "You need to come home." I was terrified. I knew they knew. So I come home, and my dad is sitting on the couch and my mom is sitting in his chair by the fireplace. My dad doesn't say anything, and my mom asks me if I'm gay. I think they knew I was struggling long before this confrontation. I kind of wavered back and forth. "Maybe… I don't know…" The only thing my dad said that night was, "Listen if you are, I need you to tell us so we can move on." But my mom took it so hard. She was like, "*NO*. You're not gay. Where did I go wrong? I failed you…" I'm not sure how hard it hit my dad. So I basically lied, and we went upstairs and called it a night.

After reviewing the cell phone bill my mom comes up to my room and she's figured out who this Dylan guy is. She says, "You need to call him and tell him you're not gay and you will never see him again…" I started shaking and I called him and I said, "I'm sorry. I'm not gay and can never talk to you again." He said, "Your mom must be standing right there," and I said, "Yes." Then he goes, "OK," and click. So she turns around and says, "Thank you. We're never talking about this again," and goes downstairs, and I'm sitting there thinking, "I just got shoved back in the closet when I've barely stepped out." So I went into my closet and grabbed the suitcase I had and crammed everything I could into it and I went into the nursery and kissed my little brother goodbye and went into my sister's room and told her I was leaving, and she started crying. She didn't really know what was going on, but I said, "Give me five minutes before you say anything to Mom and Dad." I went down the back steps and walked out the back door and got in my car and FLEW out of there as fast as I could. This was probably around ten p.m. Within minutes my cell phone started to ring—I'm sure my sister couldn't wait and ran downstairs and told them—and I just told them I was going to a friend's house.

I later found out that my dad spent the entire night driving all over town trying to find me. He wanted to make sure I was OK and wanted to bring me home. I don't think he really knew what even happened, but he was worried about me. I hate that I put him through that, but I love that he did that for me. He didn't even know where to go but he was driving around looking for me. I was mad at my mom. A few days later my dad comes up to my job and says, "Look, your mom is devastated. She's not getting out of bed. She's heartbroken. Please come over and see her and talk to her." He just wanted to mend things between all of us. He's really a loving, caring guy. He's strong and quiet and he doesn't say a lot but he's always there for everyone. My mom tells everyone that I ran away from home, but I was twenty-one at the time. I wasn't fifteen. OK, I guess I left with my suitcase in the middle of the night, but I was twenty-one. I was really touched that my dad was scared for me and ran out looking for me.

When I came out later officially at age twenty-two I felt very bitter about the way my family reacted, the way people I grew up with reacted, the way my church reacted. Because their stance seemed so hypocritical to me, I resented church and religion and I basically washed my hands of the whole thing. I was done with it and didn't want any part of it anymore. I'd come home to visit at Christmas or Easter and out of obligation I'd go to church and inside I'd be stewing, like "Get me out of here…" There would be times the pastor would shout out something about homosexuality, and it was all I could do not to storm out, but I didn't want to humiliate my parents.

One of the hardest times was when my mom did an intervention on me. Not too long after I came out she invited me over under the guise of just wanting to get together and talk. Then I get there and the preacher of our church is there and my sister and my aunt and my mom and my dad—all these people were there—to pray it out of me. I was SO angry. My dad didn't say a word. He stood in the back and didn't say one word the entire time. I don't know if he was uncomfortable with it like I was, but the second it was over I bolted. I felt so betrayed. To this day my sister even says, "I can't believe Mom did an intervention." It was horrible.

My mom and I really went through a hard time when I came out.

The rift between us was so great I thought it would never heal. We fought. We'd hang up on each other. It was ugly, and we didn't talk for a while. And I was a momma's boy. Growing up, oh my God, I wouldn't leave her arm, but boy, we had it out several times. Eventually over time we basically agreed to disagree. I wanted to spend time with my brother so I had to come home to visit. I moved in to my apartment and got a job with an insurance company, and then in 2001 they offered me a job in Dallas. I couldn't wait to take it because as far as I was concerned being gay in Tulsa was impossible. I couldn't go anywhere with a guy I was seeing or a friend without seeing someone from church, so the Dallas offer was a godsend.

Once I had moved to Dallas, I found that it was a case of "absence makes the heart grow fonder." I'd come home and see them, and we all wanted to spend time together. There was the elephant in the room that we all knew but we didn't talk about it for a long time. And here seventeen years later I still don't know how my dad feels about my being gay. I just know that deep down he loves me. He cares about me. He worries about me. I come home to visit, and he gives me gas money. I'm like, "Dad, I have a career now. You don't have to give me gas money anymore. I'm not in college…" But I'm uncertain how he feels other than I know that he loves me and I'm thankful for that. There have been times I've wanted to talk about it or say something to him but I think I've been scared to. I'm not afraid of rejection exactly. I just don't want to rock the boat anymore.

My brother is totally fine with it. He and I are close. We're best buds. I tease him and say, "When I get old, you're going to be the one taking care of me." I was nineteen when he was born. I changed his diapers and I'd take him out and about. We go shopping and people say, "Your son is so cute." He'll say, "That's my big brother." I got to do the fun stuff so I feel like I haven't missed out on being a parent because I got to watch this guy grow up.

After I came out I think it was a while before my parents told the family. My partner at the time and I bought a house, and all of a sudden I went from living in an apartment to having a house, and my mom and dad finally felt they couldn't keep it a secret from the grandparents anymore. They came out for me; I was not present for any of those discussions. But ever since my grandfather, who is eighty and old school Methodist, found out I was gay he's been very quiet and reserved with me whenever I've come home to visit. I would get a "hello" and a handshake and "good to see ya." It was like I had suddenly become invisible. This past year my grandmother got cancer and she had a tumor removed and now she's healthy and in remission. I don't know if that changed his perspective or if my grandma—who's never treated me any differently—finally had enough and said, "Be nice to your grandson!" But when I came home for Thanksgiving last year and he hugged me, that was the first time in I don't even remember how long that he's shown me any kind of affection. When they came in the entrance-way and came around the corner into the family room, my brother was standing there, and they hugged him. "Hello Andrew, how are you doin'?" As the last grandkid, they dote on and adore him. Then my grandma hugs me and goes into the kitchen with my mom. So my grandfather goes, "Well hello, Jay!", and he puts his arms out to hug me. I was shocked because it's usually a handshake, so I hug him. Then he goes, "How are you? Good to see you," and I said, "I'm good. How are you?" He goes, "I'm good," and then walks into the kitchen. So I walk into the front living room and I started to tear up. I was choked up because I don't remember the last time he hugged me. I got emotional because it was the first time he had shown me any kind of affection other than a handshake in probably ten years. But I'm thankful that I got that because I always worried that he would die and there always would have been this rift and this awkward silence between us. I hated being treated like an outsider; that's what was so difficult for me and awkward and uncomfortable.

My dad never spoke to me directly about it, but my mom would tell me that my grandfather's treatment of me bothered them. Even when my brother was younger there were a few times where my mom and dad were going to go on vacation and they would say, "Jay's going to babysit," and my grandpa didn't think it was appropriate. But they would basically stand up and defend me. So from what I understand, it bothered my dad though I don't know if he ever confronted my grandpa—his dad—about it. My dad does not share his emotions readily.

My brother noticed also. When I was home for Christmas my brother and I were talking about it and he said it really used to bother him as a kid to see how grandpa would treat me. He'd get a great big hug and a "How are ya?" and I wouldn't. It bothered him because I'm his big brother and he idolized me and wondered, "Why is grandpa so mean to Jay?" He didn't understand why, and it wasn't until Mom and Dad told him I was gay that he knew why grandpa treated me differently.

It's sad when it's your own family. With the outside world you can tune it out or just say, "They're ignorant." When it comes to your own family, that to me was so hard. It's amazing that your own family can put you through so much grief and pain because of their religious beliefs. I still to this day don't understand it.

I'm not angry with my biological dad. If he walked in the room right now I might be taken aback but I'm not angry. I almost don't care. He lives here in Dallas. I've looked up his house on the tax records so I know where he lives and I could find him in five minutes. I just have no desire to see him. He's a total stranger; I haven't seen him in twenty years. There's just nothing there. What used to bother me was the hurt he caused my mom. When I was a kid I was hurt because I didn't see him as much but I also knew there was a lot of pain and anguish he caused my mom. He really tried to make her out to be the bad one and over the years would say bad things about her. I was very close to our grandmother—his mother—but the second our last name changed to Larson, she wrote us off. She stopped speaking to my sister and me. I don't know how a grandmother can stop talking to her grandkids, but she called me and said, "You're betraying our family and so you are no longer a part of our family." I was used to my dad not being there all my life but when my grandmother turned her back on my sister and me because we let Steve adopt us—that, to me, was much more painful than what I'd already been through with him. I was used to his absence so I didn't expect more of him. But her telling me at thirteen years old that she didn't ever want to speak to me again broke my heart.

In 1996-1997 I'd just graduated high school and was still living at home and I come home from work one afternoon and I have a voicemail on my answering machine. I started crying because I hadn't heard from him in a couple years. He said, "Jay, it's your dad. I'm driving Leanne Rhymes to her bus, and she's in Tulsa this week and I want to have lunch with you." So I played the message for my mom, and she said, "It's up to you. What do you want to do?" I said, "I think I want to see him." So I met him for lunch, and he was going to give me tickets for Leanne Rhymes, but I didn't want the tickets. I just wanted to see him. But at that lunch we caught up a bit, though the conversation was just all surface stuff: "Yeah, I just graduated high school and I'm going off to junior college…" At the end of lunch I said, "Look, the ball is in your court. I haven't heard from you in a long time. I'm going to let you make the effort to keep in touch." That's exactly how I left it and then I didn't hear from him again. It was the same old thing he'd always done. So I gave him a chance, and he didn't take it.

I also, in a way, don't want to hurt my dad's feelings. If I called him up and said, "Hey, I'm going to start this new relationship with my birth dad after all these years of the silent treatment…" I almost feel like that would hurt his feelings. Maybe it wouldn't. I don't know. But I don't even want to go there.

Whenever I leave after coming home for a visit, my dad always says, "Good to see you. We miss you. We love you." Every time I leave he gives me cash. When I left at Christmas, he was like, "Here's some gas money…" He gave me $200, and I said, "Dad, I don't need $200 in gas money!" He goes, "Just take it. Just take it." I'm thirty-eight years old and my dad is giving me gas money. Two Christmases ago I remember I was leaving Dallas and driving up to Tulsa for Christmas, and the roads were icy and it was snowing and sleeting and stuff, and my dad texted me. I did a screenshot of it and put it on Facebook and I said, "This is how my dad says he loves me without actually saying I love you… He wrote, "Drive slow. Be safe. Pack a blanket and a flashlight…"—just this list of things I should have in my car with me. That text message was more of an I love you than him saying "I love you." He's always worried about his kids. Even though I'm thirty-eight years old and have my own place and my own career and I can take care of myself, I love that he does that. He does that for my sister and my mom and my brother, but it just means a lot to me when I get those texts. He'll text and say, "Did you check your tire pressure?" It was funny, I do remember one time my car was making a strange noise, and kind of under his breath he goes, "I bet none of your friends know what to do about it…" I laughed because it was like the only time he's ever made a gay joke. Last year I got a promotion at work and became a director, and my dad sent me a text saying, "I'm not surprised. It's about time. We're proud of you and we love you." For being the strong, silent type he doesn't express his emotions often, but when he does you feel it.

The day after Christmas my brother, my brother in law, my nephew and my dad and I went to the 10 a.m. Star Wars show. We were out by 12:30, and I immediately left from the movie theater in Sepulpa and got on Highway 75 to come south. About an hour and a half into the drive my cell phone starts to make the emergency alert sound. I wasn't expecting it and I was startled; I almost swerved off the road because it's so loud. I knew it was dark out and it was raining off and on, and when I rolled down my window I could hear sirens. I was in the middle of nowhere in Oklahoma and not near any town so my dad was the first person I called. I said, "Dad, can you check the radar? I don't know what I'm driving into. I'm scared…" So he stayed on the phone with me and pulled it up and said, "What town are you close to?" and I told him. He goes, "OK, it looks like it should just be going around you. You should be fine." He stayed on the phone with me for a bit. About thirty minutes later he called me back. "OK, where are you at now? What's going on and how are the roads?" Every thirty minutes or so until I got home he was calling and checking on me, and then finally as I got to Texas he said, "You should be fine until you get to Dallas." Other than some rain it was fine and it wasn't until I got to Dallas that the storms hit here.

Whether or not he approves or disapproves of my being gay, at the end of the day I know he loves me. He's never treated me differently. He never treated me like my grandfather did. He never stopped talking to me. I was always welcome in their home and he trusted me to be alone with my little brother. All that stuff, there was never any of that, ever. He's just never stopped loving me. He's a wonderful dad. I feel very blessed.

My relationship with my mom suffered for a long time. A few years ago she wanted to be my friend on Facebook. I told her, "Well, you're going to see pictures of me out with my gay friends. You're going to see brunch with friends and vacations and most of my friends are guys. The majority of people I socialize with are gay." She said, "Oh, I know. I know." I told her, "The first negative comment, whether it's on Facebook or to my face or on the phone or a text, I'm going to either unfriend or block you." I think she very much wants to know what goes on in my life, because for so long I wouldn't tell her. So this is her way of knowing. She has come a long way. When I was home for Christmas, she asked about my new boyfriend and what he does and how we met. So she's taking baby steps. I think it's still hard for her, but we're better now. I feel like I have my family back; I just don't know for sure to what extent a partner of mine will be welcome there. But regardless, I will not be pushed back in the closet again.

My dad and I never talk about it. Honestly, I'm scared to ask because it's like, "What if he really is upset with me?" But then he does all these consistently loving things, and I think, "Maybe not..." It's hard to read him, and I've been too scared to ask because I think deep down I don't want to know. It maybe sounds silly. I'm not his birth son. He adopted my brother Andrew from birth; they took him home from the hospital two days later. He met me as an eleven year old kid. I know he raised me and he loved me, but when I came out he could have very easily pulled away, stopped talking, stopped caring and treated me differently like my grandfather did. He could have but he never did. So in some ways I feel like I already have my answer.

The night they asked me if I was gay he said, "If you are, just tell us so we can move on." But my mom said, "We're not moving on..." So I really think the situation is that they're married and he has to live with her. I get to leave and go back to my apartment, but he lives with her. So I think a lot of it is his agreeing with her because it's easier just to keep the peace and not fight over it. Sometimes I wish I was privy to their private conversations because I really would love to know what he would say to her. But that night—I will never forget it—that's exactly what he said. So it made me feel that he could process it and deal with it and move on, but she couldn't or wouldn't.

You know, when I came out I wanted everyone to just accept me immediately because I had finally come to terms with being gay. But it does not work that way, and you have to be patient. Your dad may surprise you and be accepting. It's taken me all this time to think that my dad is accepting, though I don't know that 100% for sure. The best advice I could give anybody is that you may need to be patient and give them time to come out in the same way that it took you time to come out. And it's not easy to be patient. What I believe, even about my grandfather, is that even if it's hard for family members or they don't show it, at the end of the day they know that I am their son, I am their brother, I am their grandson, and they do still love me. Maybe they don't agree with me and maybe it's difficult for them, so shutting up and pushing me away a little bit is their way of dealing with it. But I choose to believe that they still love me.

Chapter 9
Ron Brunette

Ron works as a chief of design and branding in the confections industry. He lives in Michigan with his husband and their daughter.

I was born in August 1956 in Manchester, New Hampshire and grew up there. It's something of a mill town with a very heavy Catholic population and a lot of French-Canadians. I would call it a blue-collar working class town, similar to Lowell, Massachusetts and a number of other mill towns along the Merrimac River. Manchester is a pretty depressed town economically.

My dad is French-Canadian. His mother was not really that interested in child rearing, so my dad and his brother were sent to Canada, where they spent their growing up years in boarding schools. My dad attended high school there and then joined the Navy. He and my mother met and married and started a family. I'm one of seven kids and the only boy, so we were a large French-Canadian Catholic family. Neither my dad or my mom had a clue as to what "being a family" was. They loved each other and were committed to each other and they loved us, and both of these things we knew all the time. But both my parents had come from pretty dysfunctional family backgrounds. So on the plus side, you had these two people who met, fell in love and married, who—against all odds—wanted to have the family they'd each never had. And on the minus side, they were both clueless, and really didn't have the tools to deal with the challenge that they would have to create a family without any good, healthy role models at all to draw from.

My dad was a dry-cleaner and became a dry-cleaner really by default.

In the 1940's while he was in the Navy, a buddy of his borrowed some money from him and couldn't repay it so he offered my dad a store, and he took it in lieu of payment. My dad and his brother—my uncle—were trying to figure out what to do with this store and they decided to put in a laundromat, so they wouldn't have to be there all the time and could pursue other things, which they did. The place did well, and eventually my dad opened up a dry cleaning plant, and he and my uncle split up their business. Dad was in that business all of his life and worked harder than probably any human being on the planet, and did not make very much money ever. He pretty much always had adjunct jobs: driving a school bus, driving a truck, delivering newspapers to stores.... He worked constantly and was exhausted all the time, which factors into our family dynamic, I am sure.

My dad was physically a very large man, over six feet tall, much taller than I. My recollections of him are that he was a tired, hardworking, big, gregarious guy. In many ways my father was super dad: there was no favor that he wouldn't do, no request from the church or the community or the school or his family that he wouldn't fulfill. He was big, open, and unpretentious to a fault perhaps. That's the upside of my dad.

On the downside, my dad had no safety valve at all. He would bottle things up, and occasionally there would be a rage explosion. My recollection of my dad is always of the things that he would do for us, followed by the things that he would do to us. When he was in a rage he was violent, extremely so. I always found it very difficult to reconcile these "two fathers."

All the kids in our family were born two years apart. It's odd when you have a large family like ours that the oldest child does not really grow up in the same family as the youngest child. I'm right in the middle of the kids so I have the unique perspective of having been the only one in the family who remembers when the oldest and the youngest were living in the house at the same time. My oldest sisters were dating and had boyfriends and were in high school and college, and on the lower end there were dolls and play-dates, and my dad—from a financial standpoint during those years—was in very different places when my first sister was born to when my last sister was born. Society was also changing; this was the late '60s to the early '70s.

My dad didn't really know how to deal with adolescents. He was violent with my older sisters when they reached that age and with me, certainly. Though it seems to me I got pretty much the brunt of his rage, because I think even he was embarrassed about violence against girls. He didn't have that embarrassment factor with me.

It was very odd that the violence was never in response to anything predictable. We were all pretty good kids, but if you got into a fight with somebody at school, and if he was in his right frame of mind he would have looked at you and said, "OK, we have to work this out. What's going on?" He'd be there, so it wasn't about what you did; it was about what frame of mind he was in when he was making the decision about what you did. So, for instance, if you were talking back to him, and it was maybe just slightly inappropriate, if he were in a good frame of mind, that would be a joke, and it would be fine. If he was in a bad frame of mind, that would be cause for violence. In my case, he'd literally kick me around the room, kick me against the wall, throw me down the stairs. He broke my ribs. He broke my nose. It might have been that you were in the next room and perhaps were being a little bit too loud that might set him off, where at a different time you could be as loud as you wanted to be. So you were always on edge all the time because you never know what the rules were; they were ever-changing, and he was the only one who knew what they were.

My dad would take me to the emergency room and would say something like, "Oh, he fell." Now I *was* an accident-prone kid, and it really took therapy in my adult years for me to understand that in some ways my accident-prone nature was likely a cover that I created… I had been in the emergency room for legitimately falling out of trees or for cutting myself—I was an active kid—so I don't know to what extent that was my way of covering for my dad and making it indistinguishable from what might well have been a legitimate accident.

I recall bloody noses that wouldn't stop and having to have my nose cauterized. I remember not being able to take my shirt off because my back was covered with welts from a belt or black and blue marks from being kicked. The violence didn't happen that often—maybe like eight or ten or twelve times my entire life—but it was really bad when it did happen.

When I was in high school, maybe between my freshman and sophomore year, I went through one of these incidents and I actually wrote a letter to my high school guidance counselor. This counselor was a priest, and I wrote a letter to him describing what had happened to me, that my dad had beaten me up and whatever, and when I mailed it to him I was shaking the entire time. I got no response whatever from him. When I got back to high school to start my sophomore year I was called in to see my counselor, and he literally said, "This is a lie. It never happened. I know your father. He's a pillar of the community; he contributes to the church; he's a good family man; he raises money for this school; *and* if it did happen, it doesn't even matter." That was a pretty strong message to get: *There is no haven here.* As I recall, this was an incident which resulted in my not being able to take part in some social event. This counselor was also head of the marching band, which I was in, and I think we had some sort of event scheduled. I remember being incensed that I was having to call and say that I couldn't go to it due to whatever this particular incident with my dad was. I was really angry and I was sick of lying about it.

Oddly, my father's violence also served to make my sisters and me very separate from each other in some ways. We're not at all that way today. We were all hyper-involved in after school activities and working and whatever we needed to do to stay out of the house. I was also able to be alone a lot. I had school friends and whatnot, but it would not be unusual for me to leave school and go downtown and spend hours at the library reading and take the bus home late. I was on the debate team in school and was a good student and was drum major of my band. We were all pretty button-down kids.

Dad didn't specifically tell us he loved us. He was not especially physically demonstrative, and I'm not so sure he felt as comfortable demonstrating affection with me as he did with the girls. But also I think we pretty much removed ourselves from him. By the time I was in my teenage years I just hated him. There was nothing he could do or say that made me happy.

When he started to get violent with one of my younger sisters, we were then of an age where we essentially challenged him and that put a stop to it.

It made it almost impossible for him to continue because he could no longer justify it. He was fearful of what might happen and he was also profoundly embarrassed. That old notion of "that's how you discipline children" just did not hold water. When we challenged him we were terrified, but it was pretty easy because the challenge was, "This will no longer continue because if it does, we're going to tell someone." That's all we had to say, and the look of shock on my dad's face was a profound understanding—for the first time—of what would happen if we were to do that. He got the message: If a child's telling an official can put a stop to it, you cannot continue to hit your own kids and pretend it's socially acceptable, and you are going to lose your family if it continues.

This also changed our relationship to my mom. My dad was never violent with her and was incredibly in love with her for his entire life; they had a romance going on between the two of them which was really a terrific role model. However, we were understanding for the first time that she didn't really understand her own power or perhaps chose not to use it, because she could have put a stop to it in a second. She could have just walked into the room and said, "This isn't going to be happening, because if it does I'm leaving," and my dad would have stopped immediately and for all time. I'm guessing it was more a case of her not understanding her own power. My mom's response when my dad was violent was to start crying and leave the room—just the ultimate in powerlessness.

One of my sisters did say at one point that she had difficulty reconciling her relationship with my dad because she couldn't be grateful for the things he did for her because she was too shocked by the things he did *to* her. I think that really puts it in perspective. It takes a tremendous amount of inner growth to be able to be grateful for what he was and for the gifts he brought to the table when you had to deal with all the baggage that he brought with him as well.

Now he's been dead for fourteen years, and as a fifty-nine year old adult I have some perspective and can see that there truly were a lot of things that my dad was which were incredible and terrific and which showed that he loved me. I was involved in theater and did summer stock, and after my freshman year it was clear to my high school drama teacher that whatever minor theater we were doing at school was just not going to sustain my love for theater. So he got me involved in a college theater program, and because I was much younger and was slight of build, and they were always looking for kids to play kids, I then did six or seven shows a year. Not only did this help create an entirely other life for me—which was terrific—but my dad would pick me up from rehearsals at one or two in the morning on work nights, two or three times a week. I'd call home and say, "Hey, Dad, I'm ready. Can you pick me up?" He'd say, "Sure." He would get out of bed, no complaints. He'd drive there—half-asleep—and he'd pick me up and say, "How was practice?" I'd say, "It was good." He'd say, "OK," and drive me home, then, "Good night." "Good night," and that would be it. That was amazing, and even then it was uncomfortable for me in a way, because this was the same man who beat the crap out of me. But looking back on it, that was just this incredible, giving gesture on his part.

Also, even though my parents were staunch Irish-Catholic, lower middle class, non-college educated, and had very strict ideas about what families were and so on, I could stay out as late as I wanted, as long as they knew what I was doing and where I was. And I'm talking about at age thirteen, fourteen, fifteen years old. My entire crowd from then on was the college group, and my parents saw these kids that I was hanging out with for who they were, which was a really good group of creative people. I think they understood on some level how important this was to me, and they could not have probably contained it even if they had chosen to do so.

By the time I got into my adolescence I was aware that I was very attracted to boys, that I liked their bodies, but I was also having sex with girls even though I wasn't interested in girls in the same way. One time my dad had the birds and the bees talk with me, and I think I had been having sex for at least a year with a girlfriend by the time he chose to do it. It was embarrassing because my dad, true to his nature of not having a clue, sat down in the living room with me with kids traipsing in and out and people going upstairs, and my sister looking over and smirking…. My dad's idea of having the birds and the bees talk was in a public setting. I was profoundly embarrassed, and thankfully his talk was very limited, like, "When a man and a woman love each other very much…" That kind of thing. I was more mortified than I was terrified that he was going to find out that I was already sexually active; I was concerned that he already knew, and that there was another shoe that was going to drop. My dad was not a nuanced person and didn't have a lot of subtlety, but that was the extent of our talk. My mom's job was to talk with my sisters, and his job was to talk with me, and from what my sisters told me, my mother didn't do any better job with them talking about sex than he did with me.

Overall I felt like I had just landed from another planet in my family. I was interested in the arts and I liked to redecorate my room. My dad had no interest in those things and wore black pants, a white shirt, and some sort of patterned tie every day of his life. He used to joke that he got dressed in the dark, but that's actually what he did. He got up long before my mom to go to work and he would literally reach in the closet for the next pair of pants and the next shirt, and since it was always a black pair of pants and a white shirt it was always going to go with the next tie he picked. He didn't understand that one could dress according to a mood, and he ascribed such things to women. He relegated art and beauty and creativity to the feminine. He wasn't expressing that I was feminine, because I wasn't particularly effeminate or anything like that, but his lack of understanding of me was, "What the hell is this? I don't know what this is…" He was smart enough to let me indulge in it, and it was helpful that I had an uncle who was an artist and an educator to indicate that I was at least genetically somehow tied to my family.

When I was a freshman in high school I remember my dad was reading the paper, and there was a left brain/right brain survey in there, and he started taking the survey with me. We answered every single question differently. Every single one! There was one question which was, "If you could own only one chair and you could have a choice of a chair that was beautiful but not especially comfortable to sit in, or a chair that was extremely comfortable but ugly, what would your choice be?" And he read this to me, and I said, "The beautiful chair." He put his newspaper down and said, "I don't understand you at all." And he didn't. He just couldn't figure me out at all.

We were never really close. I left for college, and ironically my parents were not especially supportive of any of us going to college, though we all did. There was a sort of French-Canadian, blue-collar mindset there: "Well, the mills were good enough for me. I don't understand why they wouldn't be good enough for you…" Like, "Do you think you're better than me?" And my dad was trying to build a business—to put a dramatic spin on it—which killed him; he died of multiple myeloma, which in some circles is called the dry cleaners disease. It's like a reverse form of leukemia that attacks white blood cells. Yet my dad really wanted me to go into his business. There wasn't a ghost of a chance that that was going to happen, and he knew it on some level.

I'm a retail designer—that's my career—and for my first really climbing-the-ladder job I became a visual director for the Lord & Taylor Fifth Avenue store in New York City. During that time my dad called me in a sort of a questioning, last-gasp effort and said, "So you're not going to come into the business?" I said, "No, I'm not." He said, "Well, I just wanted to let you know that I can offer you up to $30,000 a year and two weeks vacation paid, as long as you don't take them concurrently." I said, "Dad, I'm making $65,000 a year and I get three weeks vacation now," and my dad was like, "Wow! You should keep that job. That's a good job!" I said, "Yeah, OK." And he had no understanding of what I did, up until the day he died.

I brought home a portfolio one time on a visit, and we were going through it. He's like, "Wait a minute. What do you do? Did you design this dress?" I said, "No, dad. I'm not a dress designer." There was one page which was just portfolios of windows I'd designed on Fifth Avenue. Some of them were award-winning windows—it was a big deal—and there was one that had this huge, massive, Victorian flower arrangement in the window, and he pointed to it and said, "So did you put this arrangement together?" And I actually had because I couldn't find anybody on my staff who really understood what I wanted, and I said, "Yeah, I did that." He said, "Oh, OK." Then a year later I heard him describing my job to an uncle, that I was a florist! So he thought he had finally figured it out. He knew what a florist was.

When I came out to him, he was actually fairly unemotional about it and said something like, "Well, of course, that's what you'd be." I said, "What does that mean?" He said, "It's harder. You went to college, and that was hard. You live in New York City, and that's hard. You're in a career that's very driven, and that's hard. It seems to me that you're always going to choose the harder path." He wasn't approaching my revelation from a moral stance. It was just another example of my being a person he just didn't understand.

We didn't talk much by phone; he wasn't much of a talker. I would visit New Hampshire probably every six months or so and I had started a relationship with my partner. We're now like thirty-two years together. My parents actually came to visit us in New York one time though they didn't stay very long because my dad hated the city.

About six or seven years into our relationship, Alan and I decided to have a commitment ceremony. It wasn't legal to marry back then but it was what we really count as our wedding. We'd saved up for it and we had about a hundred-and-twenty-five people and rented a jazz club and had a minister friend there and wrote a ceremony. We just sent out wedding invitations to everyone, and Dad wrote this terrible letter, a devastating letter, saying no, he wasn't going to be there and he had prayed all his life that this wasn't going to be the life that I was leading. He always loved me and I was always going to be his son and Alan was always welcome at the house, but no, this was not something he believed in or was going to attend. My mom did not attend either, of course, because she wasn't going to attend anything my dad wasn't going to attend, though we found out later that she *grilled* my sisters about what it was like and what we wore and every detail of the affair. She later said that she regretted not going. Alan and I got legally married two years ago in Portsmouth, New Hampshire, and this time not only did she attend but she actually hired a photographer because she was appalled that we hadn't hired one.

When my dad was diagnosed as being terminally ill, he was given about six months to live and he actually lived about two and a half more years and had a fair quality of life for most of that time. He had to receive a transfusion once a month, and then it was once a week, and then it was twice a week, and then it was every day. It was just progressive, and he pretty much made the call to die when he decided he had just had enough. He was at peace with leaving and he didn't want to live like that anymore, so on his last day of life he basically refused a blood transfusion. The doctor said, "You do understand that you'll probably be dead in six to twelve hours," and he said, "Yeah, I get it. But it's really time." My dad had incredible faith; he had a relationship with God and he understood it. It was unshakeable, and he felt secure that, in a very conventional way, there was room for him in heaven. I actually envy his faith. It's just not something that I have in the same way.

He spent the last day of his life calling all of his kids. We were spread out around the country and long-distance, and I'm blubbering while he's telling me, "This is it. Why are you crying? I'm the one who's dying. You're not dying." By that time I'd had years of therapy and was an adult and I had the presence of mind to ask, "Are you afraid, Dad?" He said, "No, not at all. I'm more afraid for you." I said, "What does that mean?" and he said, "Well, I know what's waiting for me and I don't know what's waiting for you." I'm quite certain he wasn't talking about me being gay. Quite certain, actually. What he was talking about was the next thirty years of my life and perhaps my lack of faith or my difference in beliefs. I'm not exactly sure, but the point was that he felt very secure about what was happening for him but he didn't necessarily feel that same security for anybody else who was going to be left on the planet. He also said to me, "If I regret anything I would tell you that I regret caring so much about what other people thought." Since my dad didn't give two cents about what he looked like or about impressing people, I truly think that what he meant was that he wished he hadn't cared so much about judging me in response to what the church told him or what other family members told him. I'm not one hundred percent sure, but I think that's what it was. It was also an invitation to me to not care so much and to live as authentically as possible, even though he didn't understand what that meant for me. That's what I felt, though maybe I'm reading too much into it.

I found a really good therapist in New York and had gone into therapy. I was with her for probably six or seven years. Interestingly I was home for a visit and had decided that I wasn't necessarily going to talk about being in therapy but I wasn't going to hide it either, and I forget what the context was, but it came up in conversation. Now having a therapist would have been as foreign to my parents as having three heads, but my mother said, "You're in therapy?" I said, "Yeah," and she said, "You're not talking about the *family* are you?"

My therapist, over the course of years, had said, "You've got to come to grips with forgiving your dad at some point." I was just angry and I said, "Why should I forgive that bastard?" She said, "Oh, I don't care about him. He's dead. The point is that if you don't figure out a way to forgive him and any damage that he's done, you will continue to be handicapped by it for the rest of your life. He has set up a very effective plan where you will continue to punish yourself, and you will never get free." That was really shocking to me, that when he was done abusing me, I would continue to rehash the abuse myself forever. I was finally able to understand just how much energy hate and anger zap, and I was finally able to forgive him, which was obviously a lot easier after he was dead. The revelation to me was that the forgiveness had nothing to do with any advantage for my dad but it had everything to do with how I was going to approach the rest of my life; that my ability to forgive him was all about and for *me*. I just didn't get that before.

My husband and I adopted a thirteen month old daughter who is now a teenager, and I was talking to my mom fairly recently about hearing myself say something which had my dad's inflection. I said, "Now that I'm a parent I find myself thinking about Dad a lot and I find that I have a conversation with him sometimes." And she said, "Me too!" I said, "Well, my conversations with him seem to go an awful lot better now." And she said, "Mine too!" It was very funny.

I just find that being a parent and going through therapy and going through the years and having the support of my partner, who comes from a very different background, helps me deal with his shit—which is very different from my own—and he can deal with mine, which is very different from his. He didn't go through my family dynamic, and he has his own. I think that has allowed me to understand how very limited my dad was and what little support he got for what he was trying to create. He and my mom were very brave in trying to create something they just didn't have any understanding of; they just knew they wanted a family and a stable marriage and they wanted to contribute to their community. My dad wanted to be a giving person and to be of service. He was involved in every charity and would do free dry-cleaning for any church or synagogue or the Boy Scouts. There were times where he was running more free dry-cleaning than he was running paid dry-cleaning, and that whole life of service was really important to my parents. So coming from the distance of time and therapy and decades together with my husband, I think I was able to really come to grips with my dad by understanding how little he had to work with.

This doesn't by the way excuse any of the abuse. Because, quite frankly, his excuse of "this is the way it's always been done" is bullshit. Whether it was the way it was always done or not, it doesn't matter; it's still wrong. I had uncles and aunts who weren't beating up their kids, and during the same time frame. I even had an aunt who came to me and said that she and my uncle, who has passed away, knew that this was going on but they just felt powerless to do anything about it.

My dad talked rather openly about having the crap beat out of him by the Christian Brothers in Canada as a kid. For the very little time he and his brother were home, there was a belt and it was used. And my dad's brother, my uncle, was my dad on steroids, so I was able to also create some distance by looking at what was going on in my uncle's family, which was the same thing that was going on in my family, but worse. I never got it into my head that I was a bad person and that this was my fault. I always thought that my dad was bonkers about this. I always felt that he was wrong. I knew he was wrong when he was doing it. I knew it was wrong when he was doing it to others. I just didn't put it together that it seemed inevitable that this is what would happen in our family given what he had gone through himself.

One time I was traveling with my thirteen month old daughter and I was totally exhausted and I was holding her and I looked in the mirror and I saw my dad staring out at me. I do look somewhat like my dad. About nine years ago I was seriously ill for a long time and in a hospital. I felt at one point that my dad was present and I felt also that I was being called not to die. I can't really describe it but I recall a feeling similar to getting wrapped in a warm blanket and in my own mind I understood it to be in some way involved with him. It was very definitely a call that "this is not your time yet."

I have a natural affinity for kids. I made a deliberate choice for parenthood, and the deliberateness by which I chose to be a dad is evident in every part of what I do. My dad had all these kids, was financially overwhelmed, was overwhelmed from a time perspective, which certainly factored into a lot of his rage and his inability to be the best of who he was. He was just exhausted, overwhelmed, couldn't financially handle things, and was utterly confused by his children all the time. So my deliberate choice to be a dad was to be financially ready to be a dad, to offer the advantages that go along with that, and to create the kind of stable home-life I would have liked to have had as a kid. My husband's and my relationship is stable and our home-life is stable. There is no violence in our home, and it's not a chaotic home. There's money enough for violin lessons and ballet and summer camp and for college. I tell my daughter that I love her, that I'm crazy about her, and that she is beautiful. I tell her all the truths that I would have loved to have been told when I was a kid. She has a great life, and I have a great life giving her a great life. We travel, and she understands other cultures. We live where we choose to live, not where we landed. I work in a career I chose. I have a lot of choices that I've been able to make that my dad did not get to make.

Chapter 10
Charlie Skinner-Waters

Charlie is a farmer and horseman living in rural Georgia. He and his husband Robbie married in May of 2016.

I was born in Leesburg, Georgia in June of 1979. My parents had four sets of twins, so I have a total of six older brothers and I have a twin sister. My dad was a full time farmer and orchard owner; we had peaches, cherries, apples, and oranges. Each of us kids had our own chores to do around the farm and in the orchard and in the house too. I helped take care of the horses and helped Mom with the chickens. Usually with the cotton or the corn or the strawberries or any of the crops we had, we were always out there to help with pickin' or pulling weeds or fertilizing or plowing. In the orchards it was always making sure they were bug-free or picking things that were ripe. This was a big place, about forty-two hundred acres of land. My parents still live there, though with Dad recently retired due to his health, the farm is all on my brother Jesse now.

I always remember my dad putting me on his lap when he was on the tractor or letting me come out and help him work on a piece of equipment. He took me fishing a lot and showed me safe ways to get around the swamps. The swamps have sinkholes, and if you're not careful you might end up twenty miles down the river. I nearly lost a horse of mine one time in one. My dad showed me where the gators usually keep their nests and how to avoid 'em and how to watch out for rattlesnakes and how to dodge those ugly, tiny lizards too.

Dad would hug us and kiss us on the top of our heads or on our ears, as much as possible. He was always telling us he loved us and always tucking us into bed at night. If there was a storm we'd come crawling into our parents' bed, and he'd always get up and say, "Get in there!" We'd always crawl in and sleep with him. If we ever got hurt, Dad was there taking care of us when Mama wasn't around. He was a pretty cool dad.

I didn't really figure out that I liked boys in a different way until I was about six or seven. When I was about nine, there was this boy I went to school with and I kept thinking, "I want to kiss him…" I was very shy at that age and I never kissed him because he moved away the following summer. When I was about eleven or twelve is when I really broke out of my shell. There was a new kid who moved to town. He was really cute. 'Course I was like, "Oooh, he's cute! I want to kiss him…." I thought, "I gotta talk to Dad about it and see what he thinks." I should have really gone to Mom first, but I went to Dad. He was working on his tractor at the time, and I think he had the alternator out in his hand doing something to it, and I walked up and said, "Dad, can I talk to you in private?" He goes, "Yeah," and chased off Jesse and Randy, and he says, "Well, sit down." I sat down next to him on the hay bale, and he goes, "What's up?" I said, "Dad, I like this boy at school." He kinda looks around and says, "You do, huh?" And I go, "Uh huh." He says, "How do you know you like a boy at school?" I go, "Because I want to kiss him." And Dad goes, "OK. Does the boy know?" I said, "*NOOO!* I'm too shy to tell him." And Dad pops me on the shoulder and goes, "Well, go tell the boy. Quit being shy and just tell him…." And I'm going, "Uh-UH! I'm scared to." So he goes, "Well, I guess we'll just have to go talk to Grandpa about it…" I went, "No!" And he goes, "Yep. C'mon."

Next thing I know he grabs me by the shirt and tosses me in the truck and we drove over to my grandparents and talked to my grandpa about it. We told Grandpa the story, and of course my grandpa goes, "Who's the kid?"

I go, "He's that Reynolds kid. They just moved into town from Atlanta." Grandpa goes, "Well, I don't know them yet." I said, "They just moved here. Nobody knows them yet!" He goes, "Well, we'll just have to find out." I'm going, "*NO!* I don't want to!" Before long we're in the truck and we're driving over there and talking to his parents, and I'm going, "Oh…

GAWD! I'm going to hide..." And the next thing I know the boy and I are dating.

This was right around my tenth birthday. I was sitting there talking with him, trying to get his name and everything, and eventually he just said, "You know, why don't you just come out and say it? I like you." I'm going, "Yeah, I like you too." He goes, "I was kind of hoping I wouldn't have no problems with that in this teeny, tiny town." And I'm like, "They don't especially like it but they don't say nothing because my family's powerful around here and everything." He said, "Cool!" Eventually he reaches over and kisses me on the cheek. And I'm going, "So this means you want to be my boyfriend?" And he said, "Yes. Do you want to be mine?" I said, "Heck yeah!" And we were together up until last summer, when we finally separated after twenty-six years. He and I lived together a long time. His family wasn't too pleased about who he was. They didn't like it. As soon as he was eighteen they told him to get out and don't come back. He still doesn't talk to them.

I actually got the birds and the bees talk from my mama. Mark and I almost got hot and heavy one night, and my dad's eyes just about popped out and he said, "Mama, you need to have a talk with him..." Dad didn't know how to say it, so he just left it up to Mama to do it. I don't recall what she said because I kinda only half-listened. I was probably about thirteen then. Most of the time Mark and I just held each other and kissed.

I've seen my dad cry a couple of times. When Aaron, one of my oldest brothers, was killed in a car accident, I was there when we got the call. I remember Dad hanging the phone up and he just busted out crying. Aaron was around twenty-eight at the time. The second time I saw him cry was a few years after that, when Grandpa passed away.

I admire my dad for his honesty and how he stands up to people, and his integrity about life. He won't give up on things. If it hadn't been for his heart condition, he'd still be working now. He has had a couple of heart attacks, and last January he had a couple of stints put in his heart. He's not the strong man he used to be and he gets tired pretty quick. We tell each other we love each other all the time.

My dad and I have a pretty good relationship. Every time I need to talk to him, he's always been there for me. Every time I get sick, he's usually there. When I had my car accident that nearly took my life, the first person I saw at the hospital was my dad sitting at my side, sleeping. But things have always been really good between us. If I've needed help with something, he's been there to help me with it. Or if I need to ask him a question, if I don't get him right away, he usually calls me back as fast as he can. When my husband-to-be and I bought this place I said, "Dad, I need my horses," And he said, "OK, I'll bring them up and bring you a few trailers that you can haul them around in and such." He's always done what he can to help me. He's a great dad.

When I was twenty-one I had this car wreck and I'd had my fiddle in the car, which I'd had for a very long time. I didn't have the case on me, and the fiddle was in the back seat, and it went flying forward and hit the floor and got a crack down it. I was upset and didn't have the money to replace it. For Christmas that year my dad walked in and goes, "I've got something for you, and you're going to love it..." I went, "What is it?" And he goes, "Here. Open it up..." So I opened it, and right there in front of me was a brand new fiddle.

Like my dad, I'm a country boy and I love to go fishing and hunting. I care a lot about Nature and animals, and he's a lot like that. I look somewhat like him when he was younger, but I hope I don't get that gut he's got!

My advice for other gay men about their fathers is to just be patient. Most of the time they'll come around eventually. Some do and some don't, but you have to give them time to accept it. If a friend of mine's dad hadn't gotten into a car accident and nearly died, my friend probably still wouldn't be talking to his dad. I had to go up there with him one day when he was at the hospital to see his dad, and his dad just looked over at him and smiled and said, "Well, there's my boy!" My buddy just about fell over, and he goes, "Well, yeah. I'm here, Dad..." From that point they just started talking again. Before that, his dad had pretty much disowned him when he found out he was gay. Now they go hang out all the time.

Chapter 11
Bobby Levithan

Bobby was a longtime HIV/AIDS activist who wrote prolifically on living with HIV and other issues related to LGBT culture. I was honored to be able to interview him for this work. Bobby died in May of 2016.

I was born on April 11, 1951 on the island of Manhattan. We moved out to the suburbs when I was two or three months old, so I actually grew up in Englewood, New Jersey, a suburban town. During my entire childhood my dad owned restaurants. Prior to that, even before he'd been in World War Two, he had been a New York City cop, which is a big part of who my father was. I'm the youngest of three sons, and my brothers were four and five years older than me.

When I think back to my earliest memories—it's funny the memory that comes up—I remember my dad lying on the floor, and me standing on his hands and him lifting me up, showing off for people. I was the different child, something I'm sure you've heard many times. My father was a jock. My brothers were jocks. I did not naturally do well in the sports which were important in my family, baseball, football, and basketball. Sports were problematic for me. I hated Little League and I think I was a big disappointment to my father. I spent more time with my mother because my father worked a lot but I wasn't necessarily closer to her. I don't know how old I was but at some point I decided I would be like my father and not like my mother so I resisted my mother quite strongly actually. She was emotional and messy, and my father was together, so I decided I wanted to be together.

Bobby Levithan

Unfortunately for my dad and me there wasn't a lot to really connect on, though I did play sports and we spent time together. I always remember one of my cousins who is two years younger than me saying as an adult that he felt it bordered on child abuse watching my father hit fly balls to me and me being unable to catch them, his more or less making me do this thing that I hated and was so bad at. The amazing thing is that as an adult I've discovered that I'm actually very athletic; I had just been in the wrong sports. I was so nervous about playing sports as a kid that I rarely performed well because of my nervousness.

There were different phases with my father over the years. When I was about fourteen both my brothers had left for college, and I was the only one still at home and during that period I started being his chum. We would go to the racetrack together though we told my mother we were going bowling. So we became very good bowlers in some make-believe world! In ninth or tenth grade I was a starting player on a winning football team, so it was like *finally*, I was doing what I was supposed to do. But a separation of sorts from my father came when I decided to not play football in my junior year. The night before we were supposed to report to football camp, my father came to me and said, "It looks like you're not planning on going," and I said, "I don't think I am…" He started giving me a lecture about what I owed football, and that was a key moment when I realized that I could no longer trust my father, in the sense that he didn't know who I was. So at age sixteen I decided that I was in charge of my life and I was no longer going to be living my life according to what he wanted. That started a very difficult four years with my father. My quitting football was a big embarrassment for him because he was an informal sponsor of the football team and friends with the coaches… I think a lot of people took it as an act of rebellion, like I was doing it to "get" him, which I wasn't.

My father may have been somewhat affectionate when I was young. But at some point, maybe when I was seven years old, we started shaking hands instead. Dad really wasn't warm and huggy, and my mother was even less so, so it was actually kind of a cold upbringing. I did have amazing aunts and uncles and cousins, and that's where I got the affection I needed. I spent a lot of time in other people's houses when I was a kid. I say to people that sometimes we don't get the nurturing we need from the people we think we're supposed to get it from, but what's important is that we get it from *somewhere.*

The most significant event with my father was one I actually did talk to him about before he died, but he just didn't get it. When I was ten years old my oldest brother was on a very successful Babe Ruth league team. They were like number two in the country that year, so we were going everywhere following the team and were in Virginia for the mid-Atlantic conference, which we won. After one of the games there was a bat-boy there who was around twelve and it looked like he was having a panic attack, and there was a bit of a general upset. People were like, "Maybe he's having a heart attack..." It turned out to be this strange experience for me because I got scared and I started to cry a little bit, and my father made me lie down in the grass, face down, in front of everybody. It was one of the most humiliating experiences of my entire life and was a very strong message: YOU DON'T CRY. It told me I couldn't be who I was because it wasn't safe to do so. When I asked him about it many years later, he said, "Well, you were hysterical..." I wasn't hysterical. I just needed to be hugged and told everything was alright. I was really worried that the kid might be sick or dying.

When I went to college my father paid for everything, room and board and tuition, although I had jobs to pay for books and clothes and things. I earned my keep by being a brilliant student; I would get 4.0's all the time. In a sense I was doing my job so well that he couldn't fault me. But there was a weird "freeze" going on between my dad and me that no one would acknowledge, and one day in the middle of my sophomore year I was coming home from college and I arrived at my parent's apartment door at the same moment as one of my brother's best friends, who grew up next door and was like a fourth son in the family. He and I walked in the door together, and my father greeted him but didn't acknowledge me. The friend looked at me and said, "What? What's going on here?" I said, "You *saw* it." It was like the first time I'd ever gotten acknowledgement that this was actually happening.

It led me to a point where, after my sophomore year in college, I went to my father and had a very serious conversation with him. I told him I could no longer take money from him because he disapproved of me so much. That actually was a big turning point in our relationship because he started talking to me about himself and his dreams and his sacrifices and the fact that he didn't do what he wanted to do with his life. My father had a Mensa I.Q. but he quit school at age fourteen. He was the oldest of seven children and he went to work and supported his family. He wanted to make sure his children got a good education, and my brothers and I are all Ivy League educated professionals. He said he actually regretted giving up being a policeman, which he gave up to make money because he had a child at that point. But he told me that day that if I stopped taking money from him that I would be breaking his heart, and I have to admit that I was deeply relieved by that. Part of me was like, "Holy shit, I don't have to go take another job and get loans and do what all my friends are doing to finish college!" But it changed my relationship with my father. I think he respected me after that because he saw I couldn't be bought.

We had a few of those times over the years, moments of vulnerability between us. Once when I was in my late twenties he picked me up after an acting class. I was studying with Stella Adler and I'd had a bad experience that day. She just totally destroyed the girl who was my partner. She didn't destroy me but seeing what she did to the girl was very unpleasant and I was kind of shaken. Somehow that night my father told me one of his biggest secrets. It was a powerful sharing moment.

When I was twenty-six I was dancing for Twyla Tharp in the movie *Hair*. A moment occurred where I got something from my father I didn't know I wanted until I actually received it. I have to give my parents great credit because when I was a performer they came to EVERYTHING. They came to weird downtown locations. They'd come to things when I was naked walking through a forest. They just came to anything. They showed up one day when we were rehearsing in Central Park and they watched the rehearsal. I was dancing professionally at that point with Twyla Tharp and I was making good money in the movie, and that day it just happened to be that Twyla had me doing extremely athletic, gymnastic sorts of things. I was being thrown in the air and landing and rolling and doing all sorts of stuff—most of which didn't end up in the choreography—but that day it was what the rehearsal was. After the rehearsal was over I walked over to my parents, and my father looked at me, and with something very close to awe said, "You're a professional athlete." It was also something of the shock of, "Of all my three sons, that you are the professional athlete is amazing…" But also there was a type of respect, something I had always wanted—an acknowledgment—and I got it.

I came out to him when I was about twenty-five or twenty-six. This was around 1977 and the alumni magazine from the University of Pennsylvania actually had a cover story on coming out. My mother was babysitting for one of my nephews uptown in Manhattan, and I went up to see her and I gave her the magazine and said, "This is something you should read, for obvious reasons. Please share this with my father." This was somewhat cowardly on my part but it was because I had come out to a lot of my family when I was twenty, and the single phrase I heard again and again was, "Oh my God, your *father*…." "Oh, my God. How is Lou going to handle this?" "Oh my God. How are you going to tell *LOU*?" From *everybody*— his siblings, my brothers—everybody was going, "You can't tell you father…" So I listened to them.

My father was working that night at the restaurant, and I went home and about ten or ten thirty the phone rang and I answered it. It was my father. The two things I remember him saying were, "Why did you wait so long to tell us?", and I said, "Well my brothers told me not to do it." He said, "You listened to them? They're a couple of prudes," which cracked me up. So my coming out to him was not a big deal.

I tested positive for HIV in 1984 but I didn't get the results until years later because at the time my doctor said they didn't even know what the test meant. So I didn't even know that I had tested positive for sure. I just knew I had been tested, and my doctor said, "Live as if you're positive. Have safe sex. Have your blood-work done regularly and we'll monitor your immune system." My parents would come and pick me up from groups that I was involved in—The Healing Circle and various things—so I felt like they might have ascertained what was going on. Then I moved out to Santa Fe, and on a visit back to New York I got my records and discovered that

I'd been positive since 1984. So I wrote my parents a letter from Santa Fe telling them the news, and their response was basically, "Well, if anyone can handle this, you can." I got no pity, no fear. Nothing but, "You'll just deal with this." That's pretty much the way my family was about illness and death. Our family motto was "The good die young, but we live forever." There were a number of people in my family who were supposed to have died from some illness or other and then they lived for another thirty more years. So my parents encouraged me to take that point of view which, ironically, is exactly what happened.

I moved back to New York from Santa Fe twenty years ago this month, one of the reasons being that my father had been widowed the year before when my mother died. My immune system had also collapsed and I had almost died from AIDS the prior year, so it was quite a difficult year. I had refused to go on AZT because my gut told me not to and luckily I didn't. I first went on meds when I won a lottery for access to the first workable AIDS cocktail in 1995 and immediately started to have good results. I've been in nearly perfect health ever since.

After moving back to New York I had a good ten years spending time with my father. People were always shocked if it ever came up that my father didn't acknowledge my existence for years at a time and that we had trouble with each other because they thought we had one of the best father/son relationships they'd ever seen. And we did; my father and I had a wonderful relationship in the end. He had been almost forty when I was born and he lived to be nearly ninety-four. In his later years my father and I would have dinner together occasionally and in his last years I would drive out and take him to lunch on Saturdays a lot. But my father was very self-sufficient and he lived on his own until five days before he died. He was unusual for a man of his generation in that he knew how to cook. When my mother was ill and had cancer for a number of years, he took care of her. So he was able to actually be very self-sufficient and take care of himself and wasn't helpless the way a lot of his contemporaries were.

My father was always a little awkward about showing affection. I'd kiss him on the cheek and hug him but it was always a bit awkward. It wasn't natural to him. But I did it anyway. He didn't dislike it, but expressing affection was always just awkward for him.

He'd had a fall. I was out of town leading a workshop, and one of my brothers went up there and had the door broken down and found him. My brother thought he was alright and left him at home, which is what my father wanted. I came home as fast as I could on Saturday evening, and Sunday morning I was going to go out and see him. Sunday morning I called and didn't get him so I hurried over there with my partner and niece and found him dazed and somewhat out of it on the bathroom floor. But he revived and I remember cooking for him while my boyfriend entertained him with my dog. I called the family doctor, and he said I should take him to the Emergency Room, so I did.

Dad was himself, flirting with the girl who was checking him in. My father liked tipping and he wondered if he should tip the orderlies who were pushing him around. They did a brain scan and came down and told my niece and me that he had a brain bleed and that the brain surgeon would be down shortly to talk to us about surgery. I said, "We're not operating." One of the things I always knew about my father was that he did not want anything like that. We left him at the hospital that night because the doctor said he might have a *grand mal* seizure. The next day my brother and my uncle, who flew up from Florida, took him home and stayed with him for the next few days until he died. I did go to visit him during those five days, but he was in dementia and was in a somewhat mean state so he was actually very nasty to me the last time I saw him, which I rarely tell people. It just wasn't him. He was in this state where he was trying to get out of his bed, and I was keeping him in the bed. So I was doing things he didn't want, and I think he was very upset with his powerlessness at that point. He had been the oldest of seven children and was used to having his way.

I miss him. His funeral is actually famous among people who were there. It was a very big funeral, and he was eulogized by my two brothers and me. There was so much laughter that I had people say to me, "It's the best funeral ever. Can I say that?" Someone said, "Would it be weird if I wrote you a thank you note for the funeral?" I remember one of my friends, who is impossible to please, said, "That was amazing and it's exactly what he would have wanted. It was so *him*." We turned it into a real celebration, and, of course, it's easy to have a celebration when somebody dies at ninety four. He had a very full life.

Being parent-less changes things. My family isn't quite the same, because my father was the moral center of the family. Some things in my family have fallen apart that wouldn't have fallen apart if he were still here. I've missed his presence and his influence. I remember on the day he died turning to my boyfriend and saying, "You know we can never break up now because I don't know how I can be with somebody who didn't know my father."

My father is such a part of me, and I've written about him. He's a big presence. People have actually said to me, "You never talk about your mother. You only talk about your father." I re-examined that at one point and I realized I needed to embrace who my mother was in my life as well. Some of my best qualities actually do come from her.

My advice is to give your father a chance to come around. I was very fortunate. I didn't go about life the way my parents wanted me to, except for going to school and getting A's. But once I was happy and had a life that worked, they were totally happy to give up how they thought I should live my life, because they wanted me to be happy and have a life that worked. So if you are fortunate enough to have parents who can let go of their own ego, give them a chance. They often will come around if you keep them in your life. I was fortunate that I had parents who went from disapproval to embracing me as the years went on.

I grew up always thinking that I would have kids. My first job was in a daycare center working with young kids. I LOVED children and I thought I'd have four or five or six of them. Then when I saw how hard that was I gave up that idea. But I always thought I'd have children and in fact when I told my mother I was gay, the first thing she said was, "Oh, you would have been such a wonderful father!" I still considered it but I did drop out of the game due to HIV. It wouldn't be fair to bring a child into the world or adopt a child and then die on them.

With both parents having passed on now, it's strange being parent-less. It changes your place in the world, and if you don't have children it's even harder. I look at my brothers who both still have a parent/child relationship, only now they're on the other side of it. I don't have that. I have something that resembles it with some of my nieces and nephews, although those relationships don't have all the baggage either. Maybe that's why we get along so well.

Chapter 12
Chi Chi La Rue

Larry Paciotti, a.k.a Chi Chi LaRue, is a celebrated drag queen and film director with hundreds of gay porn films to his credit. He divides his time between California and his home state of Minnesota.

I was born in November, 1595 in Hibbing, Minnesota, which is about two hundred miles north of Minneapolis. Bob Dylan was born there. I have a half-sister and a half-brother and am the youngest. My dad was a train engineer for the iron ore industry and worked hauling iron ore. He was Italian and very skinny. When he was thirteen years old he had a fever where he lost all of his hair so he was completely bald all over his body. He didn't have any eyebrows or any hair anywhere else on his body. I remember when I would see him get out of the shower, I always thought he looked like a baby bird and I'd tell him so. He was fine with it. I would play with his bald head like Bugs Bunny did with Elmer Fudd.

When he was young he was very insecure about his alopecia so what he did to counteract that was to excel greatly at sports. He was the star athlete in his school in football, in baseball, in hockey… Everything. He grew up in Hibbing also, in a little section of town called Brooklyn, where all the Italians lived.

My dad swore a lot—in Italian. He liked to golf and wanted us to do a lot of sports together, which I didn't care for. Up until the day he died he had very different ideas about me. When I moved to California and started working directing adult movies and stuff, he just thought that I was working at an adult bookstore. Neither of my parents had ever seen porn so they didn't really know what that was.

My brother was in the military and he was a lot more manly than me. I was a feminine kid. I liked Barbie Dolls, fashion, and Cher, where my brother was more athletic and more masculine. My dad was as supportive of me as he could be and he didn't abuse me or anything like that. I was a heavy child. I was fat, and my dad wanted me to exercise and not be heavy. It's funny how parents don't want you to be heavy yet they want you to eat a lot, and my mother was, of course, an amazing cook. My dad ate a lot and he remained skinny all the time. But I looked to food—still do—as comfort. I had gastric bypass surgery so food can't comfort me now as much as it used to! I dealt with a lot of name calling while growing up. I heard the word fem a lot, since the word fag wasn't really used back in my day. I dealt with fat-shaming also.

We were a very happy, kissy family, and that was an absolutely wonderful part of my growing up because I am still huggy and kissy. Nowadays it may not be politically correct to hug someone or show affection or touch someone—as though you're breaking some kind of boundary—but I'm the kind of person who hugs people when I meet them. Some people don't want to be hugged nowadays and that's fine, but like I said, I grew up in a happy, kissy family. My dad was very affectionate. We'd always say, "I love you" when I'd come to visit and when I'd leave. My sister and I went to a movie yesterday and before we left each other we hugged and kissed and said, "I love you."

I tried golfing with my dad. We had a family cabin and I fished with him. I would go haul rocks with him even though I hated doing it. My dad had a thing about collecting rocks and about pulling stumps out of the ground. He would take this old truck of his and we would go pull stumps out of the middle of the woods. These stumps weren't in anyone's way; he just got a kick out of getting stumps out of the ground. Then he would chop them up and we would use it as firewood at the cabin. But he just LOVED the challenge. I can't believe that he didn't wreck his truck or that we didn't flip over, but he loved doing stuff like that. He was the kind of guy who, when it snowed, couldn't wait two seconds before he was out shoveling the walk. And he would not only shovel the walk, he would shovel other people's walks. This was not with a snowblower; I'm talking with a shovel. That was my dad. I always admired my dad's work ethic and his love for my mom. Everyone just loved my dad.

I was a mama's boy definitely and I preferred the company of women as a kid. But one thing my dad and I used to do that was a ritual that I used to love was... My mother would have bridge games at the house once a month on a Wednesday. She would set up the living room for the women to play bridge, and then my dad and I would be sequestered to the basement. I was little at the time and I loved those Wednesdays because my dad and I would go downstairs and my mom would give us snacks and we would sit downstairs and watch TV while the women were upstairs playing bridge. I wasn't allowed to go upstairs when they were playing but it was great because we got chocolate covered nuts and Pretzels and little sandwiches, and it was just really cozy and nice. This was something I just really, really, really looked forward to. The women in the bridge club would all take turns hosting it at their houses, and my mom would have it once a month.

When I was about twenty-five my mom asked me one Christmas if I was gay, and I said, "Yes." Her reaction was, "Oh, but you're so cute and the girls like you so much... But I will always love you." Then I had this talk with my mom about being in drag and I brought home a tape so she could see one of my shows. She loved it. She probably told my dad that I was gay. I always felt that certain things don't need to be shared with someone who's not going to understand. It may be more harmful than helpful. Of course my life is an open book, but I did tell my dad that I performed in clubs. When I said that I had my own porn company, he still thought that I worked in a book shop. I don't think he really understood it. He and my mother were both from a different era.

My parents died five years apart at the same time of year, right before Christmas. Christmas was always a big holiday for my family, and so Christmases have been bittersweet since then. I used to go home every Christmas and then once in the summer too. I remember when my dad was up in years that he was very afraid of dying. He would get up in the middle of the night, not wanting to sleep, because he was always afraid that he was going to die in his sleep. Finally my mom had to put him in a home. He once got up from his bed in the nursing home and took off all his clothes and left the nursing home and walked down the street in the dead of winter in Hibbing, Minnesota, walking towards our house. He had dementia and just wasn't all there by that point.

My dad had gotten very sick and I flew home to Minnesota during Christmas. I picked up my nephew and we drove to Hibbing in a horrible blizzard. I really wanted to get home and see him before he went, but it didn't work out that way. The roads were very treacherous, and we didn't make it home before my dad died. I was sad about missing the chance to see him and I cried. But I was at peace about things too. He was eighty-seven.

I miss both of my parents but I don't pine over their deaths. I'm blessed and happy to have had them as parents. As parents they were pretty frickin' great. They were good to me and put up with all my shit and loved me through everything. That's really the best any kid can ask for. You see all these horror stories about kids and what they have to go through just to survive a day. Really awful. But I was fortunate to have such great parents.

If you want to tell your family that you're gay you have to be ready for any kind of response. You can't be mad at them for their response, because that's how they're feeling. Their response may be based on fear, and people are afraid of things they don't understand. So let them have their feelings and process their feelings. It's hard to do but give them time to process. Don't try to convince them of anything. Be happy with yourself and be proud of yourself. Own yourself and what you are. It can be a hard thing for people to understand. I don't think my dad really understood it so I didn't push it on him. My mom understood it and accepted it. She probably would have been happier if I were a doctor instead of a pornographer. But she loved me for everything that I am and I believe that my dad did too.

Chapter 13
Jim Bopp

Jim worked for many years in hotel and restaurant management in St. Louis. He retired and is enjoying the bright sunshine of Arizona.

I was born November 3, 1949 in St. Louis, Missouri. My dad worked for Kirkwood, the town we lived in, for forty-two years. For the bulk of that time he was an operator and then the supervisor of the water purification plant for our town. He also worked for a real estate company. I have one brother, named Randy, who is seven years older.

My overall impression of my dad then and now was of someone who was a hardworking early riser, structured and responsible. When I was young I, like many children do, took everything for granted. "I have a mom and a dad and here we are." I can't say that as a young child I felt any strong love or lack of it; I was just "perking" along.

My dad used to take me fishing with him, which wasn't my favorite thing to do. It was his way of bonding, his understanding of just what a father and son did. Sometimes he would take me with him as he was doing various tasks for the real estate company. He worked early in the morning, like from 6 until 2 pm, for the water company and then did odd jobs, like taking care of For Sale signs in the afternoons until about 6 pm. So after school sometimes or in the summers I'd ride with him occasionally. My father wasn't especially affectionate, which I always kind of chalked up to the sort of rigid, German, get-things-done, responsible type of attitude he adhered to. When he would get together with his siblings though, there seemed to be more affection expressed between them.

I was much closer with my mom. She was like my confidante, and that worked both ways. Our family attended the Missouri Synod Lutheran Church and we would go as often as possible. My mother did not drive because she had epilepsy. It was controlled, but at the time it was not a good idea for her to drive. So in the early years it all depended on my dad's schedule, because sometimes he worked on Sundays. We were very much rooted in the church. My mom enjoyed being there a lot, where I would get fidgety and really didn't get all crazy-excited about it. I was the good little kid, and later on, all through my teens, people would say, "Oh, he'd be a good candidate to go to the seminary!" I always wanted to run in the opposite direction.

Dad was good to me. He was very much the disciplinarian, but at the same time I really think he wanted the best for everyone in the family. And his way of demonstrating that was to be a good provider and proactive about being responsible and to be there when we needed him.

From my earliest recollections I was aware that I was somehow different. It was always present, but I, of course, didn't know how to express it. One day my mom said to him, "You know, it's about time you had that talk with him…" and I piped up and said, "Oh, I already know that stuff." Which I think was a relief to my dad and got him off the hook. He didn't ever pursue it after that. All I knew is what kids hear from interacting with each other, and I had already begun exploring with other boys.

I saw my dad cry when his mother died and when his father died and then a couple of times when my mother was ill. She had a lot of health problems and some emotional problems and more than once attempted suicide. So I saw him cry when he was scared for my brother and me and for himself and he felt the pain of her pain. It was tough. I was not aware of the motivation behind it, but I think one of the ways she thought that her death could look accidental is by falling down stairs, so two or three times in my preteen years she had actually thrown herself down a flight of basement stairs, which caused huge injuries but obviously not her death.

I think one of the toughest times for my dad was the most severe attempt she made. It was August and I was at the local pool with a good friend of mine from the neighborhood and we'd been swimming most of the day. It was about two o'clock, and I got this huge chill, this vacant feeling, just total discomfort. It was a feeling that something was really, really wrong. I didn't know what but I turned to my friend and said, "David, we've got to go. I've got to get home." He was like, "Oh, OK." This was back in the days when kids could hitchhike, and we did. I got home and went in the house and my mother had attempted suicide by trying to cut her throat with a butcher knife. I was totally shocked, and she *begged* me not to get help. She said, "Please don't get help. Just leave me alone. Just let me be…" The weird thing was that I came very near to obeying her because we were so close, but I didn't. I called the police, and they came and the ambulance came. Later my dad came from work. He had been contacted and he wanted to make sure that I was OK. I don't know where my brother was, but my dad was trying to cover a lot of bases at once, to make sure that I would be OK and that he could get to the hospital with my mother. It was a tough time for him. One of my aunts took me home with her to stay with her for the rest of the day, and later that day she said to me about my mom, "It's not the first time…" That's when I put two and two together about the stairs. That was hard.

My mom would deny that she was depressed, because you couldn't have a mental illness. "No, I'm not depressed. They're all wrong…" This went on for years. It was difficult, and my dad plowed through all that. He remained constant for us. There was a time after that attempt where my brother and I would be staying with different relatives, because my mother was hospitalized for a long time. And my dad would come and get us or get me and take us on various outings and things. He really did everything he could, everything he knew to do to make sure we were OK. It's another reason I am grateful to him. What I remember was that he said, "Your mom is sick, and we need to help her. We'll do everything we can to be supportive of her." I don't know that his understanding of her condition was as complete as it would have been in today's world. He just wanted to make sure we were all all right.

There for a time after she got back it was like, "Well don't leave her alone," and I was like, "Oh great…" "When I'm at work you be there…" "Oh, all right." Finally my mom said to me one day, "You know, I'm not going to do that again, and you don't have to feel like you have to babysit me," and I was like, "OK." I wanted to believe it and I mostly did believe it and as time passed I came to 100% believe it. Thankfully she did stabilize over time, and that kind of inclination and behavior subsided and eventually went away.

In my thirties I'd been working with a very skillful psychiatrist and we'd covered a lot of ground. She and I determined that it was necessary and that the time had come to actually come out to my parents. There were tears, and my dad was hurt in his own way that things just weren't what he was used to, that this was dramatically different from the way he had pictured things working out and the way he thought things should go. It was very different from the world my parents grew up in, and I understood that. I told them, "I'm doing this to be honest with you so that we can have a better relationship going forward." That they understood.

Only in later years, after the initial shock of that wore off, was there a great and close bond between my dad and myself. He had done a lot of work internally, and not with any professional help, about just who I was and who I was going to be always, and he came to a lot of acceptance. We were like two different people after that. After my mother passed away I would make a point to call every week and go visit as much as I could. I was living in Kansas City, Missouri, and he was in St. Louis, so I'd go over when I could, and he so looked forward to those meetings and weekends together. We'd have long dinners and sit and talk and go for walks in the neighborhood. Just simple pleasures. He liked to cook and was a good cook too. We just hung out and had a good time and we'd sit and talk like we never really talked when I was young. It was great.

COPD and renal failure were what eventually took him, but he was active and healthy and drove his car until he was ninety-two. When I would go visit and we would do an errand or something, I'd say, "Who's driving?" and he'd say, "Oh, I'll drive." And he was amazing; he drove like a normal person! Then one day he said, "You know, I really shouldn't drive anymore," and he stopped.

For the last six months of his life at the nursing home, I was fortunate that I was in a position where I could come and be there for extended periods, so I'd go and spend the days with him. My brother lived there locally so he could go and check on him every day, which was good. Dad was really pragmatic about the whole process. Only once or twice did he ever say, "Gee, I'd really like to go back to the house and see this or that or do this or that." He just wanted to make certain that things were taken care of, and we assured him that they were. He had done some nice things financially for my brother and myself as far as preparing for the time when he would pass away, so he continued that tradition of wanting everything to be all right for us.

It's tough to watch your dad decline. The last few weeks were really profound in that he knew there was limited time, but he wasn't morose about it. He was grateful for everything that was done for him. I was able to be there for his passing and I'm ever so grateful for that. My brother and I had been there like twenty-four hours beforehand and we would nod off and then check on him... The nurses had said, "If you see that he's flinching, that's a sign of pain, so let us know and we'll come and take care of that." He couldn't speak or act on his own, so once or twice we had to call them. At about 3:00 in the morning, with Randy on one side and me on the other, we became aware that he'd stopped breathing. We looked into each other's eyes and said, "Oh my God. That's it..." We were confused, shocked, and sad all at the same time and we embraced and cried huge tears that dripped all over our father. It was probably the most profound and moving thing that has ever happened to me in my entire life.

When I'm looking at making even some simple decisions, particularly financial ones, I'll think, "OK, what's the right thing to do here?" And I feel his influence, his guidance. I do believe in the afterlife. Probably a week or so before he died one of his sisters and his brother were visiting—my brother Randy and I were there—and the hospice chaplain was there, and my dad was sitting up saying, "Oh, they're all here..." We said, "Yeah Daddy, we're all here. Aunt Em's here..." We went through who was sitting around the room, and he said, "Oh no, no, no. I know that. But *they're* all here..." and he waved his hand around the room. Later the chaplain said it's a very common occurrence for folks who are making their transition to see their loved ones who have passed away, who are there to guide them to the other side, and I totally believe that. My dad is present in my mind and my heart a lot.

I have his chin, his big ears, and his eye structure. I like to have things in good order and in good working condition. My dad was of service to a lot of people outside of our family. I try to do what I can when I see a need.

Something that I see almost every day hanging in my closet is one of his work shirts, just a plain grey, short sleeve, button up the front work shirt from the Water Department. It's a symbol for me of everything that he did all those years to take care of his responsibilities and to be sure that we were OK. And it reminds me to be responsible too, to always try to do the right thing.

Chapter 14
Justin

Justin is the busy father of an energetic and precocious grade school age son. He lives in Denver, where he works in marketing

I was born in September 1981 and grew up in Denver, Colorado. My parents divorced right after I was born. My dad is a radiologist. He moved away to Washington state, while the rest of us were still in Colorado. I remember when I was about four years old, he came into town and took me and my brother and sister to a local amusement park. I vaguely remember riding on the little carousel with him, and then they had a potato sack slide, and I recall we were at the top and he sat down on the sack, and I was supposed to ride with him. But to me he felt like a stranger, so I was refusing to sit in his lap on the sack. Finally they picked me up and sat me down on his lap, and we went down and I realized it was fine. I kind of warmed up to him after that. I remember that night when he took us home he dropped all three of us on the front porch and didn't even knock or ring the doorbell to let Mom know we were home. We were standing there with our ice cream cones crying because we knew he was flying back to Washington. Things remained that way until I was about twelve, and he moved back to Colorado.

My sister is eight years older than I am, so I was ten when she was graduating from high school. Her graduation was probably the only time during those years that I saw him for any increment of time more than a couple of hours. He came to town and stayed for a few days, and we stayed in a hotel with him. His mother—my grandmother—came, and that was really the first big exposure we had to her as well. At one point I was supposed to get in the car with them, and it almost felt like I was at the top of the potato sack slide again. I told my mom that I didn't want to go with them. To me, for all intents and purposes, he was a stranger. I think a lot of people who come from broken homes have a curiosity about their father, but I never really did and I don't know why. I just knew he was gone and that was the way it was. So I didn't have the curiosity to want to get in the car and get to know him at that point. I did later. But when I refused to get in the car as we were being handed off, my mom said, "Look, I've got a graduation party to plan and more family flying in. I cannot take care of you. Go with him. Go see a movie. Have fun." So I did. And those few days were fine.

Being a radiologist, he obviously had a lot more money than my single mom, so he took us to a toy store and we were buying all this Teenage Mutant Ninja Turtle crap, and that broke the ice. I realized, "Hey, I don't have to wait for Christmas to ask for stuff!" But for the most part during my growing up years, my dad's entire side of the family was absent. I remember getting a few birthday cards over the years, but otherwise it was just radio silence, unless I'd hear my mom say something about him, like she was taking him back to court to get child support upped or whatever.

My mom's dad, my grandfather, who we drove to Colorado Springs to see pretty frequently, was the main male role model for me growing up. He's still alive and he just celebrated his ninetieth birthday a couple weekends ago. He's everything you'd think an alpha male born in 1925 should be; he's Roman Catholic, very family focused, very strict, very stern, but also—especially with his grandkids—very loving and very supportive in his own way. He's definitely a strong presence in my life and all of his grandkids' lives.

When I turned twelve I picked up the phone, and my dad said, "I need to talk to your mom." So I handed over the phone, and they had kind of an intense conversation. She said, "He's coming into town next weekend and he wants to take you guys out, but then he said he needs to talk to me about something…" So we spent a week trying to figure out what it was. Then he arrived and sat her down and said, "I've been offered a job about an hour away from you guys. If I move back, what are you going to do to me? Are you going to take me to court? Are you going to make my life hell?" Just very confrontational. But they ended up going ahead with it, so at twelve years of age, my dad was suddenly about forty minutes away in a suburb called Castle Rock. At that point we saw him more, and he did make more of an effort to come to town and to take us places.

We didn't see him every weekend or even probably every month. We were all old enough to decide what level of relationship we wanted to have with him, honestly. He was still a stranger to me really, so I wasn't reaching out by any means but I'd invite him to choir concerts and he'd come. Maybe in summer we'd see him a little bit more, but that wasn't very regular until he divorced his third wife, who was the wife after my mom. That was when I was about fourteen, and we started seeing him more.

He went through a period when he was single, and my older sister had left college and had moved in with him in an apartment. I was very close to my sister and I started spending a lot of time at their apartment with her. In the summertime, I'd go up and spend a month, sleeping on the floor of her bedroom in the apartment. So by proximity I started building a relationship with him slowly.

He's always been very into quarter horses and has bred and owned them, so he got me interested and we started doing some riding together and just taking care of the horses. That's kind of what started things, and I got more interested in the ranch side of his life.

He never had the birds and the bees talk with me. I remember one night we were in the apartment watching TV and it was during Mariah Carey's heyday. We were watching this show, and she was singing *Without You*, and he looks over at me and says, "She's got a nice rack…" I was like: *How the fuck would I know?* I didn't care. I think both my parents knew I was gay but they operated under the assumption that I wasn't, so when we had any conversations about sex or love—any comments—it was all pretty much geared towards that assumption, and I just pretty much backed out. So if there was a comment made about sex, I was like, *Awkward! Danger zone… They're going to figure you out…*" But we never had any in-depth conversations about sex.

He remarried and divorced again—his fourth wife—while I was in high school. We got closer through high school, and I was spending a lot of time with them. So we kept building our relationship, but there was just this noticeable wall with my dad. Even in moments where I was genuinely laughing and having fun, I'd just see something kind of click in him and he would stop and the wall would go up. It was like I was always being kept at an arm's distance.

My dad was such a Wrangler-wearing macho guy who drove pickups but who was also a white-collar physician, so he was always well dressed. I don't know that I ever related to either of those things, the macho part or the wealthy physician. Even during the horse/equine stuff, I would do things the way he would tell me to do them and would think I was doing everything right and was doing a good job, and there was just always this piece of him that had to be critical. One time I thought I did a wonderful job of saddling up a horse, and he came over and looked at it and said. "Is this your first time doing it?" I thought, *Wow...OK....* That was the sort of dynamic between us: There were the moments when he was critical. There were moments when we were just neutral and there were moments when we would genuinely start having fun, and then you'd just see him retreat.

For most of my life, especially up until that point, I felt that if something happened to me and I died, I didn't even think he would shed a tear. I just never felt like he was invested in me. There was always a sadness about him too, but you couldn't figure it out. By the time I was fourteen, he was on his fourth marriage, and it wasn't going well. So everyone kind of knew there was something bigger happening.

I came out at the end of high school, right after I turned eighteen. This was in the days of AOL, and since we weren't super close I just shot him and my step-mom an email that said, "Hope you guys are doing well. The family already knows, so just thought you should know I'm a big 'ol homosexual too. See ya later." It took a few days, but he finally called me and said all the things that parents initially say: *No big deal. We love you. You're always welcome at our house...* This was his fifth wife he was married to at this point, and she was devoutly religious, so I knew it was lip service. I went up to their place a few times after coming out. It was about forty five minutes outside of town, on a beautiful one hundred-sixty acre ranch, and I always loved going up there. But that first time visiting after coming out, there was a visible uneasiness with me being there, like they weren't sure how to talk to me or what to say or if they should hug me... So I picked up on that in a big way and I pretty much completely backed out of the relationship with him because it wasn't a relationship that I really needed to survive. I wanted to focus on the relationships that had a day-to-day impact on my life.

So we just kind of stopped talking, though we would email now and then. A few years later he had thyroid cancer, and I would see him now and then at a niece or nephew's birthday party and we'd pat each other on the back and say, "Hey, how are you doin'?" Nothing in-depth. But when he had the thyroid cancer scare and surgery, I went up and was the only one of his kids who sat there for the surgery and made sure he was OK. So we started talking more.

In 2005 I was with my first long-term partner and was taking a course at the local community college and we were doing some genealogical stuff, a little research on our family to come up with topics to write about. I knew my mom's side of the family very well. I sent him an email asking if he could tell me more information about his grandparents and great-grandparents. And I told him that if he wanted me to come up I'd be happy to, and to just let me know what time would work for him. I shut my computer off and went to sleep and the next morning when I logged on, he'd replied and said, "Here's all this information. I'm really excited that you're getting into it." He had a lot of great info and a hand-drawn family tree from the 1700's going back generation after generation... So he sent all the answers to my questions, and then his last line was, "And, by the way, I'm going to send you another email on an unrelated topic. Talk to you soon." I read that and hopped into the shower with my partner—we would shower together and then go to work—and said, "I'm surprised he replied so fast because he never really prioritized me." So I got dressed and sat down at the computer and read the second email. It said, "I don't really know how to tell you this and I understand if you can't accept me, but I'm transgender. I feel like I'm a woman living in a man's body and I've begun the process to transition. Call me if you want to talk." I always thought that it was ironic that I came out to him via email, and he later returned the favor!

This happened ten years ago, and gender identity disorder was nowhere in the news. My partner was like, "Holy shit!" I called the local equality center, and they gave me a bunch of information on cross-dressers. They didn't even know much about it.

As I sat there in the chair reading it, it just all clicked. I was like, "I get it! For the first time I get my dad…" I just immediately went to a place of putting myself in his shoes, growing up in small town Kansas… My grandparents were farmers, my grandfather was very strict and conservative, my grandmother was very cold and conservative… I just put myself in his shoes, being born in 1949 in small town Kansas, where any sissy boy in the town would just have the shit beat out of him relentlessly. My grandfather drove my dad to be a doctor, to be the best quarterback at football… There was never a time where my dad had a decision about whether he was going to be ultra-masculine or not. In that era there were standards you had to live by to survive, and he was never given that choice. I just thought immediately, "How would I have coped with being gay in that situation?" My own coming out wasn't easy, but if I had been born in an era where I couldn't come out… What if I didn't have that as an option? What kind of life would I have built for myself? You do what you're supposed to; you get married and have 2.5 kids and the white picket fence and you do your best. So the constant depression, the moments when he would laugh and I'd see him pull back, the string of failed marriages, and how I could never get close to him suddenly made more sense to me.

My stepmother at the time was very ultra-religious but still found a way to be warm to me, and I could never figure out why my dad was super-cold to me after I came out. Later he told me, "I was very resentful that you're eighteen years old and coming out and being who you are, and here I'm fifty-seven and have lived a lie my entire life, because I never had that option. You have the courage to do it, and I'm sitting here continuing to lie day to day and thinking of suicide…" But to me it clicked, and his coming out wasn't a big deal to me. It really wasn't. I also realized that it would have made me extremely hypocritical to expect acceptance from the people in my family that I'd fought so hard for, if I couldn't at least be open to my dad's journey.

Justin

A week later he came to town, and my partner left to see a movie, and we just sat in my apartment and had take-out Chinese, and it was the first time we'd had an honest conversation in my entire life. It was really difficult—I'm going to get teary-eyed—but my entire life my dad had this big, bushy mustache, and that first time he walked in after he began his transition, the mustache was gone. And it was at that moment that I realized—as accepting as I wanted to be—that this would be a grieving process as well, because my dad was fading away in front of me, and this new person who was vibrant and warm and funny was emerging, and I loved her. We were building this incredible relationship, but there was just this moment where I realized that the relationship you hope to have with your father—the one that you hear about and you hear friends have—that opportunity would be entirely lost through this transition. I would never have the traditional father-son relationship where my dad was sitting there when I graduate college, next to my mom, even if they hate each other. If I wanted to do the whole big gay wedding thing and be walked down the aisle, I wouldn't have a dad to do that. The realization of how everything was changing was incredibly difficult for me.

We had dinner and it was a great talk and we were really open and honest with each other. Like I said, it was the first real conversation with my dad I'd ever had. We went to hug goodbye, and I felt bra-straps and I froze. I didn't know what to say or what to do. My dad was always the macho cowboy, and I'm standing there hugging him and he's wearing a bra. So we made a joke about it, and I said, "It's not every day you feel your dad's bra," and we laughed it off.

After that we just started building our relationship one day at a time and figuring out what that "new normal" looked like. I knew after that meeting that my role in our family would be to be an advocate for Karen—that's the name she chose. I knew what my sister would go through. I knew my brother wouldn't accept it. I knew my mom would have things to say. So on one hand I was dealing with the loss and the grieving and the sorrow— profound sorrow—for the loss of a relationship you're told you need your entire life, in the context you're told you need it.

My dad came out to everyone, and it went exactly the way I'd expected.

My brother had a lot of anger about it, and has pretty much only called her since when he wanted to. Becoming Karen's champion in the family helped us grow extremely close. Previously my dad and I had a few things in common, and a lot of it—to be honest—was my taking an interest in things he liked, just to get his attention. Post-transition, Karen and I have a shit-ton of things in common: we love the same music, we are attracted to the same men, which is fun, and we can go out and talk about it. So like instantly there are a lot more things for us to bond over, and that relationship very quickly picked up. Part of it was that she needed to have someone in the family who was very accepting and warm and perceptive and who understood and was also an advocate for her in places where she couldn't be herself. Part of it was that we both genuinely needed that connection and that relationship but we just never could get there before because of all those walls my dad had up before.

She transitioned ten years ago, and for the past ten years she's been my rock. She's been my best friend. I'd take a bullet for her; we could not have a better relationship. We have the best relationship I could hope for. Karen's seen me through a lot of different things. I've had relationships end and I moved in with her and she completely took on the mom role where I'd be in bed crying and she'd be doing my laundry and bringing me food. The holidays shifted to where I'd spend more time with her family at the holidays. Mothers Day we celebrate with her as well as my mom, so it's been an interesting journey.

Karen has spoken publicly on gender issues as both a physician and a trans-woman and is a founding member of the National Association for Transgender Rights. She's gone on to do these incredible, world-changing things, and it's been pretty amazing to watch. She's single, and I think that instead of finding solace in a partner, she's just really busied herself in advocacy work.

I always knew I wanted kids. When you grow up gay you think it's probably not a possibility, unless you play straight. I finished high school in '99, and it still wasn't a time when gay people anticipated marriage. I never knew how I would have children but I've always had that paternal drive and have always gravitated towards kids. My sister had two kids when I was in high school, and as soon as I could drive I would spend every weekend taking care of them and spoiling them. So I always knew that being a parent was something I wanted but I didn't know if it would happen.

For myself, part of being a parent is probably the "do-over" effect. When you grew up with an absentee father, you probably go into that situation balls out, like "I'm not going to repeat their mistakes. I'm going to be there for every dance class, for every daycare, every sneeze I'm going to be there with a Kleenex." And I probably helicopter-parented pretty early on; I will own it! But having the childhood I had made it very clear to me how big of a role each parent plays in the child's life. Both parents are necessary.

I had my little boy with my closest female friend, who is a steady part of his life. He spends part of the weekend with her every weekend. She and I co-parent together. My husband Max and I have been together about a year and a half now, and just got married in New York City in March. My son is a very mellow, laid-back child, and he typically calls me Dad. Or if he's pissed off he calls me Justin: "Justin! You're being too loud…"

I saw my father cry once, when my grandmother passed away. It was at the funeral. I was sitting a few rows back, and he was in the front row and for about fifteen seconds he broke down and then immediately recomposed himself. Post-transition, Karen's a big weepy mess. Probably six months ago we were sitting there watching TV and this commercial comes on, and it's so obviously emotional porn—they're pulling on your heartstrings— and I look over, and she's just weeping quietly. I called her recently and told her I won an award at work, which is no big deal, and you could just hear her getting all choked up and she's like, "You are the best son *ever*," and she's bawling her eyes out. At serious stuff she cries. At goofy stuff she cries. So it's been interesting.

When all this happened a decade ago I talked to my mom and I said, "What are your thoughts? How are you handling this?" She goes, "Well, now everyone's going to think I'm a lesbian…" I said, "How do you figure? You've been divorced twenty-five years. I think you're in the clear." It was very uncomfortable for her obviously. I don't think they'll ever be best friends. I recently did get an OK from my mom for a joint Thanksgiving where both of them would attend, where previously she was like, "If she's there, I'm not attending." I think they are finally getting past it. The funny thing is that my bio-mom is incredible and loving as a parent, but as a person she can be a hot mess. I'll tell my friends this sometimes and I crack up, "It's amazing that my only normal parent is my tranny-dad." Karen is the textbook definition of a mother. She's very loving and maternal and always looking out for us, and before you sneeze she'll put a Kleenex up to your nose.

Growing up, I benefited a lot from having my brother, who was almost a father figure to me in my high school years. He's two-and-a-half years older than me but he's always had a "who gives a fuck" attitude. I remember coming home one day after someone had bullied me because I was never one of the guys who ran track and was always in the art classes, and he said, "Why do you care what people think? Do you like who you are?" I was like, "Yeah." He did a good job of getting that message through my head, and I think when I finally came out and said, "This is who I am," I was just kind of middle fingers to the world. I never went back in the closet or expected people would have an issue with it. But I've always felt good about myself.

After Karen transitioned she was doing this gender outreach group, and one of the nights she asked my brother and me to come in and speak to the group and give them the perspective of the family and how they would react to someone coming out and also to give advice. So we sat there, and this group of trans-people was peppering us with questions all across the board, and it's left and right, and we're not even really thinking about the answers. Now my brother has had a very different experience through all this than I have, so his answers were very different than mine. It was good for them to hear, but one of the trans-men just broke down weeping at the end of the night, and it took him a while to get his question out. He said, "My sister has completely cut me off. I don't see my nieces and nephews, and they're my entire life." And, of course, I start crying because my nieces and nephews have been so important to me. Just off the cuff I said, "Just give it time. That's all you can do. When I came out, everyone in my family said the right things at first, but then they *processed*... They started thinking about the future, and for my parents it wasn't about HIV or about promiscuity. It was about wanting the best for your children and planning that for eighteen years, and then in five seconds—even if they have suspicions—you pull the rug out from under them and everything changes. So what I did was to back out of the situation. I was there if they called and was always receptive. I answered questions, even if I found them offensive at first, and I just gave them time to re-set all of that lifetime of plans and dreams they had for me. That was probably the most successful thing I could have done, especially with my mom and sister, because continuing to be in their face about it and demanding acceptance or pushing them out of their comfort zone would have created more friction. I would have just lost them." So I tell people, just give it time. Be receptive. Grow a thick skin. They may say things that they're going to regret for years to come, and they don't mean them, but they're going to say them. So be the bigger person and be patient. It's like parenting!

When I was sixteen my dad bought me a '72 Super Beetle that we were going to fix up together. I have this recurring dream once or twice a year where we're out in front of his house working on the car, and I always wake up and I'm weeping. Those are the moments where I really realize that as grateful as I've been for this journey, it has also involved a lot of loss.

Chapter 15
Jesse Ehrenfeld

A former combat anesthesiologist, Jesse is a professor at Vanderbilt University and a Commander in the U.S. Navy. He is the co-author of Pocket Anesthesia *and other books. Jesse lives with his husband in Nashville, Tennessee.*

I was born in Wilmington, Delaware in April of 1978. My father is a dentist and worked as a dentist all his life until he retired a year ago. As a small child I always remember him coming home at the end of the workday and I remember always being excited to see my dad. I can visualize him pulling into the driveway of the house I grew up in and my older brother and I running around and running out to greet him.

I was close to both of my parents in different ways. I was always interested in science and computers and early on I actually would go in my dad's office with him when I was nine or ten years old. He'd have an emergency—a patient with a toothache on a weekend—and we would go in. Eventually I got old enough that I would assist him and help him out and be his dental assistant when he had one of those cases. He taught me everything about how to hold the suction and how to mix up the materials. I can remember playing with the casting materials for splints and making little molds and miniature sculptures out of it, and him showing me how to do that.

When I was in middle school I started to get involved with computers and I helped him with his computer system at the office. So we had a relationship that was very much centered around my dad teaching me what his work was like, and we spent a lot of time together at the office. I always enjoyed that time that we spent together. For high school I went away to boarding school and on breaks I would come home and go into the office and help out a little bit, and that remained a really a strong foundation for our relationship over the years. My brother was more into sports than I was and mostly enjoyed doing other things. My dad was always telling my brother and I how proud he was when we'd accomplish things, whether it was the computer faire in sixth grade or getting into college or graduating.

My parents had the birds and the bees talk with me together. I don't recall how old I was at the time, but there was definitely a book involved with—probably—some horrific, cartoon type illustrations. I remember that they were there together and my parents have always been pretty open about sex. I remember one time we were driving to Rehoboth Beach when my brother and I were about ten and eight. We were fighting in the back seat and I can remember at one point he was slapping me or I was punching him or something and either he called me gay or I called him gay, as young boys do. And I can distinctly recall my mother stopping us and saying, "You know, if one of you turns out to be gay, it's OK, and I don't want you to call each other that."

My dad's not really an affectionate person, and I also wouldn't describe him as a very talkative person. I was always very close to my mom and was always her baby. I also grew up being sort of bossy. At some point everyone somehow got used to me telling everyone else what to do, even when I was thirteen, fourteen years old, where my brother never took on that role. I guess I'm just someone who likes taking charge of a situation, so if we need to decide where we're going for dinner or where to go for a weekend or, later on, real estate transactions or where we should live or thinking about planning for retirement, I found that I inserted myself into those conversations and drove them much more actively than my brother did.

I didn't come out until my sophomore year in college, when I was nineteen. Prior to that I just really had very little awareness of my sexuality. It wasn't that I was closeted; I didn't date much in high school because I went to boarding school, and that just wasn't part of the culture. In college I started dating in my sophomore year and realized pretty quickly that it didn't feel right to be dating girls, so I came out not long after that.

Telling my parents was a positive experience. It was probably around January when I figured everything out and I decided to tell them the next time I went home. My mom's birthday is on March 1st, so on March 1st we were out having dinner—my college was only forty minutes away—and after we ordered and before the salads arrived I said, "Mom, Dad, I'm gay." My mom's a psychologist and my parents are pretty easygoing people, so I really wasn't nervous about telling them. It wasn't that I had sweaty palms and was worried. I knew it would be OK. I had told my brother a little bit before that, and he didn't believe me, which was actually pretty funny. But he did after I told my parents, and they were very supportive right away. My dad didn't say very much to me that night but I remember that he gave me a big hug, which meant a lot to me. My mom held it together, but I found out later that she cried a lot that night, and not in front of me. Not because she was sad or upset; she was just worried. She didn't want me to not be able to have the life that I wanted: family and kids. The hardest part for my parents was thinking that those things wouldn't happen, and obviously a lot has changed in the last ten, fifteen years, so those things just are no longer really concerns. I'm sure my life would have been very different if I had been straight. I'm not sure if it would have been better. In some ways it probably would have been easier and in some ways it would have been harder.

I knew from an early age that I wanted to be a doctor. I told my dad I didn't want to be a dentist. I think he had high hopes that I'd change my mind, but being a doctor was just always something I wanted to do, and he was always very supportive of that. When I was little and even as I got older he took me along to some of the dental conferences he went to. I always enjoyed learning and being with him and kind of tagging along.

My dad and I have gotten closer as the years have gone on. I went away to college and then medical school and residency and I would visit and we'd talk on the phone a little bit, but I always found myself on the phone talking with my mother more since my dad isn't the talkative type. But I didn't see my parents as much during that ten year period.

I moved to Nashville five years ago and then my brother moved in with me. My mom decided that if we were both here there was no sense in her staying in Delaware, so she moved in. My brother and I bought her an apartment in the same building we were living in, and then my dad came Thursday nights and went back Monday mornings, as he was only working like three and a half days a week. Eventually he retired and they bought another apartment directly across the hall from where my brother and I were living and now my partner and I live; my brother had gotten married and moved out. So my mom is in the upstairs apartment and my dad's in the downstairs apartment and I see them almost every day. I've seen my parents more in the last two years than I've seen them in the last ten and it's been wonderful to be able to have dinner on Friday nights with the whole family and be able to enjoy the kind of time together that I haven't really had since I was thirteen or fourteen years old. It's been a wonderful thing for all of us. I guess it's a pretty unusual arrangement. We tell people all the time, and they're just sort of amazed that it all works and everybody gets along. My dad loves our dog and comes over and sits with her on the couch. It's nice. It's really been great.

My partner Judd and I met at a Fourth of July party in New York. He was still in law school and then after law school he decided to move in with me. We've been together for four years and he's lived with me for two. Both of my parents just adore him. We're all pretty easygoing people. My parents never really argued or fought very much and Judd and I don't really fight or argue very much, so we all have a fairly easygoing temperament. My brother can be a bit hot-tempered sometimes though.

We were all so worried… My dad was a dentist for thirty-some years and worked very hard. He joined a group practice back in the days when dentists didn't do that. They had five dentists and a dozen hygienists… They had thirty people working for them and he was running the group. It was a lot of responsibility and a big practice and was very successful. He dedicated his life to it. We were very worried that when he retired he wouldn't know what to do with himself and he would be bored and lonely, and that hasn't been the case at all. He swims every day. He plays his guitar and has a guitar teacher. He takes photography classes and is always out and about doing something. It's been great to see that transition go so well and smoothly. He loves coming over and telling us what he's been taking pictures of and showing us his work, and I help him on the computer. It's been really nice.

He and my mom haven't slept in the same bed in years. My mom wears C-Pap, and my dad kicks. They cook together upstairs and hang out. They have two separate one-bedroom apartments, so he has his guitars set up and all of his music equipment. He probably has two dozen guitars and has a miniature recording studio set up... He has his space, and she has her space. They eat together and cook together but then they can have their own space too, and it seems to work out well for everybody.

We had another gay Jewish couple and a straight couple and my parents over for dinner. It was a lovely dinner and they were over for a few hours, and then everyone left and Judd and I were cleaning up. I didn't know this, but this young couple who are our age actually went to my dad's apartment, and the guy and my dad played guitar for an hour after they left our apartment.

My dad has been an incredible role model to me. My mom has her doctorate in psychology. She went back to school and got her masters and her doctorate after my brother and I started school. My dad supported her the whole way and made that possible and sacrificed a lot to take care of the family and pay for her to go to school. He made it possible for my brother and me to go to the best schools.

My dad has always been very sure of himself, and I think that rubbed off on me a little bit. We both have the same corny sense of humor, and in all honesty I think I got my values from him, wanting to make a difference in the world and prioritizing my partner, family and education.

In every memory I have of my dad he has a beard. Right around the time of my brother's graduation from law school he shaved it off. I actually don't know why he did it, but he decided to shave it. We all thought it looked awful, and after about six months he let it grow back and then everything went back to normal.

My dad has sort of a funny personality and every now and then he'll say something rather unexpected. As a rule we didn't take a lot of family trips to places because we had the beach house in Rehoboth which we all loved going to, and my parents sacrificed a lot to be able to have that. So instead of going on vacation, that's what we generally did. My brother and I had always wanted to go to Disney World, so as a surprise when I was thirteen, for my bar mitzvah, we went to Disney World. That was kind of my big present. Of course we got up really early and went to the airport and got down there and got to the hotel and checked in... The next morning no one wanted to get out of bed; everyone just wanted to sleep. I'll never forget, my dad said, "God damn it, we came all the way down here. We're going to go see Mickey Fucking Mouse!" It was just one of those moments that we've never let him forget. It certainly wasn't what we were expecting, but it was definitely a classic moment.

Every father and son can—even when difficult—find ways to communicate. It may not be verbal. It may not be through hugs and affection, but there are ways that we can all communicate. It's important to think about how those communication pathways can be cultivated and sustained to help relationships between father and their sons flourish. I've certainly had difficulties in my life and I know that my dad has always been there for me. He's always had his ways of communicating back to me his love and support. I make it a point to tell my dad I love him. He doesn't say I love you back so much and he doesn't hug very much, but whenever I'm flying somewhere he has always given me a hug. Somewhere along the way we got into this routine of him giving me a high-five. That's what we've done for a long time now, though I don't recall where that came from. My mom would always give me a hug and he would give me a high-five.

Chapter 16
Mike Kygar

Mike lives with his longtime partner in Oregon, where he works as a hospital revenue cycle manager.

I was born in May of 1977 in Drain, Oregon, the baby of the seven kids in our family. I was named after Mikey—"Mikey likes it!"—in the Life cereal TV commercials. In the early years my dad was a mechanic working in a gas station. Later he got into trucking and became a truck driver and was a tow truck driver for a while too. When I was a toddler, one of my sisters used to babysit me and would to walk me down the hill to where my dad worked and we would hang out at the gas station for a while. I remember my dad holding me as he would walk around and work on cars.

My brother Steven was in the Army stationed in Tennessee and he had gotten in a bad car accident, so my mother and a few of my siblings flew to Tennessee to go be with him. I was ten at the time, and this was right before my eleventh birthday. My mother decided she wasn't going to fly back because she wanted to see where her mother was born in Kansas so she took the bus back instead. She wanted to be home in time for my birthday but she ended up having a heart attack and died on the bus while she was on her way home.

My dad was the one who told me what happened. I remember being woken up in the middle of the night. My dad came into the room and said, "I need you to come out here…" He left the room, and I got up to see what was going on and walked into the dining room. My dad was on the phone, sitting down, and he was just bawling. I had never seen him cry before. Three of my sisters were standing behind him holding on to him crying too, so I knew something major had happened. After handing the phone to one of my sisters he sat me down on the couch, on his lap, and told me. After that I just shut down and I don't remember much for a couple of weeks after that. That started the big change in my world and in my dad's world.

I was very, very close with my mother. I was close with my dad, but he and I had a very different kind of relationship. My dad has kind of an ornery side to him, which I've picked up as I've gotten older too, but the way he shows his love is to tease and pick on people. So when I was a kid and it was just the two of us, he was always picking on me and teasing me and trying to start little arguments. I think it was all in the spirit of playfulness and I remember that very strongly as a child. But I always felt like I was closer with my mom because my dad was on the road a lot as a truck driver.

The next few years were very rocky for my dad and me. We actually became very close during that time but a lot of our problems started then too. When I look back on it now as an adult I can see what he was going through. He more or less broke down and shut down but still tried to be a good dad to me. I just don't think he knew how to really be a father at that point. We started arguing. During one of those arguments—we were having a disagreement in the car on a drive—he opened up to me and told me that he was really having a hard time with me. He was having a hard time because every time he looked at me he just saw my mother's face and that it was like reliving her loss over again. He said he didn't know how long he could go on reliving her loss and he started making comments about foster care maybe being in my future, which created more of a wedge between us. He just felt I would be better off if someone else took care of me. He apologized then and said, "I kind of treat you certain ways because when I look at you I see your mother so much."

I've got my mom's fair skin and hair color and her eyes. I can remember feeling really angry at him for saying that. I think at that time I had built so much anger towards him because I was blaming him for so many things, only some of which were his fault. Everyone handles grief in a different way, and as a child I felt that he could have handled it a little more responsibly. As a kid I was able to shut down my emotions and I tried to be strong for everyone around me, because all the adults around me were falling apart.

Now I see it differently; I think it's healthy to grieve and as long as people work through it, then that's what is important. But at the time I was angry and I think that just created a bigger wedge between us. My preteen and teen years with him were not good years.

My dad tried. He tried all through my teens. He always put his hand on my shoulder or on my neck and he'd rub the back of my neck and in his own way tried to show his affection. But I had built up a lot of resentment towards him in my teen years and pulled away and didn't reciprocate that affection back towards him. As I've gotten older I've realized that my dad wasn't a bad dad or a good dad; he was just who he was. He's my dad and I love him because he's my dad.

He remarried and married my step-mother the summer before my high school freshman year. They were married for only two or three years. He even told me once that he only married her because he felt like I needed a mom. I think probably because of all the turmoil we were going through in my early teens he was looking for a bandage and thought that she could provide that. I didn't really want a mom. I had a mom. I was fine with him remarrying but just didn't feel that she was the right one. Then she and I did not get along and that's how I ended up in foster care at age fifteen. That was traumatic because for me it was the experience of abandonment all over again. I had lost multiple major figures in my life to death just prior to that time—my mom, grandparents, and an uncle—and now I was just being bounced around from house to house. My dad, my parent, the one who was supposed to be there for me to the end, ended up letting me go to foster care. I harbored a lot of strong emotions and negative feelings toward him for quite some time after that.

When I was in foster care my dad had a couple of serious heart attacks so I went and visited him in the hospital. But we didn't maintain a relationship for a long period of time. Other than when he was in the hospital, we didn't talk for about ten years.

In my early twenties I got reconnected with my aunts, my dad's sisters. They were going to have a Phillips family reunion, so I decided I would go. That was the last time I saw my dad. I was really blown away when I saw him. I always saw my dad as this tall, slender, dark-haired man with dark skin, and when I saw him he was this short, pale, white haired man. By that time I had let go of the anger that I had in my teens. I had resolved myself to the fact that my dad was not in my life at that point and I was fine with him not being there. I figured that I could make a go of it on my own. But it was important for me to forgive and then let go, and so that's what that trip became for me.

We went for a long walk together. He had had a major stroke before then so he couldn't walk real well and he stuttered when he talked and didn't have the use of one arm. But we went for a walk and we just talked and let it all out. He communicated as best he could. I told him I was sorry for everything, and he said he was sorry for everything. We told each other how much we loved each other and how we wished everything had been different. We both let go of a lot of baggage that day and had a great visit. It was an awesome time. Then he went back to Montana, where he had moved several years after we had lost touch.

He wrote me a letter once that I got. I wrote a letter back but never sent it. In the letter he talked a lot about how his life was going in Montana and what he was up to. He wanted to buy me a computer. He felt that it was important that I have a computer because I was a young man and he thought it would be good for my career, whatever that meant. Then ten years ago I got a call one day from my cousin in Montana that my dad had passed away. They said, "You're his next of kin. What would you like done with him?" At that point he had made a whole different life there and I didn't really know him anymore. I didn't have any bad feelings toward him and had nothing but good memories so I said, "What do you think he would want?" They said that he'd gotten really close with their son when their son was alive—he died in a motorcycle accident—and that they were like best friends, so they said he wanted to be buried with their son. I said that was fine. My cousin and I talked for quite a while about his life over there and his relationship with their son. They said that my dad talked about me all the time, that he talked about me constantly. That made me feel good. It was nice to know that he thought about me.

When I got that call I remembered the same familiar feeling I got when my mother died. I just immediately froze emotionally. Everything became surreal, where you can see the world going on but you don't really feel like you're a part of it. It wasn't that I was surprised when he died because I knew his health was so poor. But I was shocked, because it was the end. There was no more. Even though we had made up, there was no possibility of us ever being in each other's lives as a father and son should be.

When we had gone on that walk we hugged each other and gave each other a kiss. My dad was not an unaffectionate guy and he was pretty good with his emotions and feelings. I never ever in my life heard him yell. Even when he and I had hard times and I would raise my voice, he never raised his. He was actually a mild-tempered man who would shut down more than anything. When I was really little and he and my mom would argue, he was always the quiet one sitting there listening.

I think about my dad often. A lot of times when I look in the mirror I see him. I have a big picture of him in my living room along with one of my mom. I have very fond memories of growing up in the Phillips family and have gotten back in touch with some aunts and uncles and cousins on that side and I get to hear stories about my dad. They've sent me a lot of pictures of him from when I was younger. I didn't have any pictures of my childhood through my teens and twenties; only my memories, and I remembered things differently. When I see pictures of me and my dad when I was a child, my dad was always holding me, even from when I was six, seven, eight years old, and I don't remember that. It's weird. I don't remember us watching TV and hanging on to each other, but in pictures that's what you see.

I never came out to him but I never said I wasn't gay either. The one time we connected after all those years I just didn't feel the need to tell him. At that point I was out but didn't necessarily want to bring it up while we were working through all of our differences. If he was going to be a part of my life then, yeah, I would have told him. In fact there was a period of time when I was seriously thinking about moving him back to Oregon and letting him live with me. But he seemed so happy in Montana that I just wanted him to be happy and enjoy his life there.

I always wanted to have kids, ever since I was a kid. It was always my dream to have a big family. A woman friend I've known for twenty years has an adopted son and she wanted a male role model in his life, so I signed on for that task. He's now six and he calls me Dad and he has been my son in every sense of the word since the very beginning, since before he was born. She told me that it was very important that he have a male figure in his life he could call Dad and she said that she couldn't think of anyone else who would be the kind of person that she would want to be his dad. I was honored. I want to invest all my energy into this one little boy who lives with his mother. My partner and I have had a big part in his upbringing thus far. So there's Daddy and Papa and Mama and Mommy. We live about thirty miles apart, and he comes over whenever he wants to. He spends weekends with us a lot.

Through various life experiences I began to see people differently and started questioning my memories and my thought process. I realized that people aren't perfect. After hearing horror stories of kids with really, really bad childhoods I started realizing, "Well, mine wasn't that bad. Yeah, I experienced some pretty major loss but I was not abused. My dad never laid a hand on me in a bad way. He was basically a great guy, and everyone who knew him loved him. We had a period of time where we didn't get along. Over time I found that I don't like being angry and resentful—it's a destructive force in people's lives—so I wanted to let go of all that and I did. I'm comfortable in my own skin, though I don't know how much my dad influenced that. Personality-wise I've picked up some of his traits. I playfully harass those I love. I want to make sure my son knows I love him. I think my dad tried to do that. I just don't remember it that well even though I do remember little things. My dad was a good man. If anything, it's important to be a good man and it's important to be good to people.

My dad had a thing for animals and he had a thing for bringing home strays. There was this Bassett hound on the news on Pet of the Week, and I loved Bassett hounds when I was little, and the one we'd had had passed away. I came home from school one day, and my dad told me to go to my room. I didn't know what I'd done; I thought I was in trouble for something, like, "Uh, oh...." So I went to my room and opened up the door, and there was this Bassett hound from the news hanging out on my bed, wagging his tail.

If you have any negativity or ill will towards your father it's helpful to step back and really process and think about your feelings. Remember that people aren't necessarily in our lives forever. Time can be very short, and you don't want the time to be filled with regret and negativity. It's better to hold on to those positive moments that you've had with your father and remember that, in ways good or bad, he is a part of you.

Chapter 17
Maurice Monette

Maurice is the author of Confessions of a Gay Married Priest *and other books. He lives in Mexico with his husband of twenty-four years.*

I was born and grew up in Lowell, Massachusetts in the 1940's and lived there until I left for high school seminary in 1960. My dad was a mechanic. He had learned mechanics in the war, in World War Two, and is very much a product of that generation. All his life he was a blue collar worker and worked for the city and repaired trucks. My father was glued to Lowell and he actually bought a house next to one of the houses where he had lived when he was a child, so he never really left about a four square block area. My mother was that way too, and she and he met in one of the mills where they were working, before my father left for the war. So my parents were very much a product of an industrial city and an industrial mentality.

My dad was a good, faithful father and a good husband. He wasn't a drunk or a cheater. He was a very hard worker and took care of his family. He was just always there. Compared to many other families, ours was a very secure one. I am the oldest of the three kids and have two younger sisters.

Though Dad was quite severe and strict he was basically a lovable man. My mother used to say, "He's a good man," and she'd say it especially when I was critical of him. He was a religious man, and I would say he was repressed sexually in that he never talked about sex. He was brought up in a very Catholic family where there were rules, and sex was considered mostly sinful and not to be talked about. Dad's personality was very rule-bound and righteous, so it was often difficult to meet his expectations and in relation to him then I became the good boy. I tried to figure out what his rules were—which I thought were God's rules—until I discovered that his rules shifted and changed, depending on him. But it made me very rule-oriented because that's how I earned his love and that's how I stayed out of trouble.

My father never had the birds and the bees talk with me. He made a few comments about masturbation here and there as if I was engaged in it. But I was such a good boy I wasn't even doing that.

At fourteen years of age I was accepted at high school seminary, which was up in Bucksport, Maine, about four or five hours from Lowell. This was a very honorable thing in my family, probably the very best thing I could possibly do. We did not have access to becoming a doctor or a lawyer, and even being a businessman wasn't in my purview. But becoming a priest was something I wanted to do as a young man, and my mother and father were very supportive of my going into seminary and leaving at age fourteen. It was also great for me to get away from home and away from my father because it had become so difficult for me with him being so rule-bound and strict. I was glad to get away from his critical nature.

My mother was kind of like the Virgin Mary, and I tended to lean on her. My father was more like a strict father God of the Old Testament. As a young man I felt that my mother didn't really understand me. She had completed a high school education, where my father had just gone through the first year of high school. So by the time I started exploring the world and doing things that they hadn't done, they were afraid for me I guess and were rather severe and strict about it all.

I knew there was something unusual about me, and I didn't feel very lovable. I didn't feel like the other kids at school liked me very much. I got along OK but I just didn't have the sense that I was lovable, partly because I couldn't face myself very much at that age. Doing that took me a long time.

I had been in high school seminary and college seminary and I went to the novitiate, the oblate fathers, and went through a couple years of college and finished college. At the end of college I decided I needed a break. I needed to get out of seminary because I hadn't known anything else. I had been very protected. I'd been within my own French culture with the oblates and had pursued what my father and mother applauded. My life had been guided by the oblates, and I looked ahead and thought, "You know, they're going to tell me what to do for the rest of my life," and so I began individuating. I decided to leave seminary on a leave of absence and talked with my superiors—my bosses there—and I left. I enrolled in the School of Education at Boston U. and was attracted to teaching. I actually got myself a masters in adult education and got a job working as a religious educator in a parish in Concord.

Of course when I left the seminary, my father was very disappointed. There was an instance there where I went home, and he just sat there reading his newspaper, while my mother sat in her easy chair reading her newspaper. He was ragging on me about having long hair—this was in the late '60s—and about going to Boston and "You're into drugs and all this longhair hippie stuff..." He would rag on me without really knowing what I was doing or anything about my inner life. When I look back at it now I laugh a bit because I really did have long hair. So that night he was sitting there with my mom and they were both reading the paper. My mom would try to talk with me, but my father would just put up the paper and turn on the television. At one point I just looked at him and I said, "Put down that paper..." It was the first time I had ever talked back to him and I said, "I want to tell you something. You think I'm a hippie with this terrible long hair and I'm into drugs in Boston—a profligate city—and the bottom line is that you don't trust your son." I said, "That's wrong. You brought me up and you brought me up good and here you are raggin' on me, treating me as if I'm a bad person. And you're flat out wrong." Now in my family context that was very strong for me to say, and my father was dumbfounded. He was speechless. He put his paper down and when he managed to open his mouth he said, "Now I know you're a man," which—to me—was an extremely important thing for him to say. And from that moment on I think there was a certain trust that developed, and our relationship became much more straightforward. He knew I could talk back to him at that point. I gained a certain independence and I was beginning to individualize as a person. He wouldn't have been able to say that—he didn't know those words—but he saw what I was doing. From then on we had a very good relationship.

I went back into seminary and was ordained as a priest, and Mother and Father were proud as peacocks. We got along very well. They loved it when I came home. He would give me big hugs. When I was directing a graduate program at Loyola University in New Orleans, he came to visit and he was extremely proud. I would return home as often as I could and lavish them with gifts and phone calls. The relationship was pretty smooth, and my dad and I would have some wonderful conversations, although he didn't understand too much of what I did. That went on until I was about forty-two.

Around that age I had been struggling with my sexuality and had discovered that I was gay. It took me a long time to admit it. I didn't act out, but there was a lot of internal spiritual movement going on inside of me, and on a retreat I decided that I had to make a choice. It took me some time, but I decided to leave the priesthood. I had been accepted as a visiting scholar at Harvard for a year and at the end of that year I decided to tell my mother and father. So I went to their home and I told them I was leaving the priesthood and that I was in love with a man and that I was going to be moving to California with him. They were, of course, in shock, and it was at that point that my father said, "You should hang yourself..." When that happened I stood up and just walked outside to my car without saying a thing. I was getting into the car, and my father went to the door and my mother went out the front door and over to me in the car and said, "You know we love you. Will we see you again?" I said, "Yes," and then I just left. There was nothing else to say. It was a very hurtful moment. I cried a lot after that.

At the same time I knew that telling them was what I needed to do. It was really my defining moment. I stood on my own two feet and did what I knew was right for me. I didn't want to hurt them but I also knew the truth would not please them.

I moved to California. Both my father and mother refused to meet my partner Jeff. I didn't call them nearly as often anymore but I continued to send them gifts for birthdays and Christmas. Jeff and I would visit back east each year, and we made it a point to go. We would stay in a hotel and

I would call my parents and say, "I'm around and available to see you. Will you be around on Monday—I'd give a time—at eleven o'clock? I have time between eleven and one. Can we get together?" It was my way of containing the relationship because it was so difficult for them and for me. I knew I could hold myself together, and that worked. But they never wanted to see Jeff, and this went on for thirteen years—exactly the same pattern—the gifts, the cards, the occasional phone call, the yearly visit. Jeff would always be next door at my sister's house waiting for me, and I would tell my parents at each visit, "You know, Michelle—my sister—and Jeff and I are going out to lunch after. We'd love to have you join us." My father would always speak up and say, "Oh, we have some lunch here…," which meant "No." So we would just go out. They were free to make their decision and we were free to make ours.

On these visits my dad was civil with me but he never gave me a hug during those thirteen years. We had always hugged before that. He wouldn't give me a hug, and that coldness was there, and we'd never talk about what was really happening with me. I could talk about work maybe but nothing else.

After thirteen years of this Jeff and I came east to see my mom and dad and the rest of the family. All of the rest of the family, including four aunts who are nuns, had embraced us. One or two nephews were a bit macho/reluctant, but even they came around really nicely. My sister would say things like, "Oh, Mom and Dad were ragging on you and what you're doing." I just ignored that and figured "It's their way of processing the whole thing. So I returned on one of these annual visits and my sister says, "Guess who's coming to dinner tomorrow night?" I said, "You're kidding…" They were both coming to dinner. I said, "Michelle, I don't believe you. I want to hear it from him. So when you come over and I'm there—at my parents' house—say it, because I want to hear it." So she in her typical tough fashion turned to my dad and said, "You're coming at six o'clock right?" My dad said, "Yes," and I almost just fainted right there.

So sure enough at six o'clock both my parents show up at my sister's. They were pretty old by now, in their early nineties. Jeff had been out with our nephews and when he arrived at the door he was told that not only was he cooking salmon for us on the grill but that my mother and father were there to meet him for the first time. He could hardly believe it. In any case, the introductions went very well and my mother, who by this time had had a stroke, was sitting in her chair and she looked up and saw Jeff and she straightened up a bit and a big smile came over her face. And Jeff went over and gave her a kiss. It was such a beautiful moment for me to see that, and to see him shaking hands with my dad. Dad was very civil but not warm. My mother later in a very soft voice says to me, "He's cute!" And my father's over there frowning, but she repeated that a few times because she always had a soft spot for the handsome friends I used to bring home. But the meal went well and it was a big turning point, and never again was anything said about those thirteen years. It was just a very beautiful moment. After that I told Jeff that my dad really loved playing cribbage and I said, "Why don't you go play cribbage, and I'll sit in the room with my mother. Sure enough that got my father's heart, and their relationship began to develop very nicely.

After my mom died my father would be extremely happy whenever we would come to visit and he would always welcome us both. He looked forward to playing cards with Jeff, and we would cook him meals and bring him out. The relationship just soared after that.

Dad lived three more years after my mom died. I would call him every Sunday no matter where I was. He was living alone in his own house. Jeff and I had been living in Mexico for several years, and this one Sunday morning Dad said, "Where are you?" I said, "I'm in Mexico. I'm looking at the Pacific Ocean from our apartment." He said, "I didn't remember that," and I said, "Oh, sometimes you forget. But you know that. You know we're living here and we run a guesthouse and we're doing work for a foundation..." He said, "Oh, yeah. You know, you really did a lot with your life. Your mother and I really had no idea about all this stuff you're doing and we couldn't have helped you at all. People in Lowell didn't know anything about all the stuff that you've done and what you've been through, but you know, you did it. You DID it." That took my breath away. I said to him, "Dad, you've got to know something. I'm standing on your shoulders." He said, "No, no, no. You did it. We didn't know anything about all the stuff you do." I said, "That may be true. But what I mean is that you always valued education and you supported me." I said, "You and Mom always encouraged us to learn and to grow. And look at me today. I'm fluent in Spanish and started learning it because Mom would throw a few words of Spanish at me and they got me very curious. So by the time I got in high school I started teaching myself Spanish." I said, "Look at me today. I'm teaching courses in Spanish in universities. That's what I mean, Dad. I'm standing on your shoulders and I'm very grateful to you." But he kept insisting, "Oh no. You did it yourself..." In his own simple way he really expressed an enormous amount of pride in me. I got off the phone that Sunday morning and said to myself, "He just spoke to you words that every man would love to hear from his father. And he told you this after all those thirteen years of rejection and all these ups and downs—a whole lifetime—and in your mid-sixties you got to hear it from him."

I never thought that my father and I would ever be honest with each other that way. I never thought he would accept Jeff and me as a married couple. I never thought he would accept me as a gay man. I never thought he would accept my leaving the priesthood. But you know, the old guy came around. I was just so proud of him.

He died at ninety-six years old at peace. He made peace with his other two kids and he and I were at peace. He turned to my sister the night before he died and said, "Is it OK if I die now?" She said, "Yes." Her yes was for all of us.

My father shows up in a lot of dreams. They're usually very loving dreams, and I'm really glad to see him and talk with him. Likewise with my mother. They're very peaceful dreams usually. Once in a while I get one where he's criticizing me or he's very severe. That's probably just processing old memories and processing my own personality too because I'm very much like him. My parents come in my dreams, and the dreams— even when they're challenging ones—are wonderful dreams about them. So I look forward to seeing them in dreams and I'm usually very aware of my dreams. It gives me a great deal of peace to know that the dreams are not tumultuous.

In fact, before my father became really sick as an old man I had a dream about him one night. We were in the family home, and he came down from the bedroom on the second floor. He was dressed in a bathrobe, and I went over to hug him. He was an old man in the dream and he pushed me away gently and said, "Oh, I've peed all over myself…" And in the dream I'm smelling him, and he did; he messed himself up really bad. I looked at him and looked in his eyes and said, "You know, it doesn't matter," and gave him a big, big hug and held onto him. That was the dream and when I had that dream I just knew within my own unconscious I had made real peace with him. He must have been around ninety when I had the dream, and it prepared me to deal with his old age, his illness, and his dying. But it was a fabulous dream.

I do consider myself extraordinarily fortunate to have had such a good father who hung in there, even till the very end, and who gradually came to some acceptance within himself of his relationship with me—and with Jeff—very beautifully. And who gave us more than we could have dreamed to have.

I saw Dad cry several times. When he talked about World War Two he cried a lot. He had been over there from the beginning and was in the Battle of the Bulge and also saw concentration camps. Jeff and I went to visit Matthausen this last fall, which was a work camp just outside of Vienna. My dad was one of the people who went in there as a liberator within the first few weeks. We went there as a pilgrimage to honor my dad because he had talked to me about it and had shown me some photos. But he could never talk much about the place because he always cried when he did. He cried when my mother died and he cried around her because he was very much in love with her.

I have an oil painting that he painted and gave to me that I almost returned to him once. It's a picture of a typical New England seacoast, with three boats in a harbor. Each boat has the name of one of his children, and my boat is the biggest and it's in the front. I still have that painting with me, and it just reminds me how much he loved us. I found in my old age I've started to paint, so in a way I'm taking after him.

One piece of advice… Try to be loving to your father, and your mother, no matter what they do to you. Don't treat you dad's opinion, his feelings, his tantrums, his rejection, or whatever he does to you that you don't like as if that's who he is. Focus on the person underneath all of that. He is not his feelings. He is not his thoughts. He's not his nasty actions. Underneath all that he's a person who has choices and he's a human being created by God, if you will. In any case, he's a human being who has dignity and honor. Appeal to that part of your dad and love that part of your dad and expect that part of your dad to show up. And don't take the rest of it too seriously. That's my advice.

There's a real intersection between spirituality and father/son relationships. I think there's a lot there. It seems to me that for so many men their relationship with their father has a lot to do with their relationship to the universe and how they relate to the universe or to God; whatever you want to call that. There are very direct links there for many of us. Some might link more with the mother, but in my observations I've noticed that there's often a lot going on there with the father. And if we can work out our relationship with our father oftentimes we can relate better with the universe and with the mystery behind it.

Chapter 18
Jesse Torres

Jesse is a busy single dad raising his young son. He works as a restaurant manager in southern California.

I was born in Los Angeles, CA in January of 1978. I have an older sister from the same dad, a younger brother from a different mother, and I have a younger sister from a different father. My older sister and I have the same parents, and she has been my rock ever since we were kids. We have a great relationship. We grew up in the L.A. area until I was about thirteen and then we moved out to the Inland Empire, about thirty miles east of L.A. We moved around a lot.

My parents split up when I was about a month old. My dad cheated on my mom and used to get physically abusive with her, so she left him. My father was a warehouse worker for a number of years. I remember when I was about three or four years old that my dad drove a blue VW Beetle, and he and his girlfriend would pick me and my sister up every other weekend and we would go to Dodger games and Raider games. We would go visit family and we'd sometimes spend the holidays with them. Dad was a drinker and he would end up getting into arguments with the family or with his girlfriend Debbie. I remember him drinking and driving a lot. One time he was driving my uncle's Oldsmobile, which had one of those front bench seats. I sat in the middle, and my uncle sat to the right and there were a couple of people in the back. My dad was drunk and really angry with Debbie, and I remember him jumping on the freeway and speeding, and we got pulled over. The cop gave him a speeding ticket and then let him go. We drove away and I just remember my dad ripping up the ticket and throwing it out the window. He kept speeding and driving erratically, and I remember being very scared. Nothing happened fortunately and we made it to our destination safely, and then he and Debbie got into a big argument because she was upset that he drove drunk with me in the car.

Still he was my dad and he was my hero and I looked up to him. On the weekends we would get up, and he would make breakfast. Dad was a jokester and he liked to have fun. He'd play pranks. He would make me read, and sometimes when everyone was watching movies I would get bored and I'd go read by myself. My dad was very into sports so he was always trying to get me into sports, which weren't really my thing. When he was sober he had the personality of someone who was just pleasant to be around. On weekends he was always drinking at night, so on Friday nights he would drink and on Saturday nights he would drink. Sunday day he would drink and then get us home. Even while drinking he usually wouldn't yell at us. The only time he would yell at us is when we'd ask him to stop yelling at Debbie, and then he'd tell us to "Shut the fuck up! This is none of your business…" He was never really mean or mean-spirited towards us. If he was upset he wouldn't take it out on us.

When I was four or five years old, he and I would take showers together to get ready to rush through the day. When we were out and about he was proud and would say to people, "This is my son." So that was good but that lasted only until I was about seven or eight years old. When I was about five or six years old he started skipping weekends. Then every other weekend turned into once a month, then every few months… What ended up happening was that he beat the crap out of Debbie and put her in the hospital. Then when she left him he pretty much disappeared from our lives, which told me that she was the only reason he was coming around and being a father. She had been the one encouraging him to see us and once she was gone from his life, he was gone from ours.

None of this was explained to us, and at the same time that he vanished my mom took off, so we were left with our grandparents. My grandma— my mom's mom—prided herself on being a great mother and she wanted my mom to be a great mother too, but she and my mother just didn't see eye to eye, so they would fight a lot. When we were living with my mom we were living in conditions that were pretty much uninhabitable so my sister and I actually made the decision to go live with our grandparents. We called our grandfather up and told him that we didn't want to go back home and asked him to pick us up. I was in fourth grade then and by that time my dad had already been gone for a couple of years. I felt abandoned by both parents and just really felt lost. I had a bunch of cousins my age and their dads were still around, so it was like, "OK, where's my dad at?"

My grandfather and my grandmother fought every day, and at some point they even separated. My grandmother moved out and moved in with my aunt. She took me with her, and then my sister went back with my mom. At my aunt's house, the only time my dad would come around was to buy weed from my uncle. He would come by, he would buy weed, say hi, and then he would leave. My uncle also sold cocaine and other drugs, so I think my dad was into more than just weed. I know he was also into meth. My uncle became my father figure in a sense. I looked up to him, and he treated me like his own kid. We got pretty close, but that was a rough relationship too because of the drug dealing. At some point I started calling him Dad, and he told my dad I'd called him Dad, and then my dad unleashed on me. He was very upset and couldn't believe that I would betray him like that. At that point, he'd already been in and out of my life—mostly out—for years, so I didn't understand why he was so upset. I moved in with my aunt and uncle when I was about thirteen and was there for a few years. When I came out I was asked to leave.

I had met someone older. He was twenty, and I was fifteen. I dropped out of school and got a job and moved in with him. He turned out to be the most abusive person I've ever dealt with in my entire life. To this day I've never had anyone beat the shit out of me like he did, and that relationship lasted for about two and a half years. At that point I didn't have anywhere else to go so I just dealt with it. My dad was in and out of my life here and there during this period but I hadn't come out to him yet and he didn't know I was gay.

At seventeen I was diagnosed with a heart condition, and my dad came to a surgery I had for it. After the surgery I was high on the painkillers and I was speaking freely and I didn't know my dad was in the room but I was telling my boyfriend, who had left me to go be with someone else but who was there for the surgery, how much I loved him and that I wanted him to come back home to me. That's how my dad found out I was gay, and he had asked my mom if he could speak with her in the hallway, and she agreed. He asked her, "Is my son gay?" She said, "Yes he is." He goes, "Who all knows?" And she said, "Everybody." He goes, "My family? My mom knows?" And she said, "Your mom knows." He said, "Why didn't anyone tell me?" She told him, "Because you haven't been around for years, and he doesn't need you." Then he said, "I fought off those urges. Why can't he? He can do the same...." And my mom goes, "He is who he is. You either accept him for who he is or you leave and you don't come back, because he doesn't need you in his life." He goes, "No, no. I'll accept him."

But he didn't. He would always ask, "How's your girlfriend? Do you have a girlfriend?" I'd be like, "Dad, I'm gay. I don't have a girlfriend and I'm not going to get a girlfriend. It's not going to happen." He and I would go months without communicating, to the point that we only saw each other on Christmas, because that's when I would go to see my grandmother. And seeing her I had to run into him because that's where he lived. That's when I realized just how heavily he was into drugs and drinking and that he just didn't care about life anymore. When my grandfather—his father—passed away, I saw the way he responded and reacted. When the coffin was going down he threw a rock at the coffin and was just drunk and stupid, so I left. I didn't want to be around him. I found out later that my grandfather used to abuse my dad and beat the shit out of him and beat the shit out of my grandmother too.

Over the years I came to understand that I'm just like my father. That was hard to take in, because I don't like my dad at all as a person. I love him as my father but it's really hard to take in that I'm just like this person I despise. We have the same name, we almost have the same birthday—one day apart—and we have the same habits. Our signatures are almost identical, which I didn't realize for the longest time. I even changed my signature when I realized how incredibly similar they look. I ended up being not a womanizer as he was, but I was a male whore. I got into drugs when I was twenty-three, into cocaine and Ecstasy and meth, and my life became a big party.

In August of 2012 I adopted my son. I promised to be a better father to him than I had ever had, and that's the kind of dad I try to be. I've had my fair share of hiccups. I've gotten busted for drugs and I've been busted for a D.U.I. But I've always been honest with my son and I've always talked to him about life and things, and my son knows I'm gay. He doesn't know yet that he's adopted. He knows who his mom is; we have open communication and he gets to talk with her when he wants. I just try to be the best father that I can be to him, and he respects me and loves me unconditionally, and that's what I live for.

When I was twenty-four I remember mentioning to my dad that he was dead to me and that I didn't want anything more to do with him. I was just done with him. Then I made all the mistakes I made with the drugs and the D.U.I. and getting a drug charge. In 2012 I took a deep breath and I let it all go of all the resentment I had toward my father. My grandma had passed away, and I didn't know where my dad was at or where he was living or what was going on with him. We finally found him in an alley in a tent, and I told him that I had room if he wanted to come home. I just wanted to let him know that no matter what happened in the past that I forgave him. I cried and I told him, "I forgive you. Let's just move forward from here…" I stopped expecting anything from him, so that way I wouldn't be disappointed.

My father lives in a park in L.A. now. I try to go visit him once a month. It's hard because it's a repetitive visit; his mind is so gone from the meth that it's basically the same visit over and over again. Every time it's the same conversation: "Come look at my tent." "Look at this necklace; it's worth thousands of dollars." I have to tell him, "It's costume jewelry, Dad. It's not worth anything." Then it's, "Here, take this bike. Take this jacket…" "I don't want your bike or your jacket." Then he says, "How's your Uncle Rudy doing?" "Uncle Rudy passed away last year." "Oh, I didn't know that," though I told him that last month and the month before that too. Then he starts talking about conspiracy theories with the government and how the government is going to give him an apartment but he doesn't want it because they will bug the apartment and then they will know what he's doing.

The park he lives in is right next door to a shelter, but he refuses to stay in the shelter because the shelter has rules, and he says he doesn't like to follow rules. He chooses to live this way. This is how he likes to live and how he wants to live. A large number of homeless adults aren't homeless because they're not loved; they're homeless because that's how they want to live. I love my dad, and if it were my choice he wouldn't be homeless. But it's not my choice, it's his, and that's how he wants to live his life.

I always hug him. He's not dirty and he doesn't smell because he goes to the shelter and showers every single day. He never shaves, and I'll tease him, "Hey, let's get you a haircut and a shave," and he'll say, "Nah, I don't want to do that. You're crazy." My aunts—his sisters—they're all homeless with him. I have three aunts who are homeless, so when I go visit him I visit them too, by default. And that's why he won't leave, because they're there. He won't leave his sisters behind. He got caught operating a meth lab with one of his sisters a couple years ago and was put in jail for it because it was like his fifth or sixth offense. He's been in rehabs but he just really isn't interested in giving up drugs.

I'm close to one of my cousins whose mother lives with my dad. He lives in the area there so he sees them more, usually on a weekly basis. Sometimes I'll just shoot him a text: "Hey, have you seen my dad? How's he doing?" "Oh, he's fine. Same old, same old..." "Alright, cool. Tell him I said hi and I'll see him soon." My father doesn't know my son, and my son doesn't know him. I explained to my son why I don't take him along on these visits, and he's OK with it.

I'm sure my dad has regrets. I don't have any regrets because if I did that would mean that I haven't forgiven him and I've truly forgiven him. I've accepted him for exactly who he is and I stopped passing judgment on him because I went through the same trials and tribulations. Fortunately I got out of the drugs and all that turmoil I was going through. Unfortunately for my dad he didn't, and I'm sure that his regrets are that he wasn't a better father and that he wasn't a better human. He took advantage of my grandma by freeloading off her for the last twenty years of her life. He did nothing with himself—no college, no career—though he had every opportunity to do those things.

Be grateful if you have a good relationship with your father. If you don't have a good relationship, my advice would be to expect less and try to love more and to be the bigger person. And forgive. It's that old cliché saying, but forgive them not because they deserve it but because you deserve to be free. That's a true statement, and I live by it. I didn't forgive my dad because he deserves it. I forgave him because I deserve peace in my life and I'm at peace with that relationship. We're good.

I never brought up to my dad the comment he made to my mom about his gay tendencies. I was always afraid to, because of his anger problems. I don't think he even knows that I know he made that comment. When my mom shared it with me I was surprised, but it made sense; that he was always unhappy with himself because he could never be who he really is. When you fight off your true self you're never going to be happy, and it's sad that my father never got to be true to himself. I believe that, like me, he was born a gay man but he was just trying hard to live up to his father's expectations. That happens a lot. Still if he hadn't fought his urges I also wouldn't be here, so I'm not mad at him for taking the path he did.

Chapter 19
Matt

Matt lives in Los Angeles where he works as an actor and stand-up comedian. He lives with his boyfriend of several years and their dog.

I was born in March 1979 in Oklahoma City and lived there until I was eighteen. I have an older brother named Bryan, who is two years older than me. My father comes from a big, loud Southern family and is a plumber and plumbing contractor, and the thing I remember very vividly from my childhood about my father is his hands. He worked outside a lot and his hands have always been calloused and rough. I remember being a little boy and sitting on his lap and him patting my leg, and feeling the roughness in his hands as compared to my mom's. I do remember feeling very loved.

My father loved tractors and things; I remember the smell of diesel from a very young age. That smell makes me think of my father and of playing on his tractors while they were turned off, and I recall wanting to be like him. One of my earliest memories also is of being a little kid and being obsessed with Wonder Woman. I loved her! At two and three years old, I would have a diaper on and red galoshes and I'd walk around with a jump rope telling people they had to tell the truth, with my big lisp. I remember the way I would stand; I would stand on one leg and shift my weight and kind of pop my hip out and I'd hold my hand out with a limp wrist. And I remember my dad always yelling at me, saying, "Matthew, get your goddam sissy wrist down," because that's the way I stood all the time. It never hurt me or made me feel that I was being picked on or anything because I knew my father loved me.

My father didn't have a father. He grew up with five siblings, and his own father, for various reasons, left the family when my dad was five years old. So my dad grew up without a father, and I still think that's his deepest wound, that he didn't have that. Especially for a kid who loved baseball; he was a star pitcher who had to quit baseball and go to work at age fourteen, along with the rest of his siblings, to help keep the family going. They grew up very poor, and would often go to bed hungry at night. My dad would say, "My whole life I didn't have a father who gave a fuck, so even if I do nothing else with my life I'm going to be a goddam good dad!" That's kind of his mantra, and he's always wanted to be present in our lives. Even looking back on it now, I know the reason he was telling me to get my wrists down and all that was that he loved me and he was just protecting me from the sorts of negative reactions I might get from others. I think on a subconscious level I knew that.

I definitely felt growing up at home that I was in a "love bubble." Did my parents love the fact that I was running around playing Wonder Woman? Probably not. But I remember my dad letting me lasso him, and him laughing with me. Would he distract me and try to play Popeye instead of Wonder Woman? Yes, but he never told me I couldn't play Wonder Woman. So I kind of felt that I had this love bubble around me, and then when I got older and went to school that's when the love bubble popped because I started hearing the negative narratives of all the peers around me.

My dad was a sports guy, and my older brother Brian was super into sports, while I really wasn't into it. I remember I was the bat-boy on my brother's baseball team, and my dad was the coach. This would have been when my brother was around nine years old, so I was probably around six or seven. At the end of the season my brother and the other guys all got trophies. I did not get a trophy and I remember being so hurt and crying and upset. When I came home from school the next day, my dad had gotten me a little trophy. For some reason my dad always called me Matthew Doofloppy—that was like his nickname for me—and the trophy said "MATTHEW DOOFLOPPY, NUMBER 1 BATBOY" on it. He went and paid for that trophy himself, and I remember at the time being very touched by that, that my dad would go out of his way to make me feel included.

Bless his heart, my dad really wanted us to play baseball, and I was very concerned about how my baseball outfit looked and my shorts and socks; I always wanted my socks to be pulled up tight and high. My father's plumbing company sponsored the team, so his name was on all our shirts. I really liked to play center field and I loved to dance in the outfield. In one game someone hit a line drive out to center field, and I literally was turned around the other way, dancing, I think, to a Debbie Gibson song playing in my head, like "Out of the Blue." The ball just went totally past me. I didn't even see it, and people were yelling at me... "*Matt*!" I remember my dad going, "MATT! *MATT!* GET YOUR HEAD OUT OF YOUR ASS, GODDAM IT!!!!!", just screaming in front of everybody. That's the last time I remember really doing any sports stuff.

I did eventually play tennis a very little bit too, but only because I liked the outfits. I love tennis now, but that's really what pulled me into it. I knew at the age of five that I wanted to sing and act, and my father was always supportive of that, always telling me: "Do what you want to do." He never let us work in middle school or high school because he said, "I did that my entire life. I make money so you can be a *kid*. He would always want us to be a kid. I definitely felt encouraged.

My father was very affectionate, always telling me that he loved me. He would kiss me on the lips and tell me he loved me, he and my mom both. Neither of them had great childhoods but they very much made a choice to not only be emotionally nurturing but physically nurturing as well. Even my boyfriend says to me, "Oh my gosh, your family is always so touchy and loving..." And we are that. One of my earliest memories of my father is when we would be at a movie theater, he would put his calloused, strong hands on the back of my neck and just hold my neck; kind of wrap his forefinger and his thumb around the base of my neck, and I loved that. I remember feeling like I was being protected from everyone in the world and I was with my dad.

He was also very goofy and always wanting to make us laugh. I think I get a lot of my comedy and stand-up humor from seeing my dad walk through the room and hike up his pants and walk funny and make a funny face to make us giggle and laugh. He would do pretty much anything to get my brother and me to cut-up. He's always been a really, really great dad in that regard.

My dad and I never had the birds and the bees talk, but I did learn a lot from my older brother's experiences. He was a horny little boy who went through puberty early. Now my dad was very loving but he also had a temper and would get pissed off, and I remember him walking into my brother's room and tossing some condoms on the bed and saying, "You better fucking use these, because I'm kicking your ass if you have a goddam baby!" That's my dad, very loving but not the most subtle with his words.

My dad and I talked about sex later, after I came out, and then my father is asking me if I'm a top or a bottom and that kind of stuff. That was *not* a conversation I'd planned on having in my thirties with my father. My dad said, "I just want to know. Do you take it or give it? Do you feel like less of a dude?" And I'm like, "Dad... *DAD*, it's not about that..." But he's just wondering so he wanted to ask!

My parents got divorced when I was a sophomore in high school, which was probably actually the best thing for my family in a lot of ways. My dad is a fantastic father but not necessarily the best at being married. My dad was always active in my life, but when my parents got divorced, then he really had to be, and he started to go to things more. I'm a singer, and when I was in second grade I sang "Rocky Top" in our little community talent show. I ended up winning in both the youth category and was also the overall champion and got this big trophy. My father didn't really know I could sing, so when I got off that stage I remember him being shocked. My dad is also the type where, if one of his sons does something well, he's like, "My son's the best fuckin' singer in the world! No one's better than my son..." He becomes like super arrogant-prideful almost. But I remember him being so proud of that talent show, and he bragged about that for *years*, and I'm talking like ten years. When I was seventeen years old and we would meet somebody he would say, "Oh, this is my son Matthew," and they'd say, "Nice to meet you." And he'd say, "Maybe you've heard of him. He won the talent show, singing Rocky Top." And I was like, "Dad, I'm seventeen. I was eight years old then...." But it's so funny because I'm from a small town, and people are like, "Oh yeah, I remember that," and then they'd talk about it.

My mom was gone the day of the talent show and didn't get back until late. I remember my dad saying, "OK, put your trophy out on the table and make it look good for your mom." I remember going to bed and hearing my mom come home, and falling asleep to him laughing and bragging about how well I did at the talent show.

When I think of my father and his love for me, that's kind of at the core, because he was not only supporting me but also supporting something I loved. Very much so, and he's really done that throughout my life. I got my undergraduate in music school, and he paid for all my school. My degree is in opera, and my father is a country music lover. I was recently speaking at an arts camp I went to, which was about three hours away from where he lives in Oklahoma. I said, "Dad, do you want to go?" and he said, "Matt, I paid for your whole undergraduate school and I had to listen to your recital, where you sang pretty much a whole fuckin' Italian opera without one goddam country song. I think I'm good. I paid for your whole schooling so you'd think you would have sang a little bit of Garth Brooks for me…" That's my dad.

In eighth grade in middle school I was in *Cinderella*. I got to play Prince Charming, and, of course, Prince Charming has to wear this tunic and these tights. My dad said, "Matt, you're going to high school next year, so here's a sure-fire way to get those girls a droolin'… Son, we just take a sausage and tape it to the inside of your leg, and when you put on those tights and walk out there, they won't know what hit 'em!" It might not have been the exact sort of support I wanted, but it was my dad's way. And even though I skipped the sausage, Cinderella and I ended up dating for two years, though we never did get physical.

There are two things important to my father in life: work and children. My dad is a Virgo and he's the hardest working person I have ever met. He's worked his ass off for years with physical labor and still does, even though he's sixty-six now. He's also not the most patient man. My brother called me about a year ago, all emotional, and I said, "What's wrong?" He said, "Our dad is all fucked up." I said, "What do you mean?" and he goes, "I just sent you a picture." He sent me a picture of my father's tombstone, and I said, "What the hell is that?" He said, "I came out to see grandma's grave, and dad went ahead and put up his fuckin' tombstone." I called my dad and I was like, "Dad! You didn't tell us you did that," and he said, "You and your brother probably would have messed it up and spelled my name wrong, so I just thought I'd get it done." And on his tombstone he actually has a logo of his plumbing company on there, which shows how important work and being a hard worker is to him. He's worked nonstop since the age of fourteen.

My dad is super social and super gregarious, and we get that from him. My brother is pretty popular in the community and he announces the local football games. I was always performing and doing stuff, so we get that from our father. He's a great storyteller as well. I remember as a kid, it would take us two hours just to go to Wal-Mart because he would know so many people and would want to sit and talk with them. My brother and I were just like, "*DAD…* ," because he just liked to talk and tell stories. I'm an actor and I've been on a couple of game shows. One of the things I shared on the game shows is about one of the camps I founded, called Brave Trails, which is a leadership camp for LGBT youth, ages twelve to twenty. I'm very vocal about being out and being an advocate and an activist in the LGBTQ community, and my father's been very proud about that.

If the south is the Bible Belt, I think Oklahoma must be the buckle, because of how conservative it is. My brother called me one day and said, "Dad walked off a job. We were roughin' in a house, and a guy—one of the hands—was making a joke and he told a gay joke." Now some of these guys do know who I am because I've been on TV and stuff, but a lot of them don't. So he tells this gay joke, and my dad just looks at him and says, "Fuck you, motherfucker!," and throws down his tools and walks off. My brother says, "This guy had no idea what he did to piss dad off, and dad's walking to his truck…" So my brother says to him, "Dad! They don't know about Matthew," and he says, "I don't fucking care. They shouldn't say stuff like that." Then, of course, when I call my dad, I'm like, "Dad, you don't have to do that." He goes, "Matthew, that shit just pisses me off." Then he pauses for a second and says, "It was a good joke. Do you want to hear it? It's pretty funny." And he tells me the joke.

When he got remarried to his last wife, she wanted to get married in a church, and he said, "I'm not going to get married in any so-called house of God that thinks that my son, who is volunteering for suicide help-lines and is starting a camp and is trying to help people, is less than any of those sacrilegious motherfuckers who are preaching the Bible and sleeping with a million women." So I think it's really cool that I have this dad who's this southern Oklahoma plumber who you would think would be the least enlightened and supportive, but I'm his son and he loves me. He loves me and he LOVES my boyfriend. My boyfriend is black and is my first long-term boyfriend and I remember thinking when I first brought him home, "How's this going to go…" My dad was great, and now he's like, "Y'all live together and he's practically your husband. When are y'all going to have kids? I need a little Matthew." I said, "Well, Dad, having a kid of my own is kind of expensive for me," and he said, "Matthew, Matthew, Matthew…. Here's what you do, son. Just get yourself a woman. Make it a blonde, and just pretend it's Burt Reynolds. Then if she needs any compensation, I'll give her twenty grand." I'm like, "*Dad*!" But he's full-on, dead serious. "Hey, I want a little Matthew. Let's go!" He's a mess.

North Texas State, where I went to school, had a summer program in Crested Butte, Colorado, and we went there the summer after my freshman year. I was with all my college mates and we were all staying on one floor of a hotel and we were playing drinking games and got really drunk. This one guy and I were talking in his room, and he said to me, "Aren't you tired?" I was like, "Tired of what?" And he goes, "Tired of lying." So I ended up coming out to him. But his roommate, who was also gay, came into the room to find out what was happening, and he ended up telling *everybody* that I'd come out. So I came out to one friend, went back to my room, and then I got up the next morning and had all these people coming up to me saying, "Congratulations! We're so happy for you!" A voice teacher came up to me and said, "Hey Matt, I heard last night was a night of true confessions," and she just saw the color drain from my face. Later that day she apologized and said, "I really didn't mean to startle you. You're going to be so much happier…" Everything she said was right, but still it was difficult. It was also good in that I ended up being out at school but not at home. So I had about two years to get used to the idea and then ironically enough I came out to my sister-in-law after a friend's wedding. Later I told my mother, and then we waited to tell my dad. I will totally own the reason why: honestly, it's because he paid for all my undergraduate education. I couldn't pay for college myself and I was almost done and I was worried about how he might react and just didn't know what to do. But I also couldn't wait until I got out of school, so I was twenty-one and in my senior year of college when I told my dad in person. I'd spent the whole day hanging out with him, and it was at the very end of the day, and I was thinking, "I gotta do this..." I said, "Dad, I've got to tell you something," and he goes, "Matt, I don't want to know..." I said, "Dad, you've got to know," and he says, "Matt, I don't want you to say it." I was like, "Dad, I've got to say it..."

I'd only seen my father cry two other times; once on the day I helped him move out of my childhood home, when he left my mother, and then the day that his mother died. So this was the third time that I'd seen him start crying, and it made me really sad to see my father actually plead with me and say, "Please don't say it." I told him, "I won't say it, but we still know the truth and we know that it's there." He said, "I love you," and I said, "I love you too." We each went off to bed and then the next day I was just hanging out at his house—I was on summer break and they had a pool and stuff—and I'll just never forget... Normally when I'd stay with my dad, he'd always come by from work and say, "Hey, just wanted to see if you wanted to go to Monte's"—this little diner—"and see if you wanted to go grab lunch." But I'll never forget; that next day I was standing outside and I saw his work truck come down the hill with the dust coming behind it and pull in the drive and thinking, "What's he doing? I guess he needs to get some tools or something like that..." But he just pulled up and said, "What are you doing?" I said, "Oh, nothin'. I was going to go visit my friend Shaun." He said, "Oh, I just came by to see if you wanted to go to lunch." It was the best way for me to feel that nothing was going to change between us. And we did, we went and got lunch. We didn't talk about it at the time, because with any parent, they've got to have their coming out process as well. I didn't even say anything during the lunch, just sat and listened to him tell stories and tell dirty jokes with me and his other friends, and then he came and dropped me off, and I went and saw my friend. That was it. But I was at peace with it. I knew he loved me and I knew everything was OK. When I left he said, "Do you need money?" And I said, "No Dad, I'm good." He said, "Oh fuck it. You're taking my money. Here."

Then we didn't really talk about it for like a year. He knew I loved Shania Twain and he'd call me and say, "Matt, I'm watching a Shania Twain video. Really? You really like her just for her music? You wouldn't fuck that at all?" And I'm like, "Nope, dad. Wouldn't do it." He's like, "Well shit…" He'd go, "Are you sure it's not a phase?" And I'd say, "Dad, it's not a phase."

About five years in he was totally accepting of it. In my standup I tell people that both of my parents are so much involved in my gay life. My dad is remarried now, but when he was single he would tell me, "Matt, I'm dating this one woman. I wish you would teach her a thing or two about BJ's, because she didn't get the memo!" I'm like, *Dad…* So he's definitely come around.

I'd like to be a father. The two things I've known I have wanted to do since I was probably five years old were to be a performer and to be a father. I'm now thirty-seven and I'm just now in a place where, thankfully, my acting career is starting to take off. My boyfriend is younger, thirty-one, and being parents is something we want to do, though I don't know the logistics of how it would happen. We're not there yet. I just know that it's something that I want. Obviously I would like to do it sooner than later because I want to make sure that both my parents will be around for it. I'd want to have children for myself but also would love to give my parents grandchildren.

In 1998 he surprised me with fourth-row Shania Twain tickets, to see a concert of hers in Oklahoma City. It was him and my stepmom and me. During the concert Shania saw how into her music I was and she asked me to come onstage. She said, "Would you like to sing a song with me?" And I said, "Sure!" Now I'm not the best singer in the world but I do have a degree in opera and I knew all the words to this song because I'm a huge fan. So I'll never forget her putting the microphone up to my mouth, and I couldn't hear anything because I didn't have a monitor, but just seeing her mouth drop and her eyes get big and the audience standing and cheering and the flash bulbs and lights going off... But equally cool was when I got back from the stage, seeing my father, just floored. He said afterwards, "Matt, I didn't know you could do that!" I was dancing and moving around and playing with the audience and just being a singer and a performer—what I do! My dad has always believed in me, but that's when he saw, "Oh, he could do this..." So that was great. He surprised me, and I really surprised him. The only thing he ever dragged me to that I went along with because I love my father is NASCAR. I went once and thought, "I'm never going to do that shit again!" But thankfully my father is finished with his NASCAR phase.

My dad and I talk once or twice a week, usually every Sunday night and then maybe some other time during the week if we have something specific to talk about. All the time I get these questions from my dad out of the blue... "Hey, I was watching a porno the other day and I saw a girl deep-throatin', and for some reason I thought, "Can Matt do that?" He said, "Do you have to learn to do that?" I'm like, "DAD... I'm not talking to you about this." "Son, I don't care. I'm just wonderin'..." So it's definitely like, "Dad... *NO*, I do not want to talk about this!!!"

I think that in dealing with any parent, certainly in dealing with your dad, two things are important. First and foremost—and I say this as a gay man and as a therapist—get yourself right. Be the one person who supports yourself initially. Love yourself first. In coming out to anyone and dealing with other people's reactions, be the only person who judges you, the only one whose judgment matters. Then in dealing with your father, whether his response is good or negative, try to see him as a person, a person who has faults and who is—hopefully—trying. Know that it's OK if you don't have a relationship with your father, because some fathers aren't going to be able to be accepting, sadly. If you love yourself and support yourself first, even though it's hurtful that you don't have a relationship with your father, it's OK. It's livable. Overall, have realistic expectations of yourself and of others, and try not to get fixated on what people should be, because you'll always find yourself disappointed when you do.

Chapter 20
George Morris

George lives in the Pacific Northwest where he works in technology sales.

I was born in Birmingham, Alabama in 1968. I was an illegitimate child, and my mother married my stepfather when I was a year old. Then along came two sisters. My stepfather was an extremely physically and verbally abusive man, so I would get shipped to my aunt and uncle's for a time and then shipped back home. I did that on and off until I was sixteen. He resented me tremendously, and I seemed to be the "problem" and was always the one who took the brunt of his abuse. I never could figure out why he resented me, and when I say abusive I'm talking whipped with whips and chains and boards and fists—you name it—so that I couldn't go to school some days. Anything I said or did was ALWAYS wrong so I was a very quiet child up until I was probably seventeen.

At my aunt and uncle's house I had an aunt who was very psychotic in her behavior. My mother's sister, she was a pathological liar and a hypochondriac, and everyone appeased her except me. My uncle was a pacifier. He overcompensated and kind of doted on me a bit. He was easygoing and always wanted me to be involved in whatever he was doing, and up until I was twenty-one if I had imagined wanting a true biological father it would have really been him. He was the closest thing to a father figure that I ever had.

As a kid I did ask my mother from time to time who my dad was, but it always made her cry so I didn't ask often. I was told that my biological father had joined the service and he was killed in Vietnam. So I was given the name of the person who was supposed to be my biological father. I had known that her husband was not my real dad from as far back as I can remember, and it was made very evident to me that I didn't belong to him. My sisters both fared better with him.

My mother came from a very large family, and there was one particular uncle I had who I just adored. He was a self-made man, had his own business, had all the things that I thought I wanted out of life, and was extremely affectionate and always made it known that he loved you and that it was OK to show another male outwardly that you loved him. Uncle CJ always made me feel very special and very included on anything that was happening. My stepfather rarely went to events on that side of the family because, well, nobody liked him, so that gave me more freedom there. But Uncle CJ was one of my "sanity heroes." He was an island in the middle of chaos and he would say things like, "I know things aren't easy where you are, but know that I always love you."

I was very withdrawn all through school and got straight A's. After I turned fifteen I was told that if I got in any trouble at school or if I didn't get good grades that I could quit school and go to work. So at seventeen I joined the Army; I got the parents to let me do early enlistment. Everything began to change at that moment in time for me. There is not enough money on the face of the earth to get me to want to relive those years between ages seventeen and twenty one again. I was dealing with the gay thing and had no one to turn to. It was extremely difficult having to come to grips with my sexual orientation and how life outside of what I'd always known was so different. It was very difficult, and I actually attempted suicide three times while I was in the military. I overdosed. Looking back, I don't think I ever wanted to die; I just wanted to escape the demons.

By age eighteen or nineteen I had found my voice, and it was an angry voice, and I took it out on anyone who crossed me. I was a Billy Badass. I had to be tough. That was my mentality; if I wasn't strong I was weak. And, of course, military training didn't help. It's kind of unusual that I started out being a weapons specialist when I went in the service and I ended up being a medic. I graduated basic training and came home for a short time before I went to my MOS school. At that time my mother had left my stepfather and was divorcing. Needless to say I was no longer a shy, small child; I was 6'3, weighed two hundred twenty and, having just come out of basic training, was solid muscle. For thirteen weeks I had just been trained to kill. So things didn't bode well for my stepfather.

In my youth I didn't know any different and I didn't know what child abuse was. Growing up, there was no such thing that I had heard about, and I didn't know that all the adults who were in any way connected with me knew what was going on and never stopped it. But the first time I beat him up I beat him up pretty bad and to the point where my mother hit me in the head with a cast iron skillet to keep me from killing him, because he had already stopped moving by that point. I don't remember the fight much but it devastated me that I could actually do that to another human being.

Then add to that the gay thing and the struggle not to tell anyone and to make sure that all of my encounters were out of town… I kept it all well hidden until I was twenty-one. At twenty-one I met the first guy that I fell in love with. At that time it was just sex—there was no kissing or affection— and right in the middle of it, this guy says, "I love you." I said, "Stop that. You don't love me. You may love what we're doing but you don't love me." That was kind of the beginning of the end of my closet. This guy broke my heart, of course; I was young and dumb, and he already had a boyfriend. I always liked older guys and never went for anyone my age. Looking back on it now, I can see that for so many years I was always looking for a father figure.

By twenty-one I had come to terms with the fact that I had never really fit anywhere my entire life. Everywhere I went I was a lone wolf. I was a source of contention no matter what household I was in. I was determined to find my biological father. Even if he was dead at least I could see the family and see people who I looked like and maybe by some chance have some siblings who wanted a relationship. By twenty-one I had reached a high enough security level in the Army to have access to medical records for Vietnam. So right before my twenty-first birthday I said to my mother, "I don't want to cause you any pain or grief but I have decided that I'm going to look up this guy and I need a little bit more information. I've pulled military records and there are five of these names in the areas that you said you were in. Was he black?" She said, "No, he wouldn't be black." So I'm trying to narrow this down, and she's being very evasive. I said, "Were you raped?" I was trying to put the pieces together, and Mother was answering without answering, something she was very practiced at.

So on my twenty-first birthday my mother comes over. I will never forget it. She came over and shut the door and said, "We need to talk. I don't want to do this on your birthday but I know that if I don't do it now I'll never do it." I said, "OK." She said, "I think you know who your biological father is..." I said, "I've heard rumors but I want to hear you say it." Without missing a beat she said, "Your Uncle Red is your father." That was the uncle and aunt I had lived with all of those years. I remember one particular time as a kid when I was living with them, my aunt got mad at me for some reason and was screaming and said, "You should go downstairs and ask him who your father is. He knows who your father is, so you should ask him..." My uncle did some mechanic work in his spare time in the basement, so I went down and I asked him. I was a boy at the time, probably nine years old, and I just remember him taking off his welding gloves and his welding cap and setting them down and saying, "Do not come upstairs. You stay down here." Then he bolted upstairs and all I could hear was screaming and yelling. I had never heard them fight before and could just hear this horrible fighting. In a few minutes he came back down, so I asked again. Looking back now it all makes sense, but he sheepishly said, "George, I don't know. I really don't know. I don't know why she would say something like that. You know how she is..." So I thought, "OK. Mean old woman. No big deal." But when my mother tells me this, I'm not shocked. A lot of the pieces of the puzzle sort of fell together. He had children, a son and a daughter. The son was three years older than I was, and when I attended school there—they lived an hour away—everybody there kept thinking that he and I were brothers.

So I decide that now I'm pissed at him, thinking, how could you let go through all of what I went through? Why didn't you stand up for me? Now it's all his fault. My mother goes, "I've called and told him. He knows I'm going to tell you, and he wants to talk to you..." It took me probably a month before I could finally gather it up enough to have a conversation.

So I drive up to the house, and he's working with a tractor in a field. I go out there in my truck, and he gets off the tractor, and I say, "So Mother said she called you. She said you want to talk. She said you're my father, and I want to know if that's true." He said, "Your mother was a whore and yeah, I had sex with her but I don't believe you're mine. I never have thought that. She's always said you were, but I never have thought that." So needless to say, being a hothead with a chip on my shoulder, a fight ensued which did not go well really for either one of us. He had to go back and tell the story of why he had black eyes, a broken arm, and a bloody nose.

After that I didn't have anything to do with anybody really for probably six months. I was just angry and I was getting in bar fights and fist fights; every chance I had to be violent I was. This was when I was off on personal time. No one in the military had a clue that anything was wrong in my world because I did my job well and kept my nose clean.

Three days after I had beat up my stepfather the first time, he signed a warrant for my arrest once he got out of the hospital and had me arrested. And I will never forget it… I had known the sheriff who picked me up my whole life, and he says to me, "George, I know what your life has been like. I'm very aware of what has gone on in your life. You need to keep your military career, and I'm going to help you with this and let you sign out your own bond. I'll make this go away. I will go talk to Jerry myself, and this will go away." So I'm looking at this deputy and I said, "So you knew what was happening and you didn't do anything?" He just dropped his head, and I said, "I'd always had so much respect for you, until this very moment. I appreciate what you're doing today but that's pretty shitty of you—as a law enforcement officer—to turn your head to the hell I was living in." He said, "If I'd have said anything they would have took you from your mother." I said, "You know, I get it. But I don't like it."

I always looked for male approval, so the military thing went really well for me. I did my four years and got out and went to school. I loved numbers but hated history and English and I was having a lot of problems with a particular history course. There was one visiting professor who had told me, "If you can help me in my antique store on the weekends with inventory and set up estate sales, I will tutor you." Anything I could do to get through school I was good with so I did strike up a business relationship with this man, and he did help me. It was never a sexual thing. He was like seventy and I was twenty-one. Walter was the first person I ever met who was wealthy. My family was poor. We had nothing, and people of means just were not in the circle I ran in. Walter and I did estate sales, and I worked at the shop. I would spend weekends at his house, and he had this beautiful antebellum antique home.

One day Walter came in the kitchen and said, "If you don't mind, would you do me a favor? I want you to cook tonight. I'm having a little party and I have some people coming over and I'd appreciate it if you'd run the grill." When I said I'd rather not mix and mingle with his guests, he said, "No, no, no. It's a bar-b-que. It's not a big deal and it will be fine." Of course I hadn't come out to him yet and I was still in the closet socially but I asked him, "Well Walter, who's coming to this party?" He starts pairing names together like, "So and so, and so and so, and so and so…," and all of these are men. After about the tenth couple I looked at him and said, "Walter, are you gay?" He goes, "Lord yes, George. You haven't figured that out by now?" Inside I was in panic mode; I didn't have my car there and I couldn't leave and I didn't know how I was going to get out of there and I was literally falling apart, so I began to drink heavily. He said, "Oh, and there are two people coming from your hometown." He named them off and I didn't know them but I panicked at that point, thinking "Oh crap! Now they're going to tie me with gay people, and that can't work…" But I began to drink and thank goodness, I didn't know who they were. So I'm at the party and I'm handling things pretty well or feel like I am. I've told everyone that I'm straight and so don't be trying any crap—trying to be this big, bad, bully, butch guy and survive this party—and I will never forget… Right before dinner was served, there were these two guys there, and I thought, "My God, you look like regular guys. You're not effeminate and you own a farm and I know your dad who owns the lumber mill…" They were just two regular, everyday guys who were extremely attractive and I will never forget seeing them kiss each other. I had never seen a man kiss another man in my life. I remember I was holding a glass drink and I dropped it on the tile floor and it burst into a thousand pieces, and everyone looked at me and I was mortified. Needless to say I survived the party up until the moment Walter came downstairs in drag and I just freaked the hell out. I didn't know until much later that Walter had been telling all these gay guys that he and I were an item, which was not true.

That party turned out to be a pivotal moment in my life. The biggest thing I took away from it was, "Hey, it might be OK to be gay because these two guys are gay and they're just normal, regular guys. They're not wanting to be females. They're just two dudes and they're not much older than I am." I was just amazed by them. Over time the older of the two guys helped my mental stability more than any person on the face of the earth ever has. I've even tried to take the time to make him understand how much he's helped me, and he just kind of blows it off. But that relationship and seeing their interaction was the changing point in my understanding that being gay was not synonymous with being effeminate.

From that moment forward up until just before I turned thirty, I had many, many friends, and they were always older guys. These were men I wanted to impress. Because I had never had a father I wanted them to respect and think highly of me. I cut all relationship with the biological father and found solace in the people I adopted, in people who would spend time with me and show me how to do things and teach me how to be a man. I was drawn to older guys I would meet at the bar who had means and a career and who worked for their money. Not for sex or for what they could do for me but just, "How did you get what you have? I don't mind working for it but I don't know how to get there from here..." So over the years I had tons of good gay men who sheltered me and gave me guidance and who were my role models and who were people I wanted to emulate and be like. I ended up striking up a friendship with the two guys I mentioned earlier who were from my hometown at the party. Larry was much older than myself and was a hospital administrator and had a career and a boyfriend, and so I wanted to be just like him.

Up until I was twenty-seven or twenty-eight years old I really had some disastrous relationships with guys and I was jealous and petty and had gotten really heavily into drinking and partying and sexual experimentation. Of course, I was working and holding down a job the whole time while I was out nights till four in the morning at a sex club in Atlanta. But to get back to the point, I largely had to raise myself. I had to figure out first and foremost how to be a gay man, which was certainly not something I learned at home. I had to learn how to be a respectful gay man and to not be so closed-minded to others.

When I turned forty-six my mother told me that my biological father would really like to talk with me. Before that, for many years at funerals or any family event I could walk by that whole family as if they didn't even exist, as though they were invisible. For years that's the way it had been. I hadn't spoken to them and I didn't want to know about them. My mother knew not to bring them up around me because she would not like the response she would get. But when I was forty-six this man, who is elderly now, decides he wants to talk with me. So I tell Mother—here I go drawing a line in the sand—"I'll tell you what. You tell him that I said if he will go and have a DNA test done, then I will agree to talk to him after the test is done." And I'm thinking to myself, "This will end THAT conversation because he will never accept responsibility for me to anyone. Then I was told he agreed to the DNA test, and I'm going, "What? Crap…." But since I've always been a man of my word I said, "OK, let's get it done." So we do it. Mother came to my place in Florida, and I paid for him to go to the designated place near where he lived to have his done. The test results take two weeks, and I just really didn't give it any more thought.

Two weeks later the lab calls and the results are in but they won't give me the answers over the phone. So I go in to the lab, and the guy is rattling off the results and he says, "And the test came back negative for your father." I said, "Stop. What did you say?" He said, "There's no way that the gentleman you had tested is your biological father…" I just remember standing there dumbfounded. So I'm left with this information and I'm wondering if there has been a mistake. I said, "I want the test re-done. Hell, maybe Mother's not my biological mother. I mean, who knows now?" I was at the point of "Wow, who the hell am I?" So they ran mother's DNA, and hers came back 100% that she was the mother. I waited two weeks for that and then I confronted Mother with it. I said, "He is definitely not my father. It is black and white. DNA testing does not lie. So what are we going to do now?"

Now I've put him through hell all these years and now I'm having to deal with the fact that—holy crap—he was right and I was wrong. I trusted my mother 100% and never questioned her. But we flew home and we drove up to see him, Mother and I and my husband Andy. I took Andy because he's the only one who can keep me calm. We arrived and we had this conversation, and it was idiotic and stupid and childish. I said to him, "I was told you wanted to speak with me." He said, "I didn't ask to speak with you. I thought you wanted to talk to me; that's why you were coming up here…" So I had Mother come in the house and I said, "Mother, what the hell? Here I've spent all this money and used vacation time to take time off from my job to come up here because you said this man wanted to see me, and he's saying he knows nothing about it." Then we got to arguing, and I said, "You know what? Just stop. Everybody. STOP. Mother, get your coat. We're going. This is over. I'm done." So we left. I was backing the car up off the property onto the main road, and as I pulled away I literally put that whole portion of my life away. It was done. The final chapter was finished. I have no idea who my father is. If my mother chose not to tell me, that's it. I don't trust her anymore and I'm not angry. I'm just totally done with the whole thing.

I'm forty-seven now. My husband Andy is ten years older than I am, but I have always been the more mature of the two of us. I met him in my late twenties, and we've been together almost nineteen years. If I've ever had any functional relationship in my life, this would be the one that I've had, and it has been a lot of work. Andy was going through a divorce at the time we met and had two young children. I wanted no kids and wanted nothing to do with children. I was single and happy and sleeping with anybody I wanted to. How the hell we ended up together I still don't know but we were living together within two weeks of knowing each other. I was giving up my freedom and my own way. And all the things I worked so hard to have just went right out the window when I met this guy. I just fell head over heels.

For someone who originally wanted nothing to do with kids I'm here to tell you I've got four wonderful grandchildren and my son and daughter—

Andy's biological and my adopted children—and I couldn't love them any more. Amazingly Andy and I have had only three arguments in nineteen years. My one rule is that if I have to scream at you or hit you or track you down, that is not a relationship I want to be in. I would rather be by myself and be lonely than to be in a relationship like that. But Andy wanted peace and a place of safety for him and his kids. Andy has seen me at my worst and at my best. I credit him for showing me that it's OK, to be tender, to be soft, to cry, to be human. He's the person I want to lay down with at night, and the one I want to get up with in the morning.

Andy's daughter is older and his son and I have always been really close. I've always doted on both kids, but Jordan was special. A peacemaker, he's always had a calming influence on anyone who is around him. He would come to me before his father when anything was wrong or when something was on his mind. I was chosen to have the sex talk with Jordan on his twelfth birthday, so we went and made a boys' day of it. It was all the things I thought my father should have done. I always said, "Being a stepdad I'm going to break the cycle. I'm not going to be that arrogant, stupid, backwoods, abusive bastard my stepfather was. I'm going to show a child that... 1. It's OK to love someone else openly. 2. You're allowed to have an opinion. Not a smart mouth, but an opinion. And 3. We can talk about anything on the face of the earth. Anything." So Jordan and I had the sex talk and went rock climbing and I took him to the river and we went swimming; all these things that I always wanted someone to do with me when I was a kid.

So we're on the way back home and we're almost there and Jordan puts his hand on my knee and says, "George, can I tell you something?" I said, "Of course. You can tell me anything." He says, "I just want to find somebody who loves me like you and Daddy love each other." And I'm looking out the window with big tears running down my face thinking, "How did you figure this out at twelve years old?" Finally I got up the guts to ask him and I said, "What do you mean, son?," and he said, "You and Dad don't fight. You're respectful of each other and you both make me feel safe. I want to be that for somebody and I want somebody to be that for me when I get older." He just came out of the blue with that statement.

So many of our gay brothers think, "If I don't have my father's approval, my whole life is just crap." And that's just not true. Your self-worth is not tied to your parents. If their approval and their acceptance of you is the driving factor in your happiness, then you need to look at yourself and your happiness. You can't force somebody to love you. That's not what love is.

I didn't know or have a father growing up but I think I turned out pretty damn well OK. I have a very successful career. I have a family and friends who love me for me. I'm not perfect and I'm still striving to be a better person. But I made it despite all of the hurdles placed in front of me. And if I can do it, anyone can.

Chapter 21
Darrell Schramm

Darrell is a recently retired professor of poetry and composition at San Francisco State. His moving essay about his father is a highlight of the 1994 John Preston book, A Member of the Family.

I was born in a tiny, two-room house in Hazen, North Dakota in the dead of winter in 1943. My grandmother was the midwife for my birth. I grew up with three brothers and one sister and I'm the oldest of us. I can remember when I was about four years old that we had been invited to the farm about a mile down the road. My parents almost left me and my brother at home, and at the last minute they decided to take us. But I remember we had just sat down to dinner where we were invited, and somebody said, "My gosh! There's a fire out there..." I guess they were looking out the window, and I remember all the adults jumping up from the table and going outside. I just remember standing next to my father and I remember him saying, "That's our house..." If they hadn't brought my brother and me along, we'd have been in that fire.

One time my dad was trying to get one of our horses out of a corral. Even though the gate was open the horse just would not leave, and my dad grabbed a large stick and tossed it at the horse. At just that very moment the horse turned, and the stick gouged its eye. That was a horrible thing to see and hear. I think I understood that my dad didn't intend to do that, but I was just so horrified that it happened. I was about five years old then and I can still remember the shock that I felt at the time.

My dad worked hard. When we were on the farm he was up early doing chores and then going out into the fields and—depending on the time of year—cultivating or harvesting, and then he'd come back and milk the cows again… So he was always out doing things. I do remember sometimes my mom would say, "Here, take this little cream can full of cold water out to your dad in the fields." I remember doing that sort of thing.

The thing that tells me that my dad had a lot of affection for me is that he really just let me be who I was. I took to wearing aprons as a kid because I think I wanted to be a girl. I knew that I was different, but it's not something you can really articulate when you're six. So I wanted to wear aprons and I wore two aprons, one around my waist and one over my head, to pretend I had long hair. My dad let me do that. He never said, "Don't do that. You're a boy. That's girl-y stuff…" He never stopped me. When we'd go over to my cousins', who were girls, I would spend the whole time playing with their dolls. My father never reprimanded me or said, "Go play with the trucks." Even when the girls got bored with that and went off and did other things, I remained playing with the dolls. I was dressing them and all that kind of stuff. What my father wanted was for his children to be happy and he let them choose what it is that they wanted. My mother didn't object to a lot of these things until later, and I think she then thought that I might be an embarrassment to my father. She was wrong about that, but I didn't know that until much later.

My dad didn't have the birds and the bees talk with me, and in fact I was the one who actually approached him and I did it in a very awkward kind of way. This is almost embarrassing, but I was twelve years old and one day my dad was coming out of the shower and he was wearing his underwear and I just said to him, "Dad, how come I've never seen your cock?" And he just whipped it out and said, "There. Now you've seen it. OK?" I was really quite surprised and embarrassed. I did not think that's how he would answer my question. My dad came from a family that was very modest and very reticent about matters of sex. My mother's side was just the opposite, where they talked about everything and were all loudness and drama. He would tell me, "You're of the age now where you might want to consider shaving. Your face is getting more hairy," and, "This is how you would do it. Here's how you shave yourself…," and he'd ask me to watch him. He would give me instructions on this and other things but he wouldn't talk about sex.

Secretly I was messing around with guys like my uncle, who was my mother's youngest brother. My mother was the oldest of twelve children, and this brother of hers was child number eleven so he was only two or three years older than me. I was in the fifth grade when we started messing around together, and then when we moved to California the following year, he came to California and stayed with us, and at night I'd be creeping into his bed… So here I am messing around with my uncle who didn't seem like an uncle, with our being so close in age. There were other times I carried on with guys on the sly too.

My sister died while I was in college. She was only sixteen, and it was really devastating to the whole family, especially my mother. In college I was out to a couple of my friends, and one of them said something to me like, "Well maybe it's because of your sinful lifestyle that your sister died. Maybe that's God's punishment to you…" At first I thought, "I just don't think I'm a bad person, and that's just not so." But he and then a couple of other friends got on my case a bit and said, "You really ought to change your life" and all of that, and then I thought, "What if they're right? Why did my sister die at age sixteen? That's so young…" I struggled for a whole semester with that and tried to change my mind and feelings, so I started dating. I dated three different girls in college. One was always dropping her pants and wanting to fuck immediately, and I just wouldn't. It just didn't interest me. So my parents did see me bring a girl home a few times, but of course that didn't last.

When I lost my first love as a sophomore in college, I was heartbroken. It distressed me so much that I was not functioning very well in college and I started to miss classes. I got into my junior year and in the middle of the semester I called my dad up and said, "Dad, I'm coming home." This was mainly because my heart was broken; I couldn't concentrate on my classes and my homework and I was missing classes because I was so depressed. My dad was very patient with me over the phone and he said, "Darrell, you're the only member of this entire Schramm and Rinehart family—both sides—who has gone to college, and I have been so proud of that fact. You worked summers to put yourself through, and I really don't want you to drop out." I said, "I just can't do it, Dad." Basically all I would tell him was that I was unhappy; I didn't say why. He said, "I'll tell you what. Stick it out through the semester. Don't lose all these credits and units. Then you can come home at the end of the semester and live with us, and we'll take care of you, and if you want you can enroll at Chico State," which was about thirty miles from where they lived. So I finally agreed. He persuaded me, and I finished up the semester and then I was out of there and came home. I lived at home for a semester and enrolled at Chico State. I did want to please my father, so I went along with his suggestions. He may have suspected why I was depressed, but I really don't know.

When I did come out to him in my early thirties it wasn't like the sky fell or anything like that. Not at all. I had gone home for Thanksgiving and I had been thinking about talking with him and coming out to him. My two younger brothers were the jocks of the family, so they connected with my dad a lot. They'd talk about cars and football, and I just never engaged in those conversations because I didn't care about those things. That's when I found out that my father was distressed that I didn't talk to him about things. He and I were sitting on the sofa in the living room while Mother was fixing dinner, and I was just quietly flipping through a magazine. Suddenly he jumped up from the sofa and said, "Why in the hell don't you talk to me like my other sons do?" and left the room. I realized that he really did want to connect with me, but I didn't know how to. The only way I could think of doing it was to come out to him, so I believe it was the next day when I said, "Dad, there's something I want to tell you." He said, "Well, tell me now." I said, "No. No, I can't. I'm too scared. But I will let you know and I want to talk with you before I leave to go back to San Francisco."

I was rehearsing exactly what I wanted to say before I called him into the bedroom but, of course, the minute I saw him I panicked and just said, "Dad, I'm gay." I was going to lead up to it but instead I just blurted it out. I told him that I was in love with another man, my partner Chris. That's when he opened his arms and just pulled me to him and said, "You're my son. I love you. As long as you don't disown us, I shall always keep you in my family." It was an amazing moment. I had come out to my mother previously, and she had led me to believe that my dad would be disappointed if he found out. She would always say, "Well, don't tell your father," and made me feel that he would be very upset about it. But when he hugged me, I just started to cry, and he held me. I cried on his shoulder. I just had no idea that he would be so accepting.

I saw my dad cry when his father died. My father was a very quiet man, but I knew he felt things intensely. I have a beautiful photo of the four generations: my great grandfather sitting next to my grandfather, who's sitting next to my father, who is sitting next to me. My dad was very close to his father. When we'd go visit them, he and Grandpa would get up early and the first thing they would do is walk into the kitchen and my grandfather would pour two little jiggers of Schnapps—German whiskey—and he and Dad would each down a jigger in one gulp. That started their morning. Then they would have their coffee and their bacon and eggs and all of that. But they always did that little ceremony, which I thought was so wonderful.

When I brought Chris to meet my parents for the first time I was a little nervous about it—"How's this going to turn out?"—and my father took to him immediately. It was a tradition that whenever I'd go down to my parent's place, my dad and I would go out to this farm where my parents always bought their eggs. This time the three of us sat in the front seat. My dad was driving, and Chris sat in between us, and at one point in the conversation my dad put his hand on Chris's knee. I just thought that was the greatest thing; he was clearly telling Chris, "You're OK." It just warmed me inside. I think he did that because he was trying to show him that he was accepted in the family. My mother on the other hand was very jealous of Chris. For years! Whenever we'd visit, she'd call him every name but Chris. She would call him John or Phil, all kinds of names. And Chris tried everything. He sewed her a blouse, wove something for her, made drawings for her... None of it really persuaded her. It was a long, long time before she finally accepted him.

I'd call home every week, and it was usually my dad who answered the phone and we would speak. But he was not a talker so we would say a few things, and if there was the slightest pause he would say, "Well, here's your mom!" I couldn't even say, "But, Dad, I want to talk to you some more," because he'd already be handing her the phone. That happened a lot.

His health started going downhill. He had worked in tunnels and had emphysema from it. Not from smoking but because he had worked in these tunnels for years and years, in construction, blasting tunnels and stuff. He had really bad lung problems. Sometimes I'd call home and I could just hear that his breath was raspy. There were a few times that I drove down and said, "I'll take you guys to the county fair," which was about an hour away from their place. So we'd get there and then my dad would say, "I'm just going to sit here…," and he'd find a bench in the shade. "You and Mom just go and do what you want. I'll be here." It was just hard for him to breathe, especially if he walked for a long time. I was getting more and more concerned about him, but there wasn't anything I could do.

The last time I saw him I was down at their place in the late 1980s, just before Chris and I were heading off on a trip we had planned to Scotland. Dad just wasn't looking very good; he was very pale and he was having a hard time breathing. Apparently he was also having heart problems which I didn't know about. I said, "Dad, I'm going to postpone the trip," and he said, "No!" I said, "Well, you're not well," and he said, "Look. You have been planning this trip for a long time. You and Chris go and enjoy the trip and do what you have to do to make it a wonderful vacation, and I'll be here when you get back."

We got to Scotland and at some point I called home, and learned that he had been in the hospital. I rang up the hospital and talked to him there. They said it was his heart but it was cardiac-pulmonary, both heart and lungs. We spoke and I told him a little bit about our trip and what we were doing and so forth. I told him that I loved him, and he told me that he loved me too, and I still remember this kind of crack in his voice when he said it. It was scary. I remember leaving the phone booth and just crying. I told Chris, "It sounds like I will never talk to my dad again…" Chris said, "Oh, he'll be OK. Don't worry about it. They'll take good care of him." Then Chris went home, and I had taken off the semester from teaching to stay and spend a couple months writing in Spain. I was in Spain when the Loma Prieta earthquake hit the San Francisco area and I was trying frantically to call home and couldn't get through. All the phone lines were jammed because, of course, everybody was on the phone calling from across the world. I tried for two days and then finally on the third day I was able to get through to Chris's family in Sacramento, and that's when I found out that my dad had died. By then it was too late to come home, of course. My mother had tried to locate me and couldn't. I just sat and wept.

My dad has shown up in a lot of my dreams since then, though not so much in the last year or two. There's always a body of water present and we are always on the same side of the body of water. Sometimes we're walking together, like on a shore, with little ripples coming in. He would never be completely at my side but would always be a little ways away. But these were always happy dreams, and I was always so glad to be with him. When I'd awaken from these dreams I would feel so good. They were always very positive.

I think I have a lot of the old values that my father had, though not all of them by any means. I'm more apt to talk about sex and all of that. I do know that my parents carried on very late in life, so I know that my father was sexual, and that's definitely true of me too. So I'm very much like my father in that sense. My father just taught me a lot about how to live well and how to be a good person. That to me is the paradise I have and I am still a very happy man, and I think I owe much of that to my parents, especially my father.

I knew I was old when I looked in the mirror to shave one day and I practically jumped out of my skin; I thought it was my father looking at me. I was just astonished. Then two things struck me: Well, how wonderful that I look so much like my father, and gee, I'm old! I still wear my dad's wedding ring. He had big fingers. I have tiny fingers, so I had to have the ring resized and made a bit smaller. But now I can't get it off my finger, and that's fine. I keep photos of my dad around and I enjoy looking at them.

My advice to other gay men is that if your father dies, don't close yourself off to other possible surrogate fathers. Chris's dad became my surrogate father, and we'd go over there and visit. They had this long kitchen counter where everyone would sit, and Charlie—Chris's father—would come up behind me every time and he'd put his hands on my shoulders and knead my back or my neck a little bit. He was showing his affection, and he and I just became very, very close. Even though he was a bit of a bigot,

I valued the good side of him. And it felt so good that he kind of stepped in and was like a father to me.

I can see how for some people they may feel that, "That was my dad and that's the only dad I will ever have..." My dad was always willing to be open, and that's one of the important things that he taught me. I loved how open he was and how he just let me be who I was. I always want to be that open too.

Chapter 22
Dale

Dale lives in Fort Worth, Texas where he works in healthcare. He and his husband Marty married earlier this year.

I was born in 1976 in Decatur, Texas, a fairly rural town. My dad is a dairyman and a fifth generation Texan, so our family lived here before Texas was even a state. I am the oldest son, and have one brother, who is two years younger than me.

I loved to play with Barbie dolls when I was four or five years old, and my dad would sit on the floor and play along with me, and we would fix their hair. He had no problem with that, and it was no issue. I remember when I was six years old, he got us motorcycles, and I rode a motorcycle before I could ride a bicycle. I had a little Yamaha 50 and no helmet, no pads, no anything. I wouldn't even considering allowing that with my kids now, but that's a good memory of mine. We always had motorcycles around on the farm. It's funny that I still had a bicycle with training wheels on it, but I could ride a motorcycle!

I can remember when I was four or five, my dad would take me in the hay truck and put in into low gear and let me stand on the seat and drive around in the pasture while he threw hay out for the cattle. He would tell me just to drive in circles in the field, and I thought that was great fun. He would jump down and run alongside the pickup whenever he was done, because there was no way I could stop it. I can remember my brother being six or seven and driving the truck so I could throw hay off the back. All of that sounds terribly unsafe, but we were farm kids, and you had to do what you had to do. I remember helping milk the cows in the afternoons.

Neither of my parents are real affectionate. I recall Dad being a lot of fun and tickling me and throwing me around and wrestling. My dad was loving, but he's never been the type to say that he loves you. Of course as a kid you don't know how to ask for affection really, but as a dad now I'm way different than my dad because I think I needed that affirmation as a kid. But I can't say that I ever doubted that he loved me, even if he's not a hugger and he doesn't say that he loves you.

My family was very close, and I felt very secure. I look back now and realize my parents really didn't have the same defined gender roles that you would expect of people who are very traditional and very rural. My dad did a lot of our cooking. My mother worked outside of the home; she was a teacher and then became a principal and later on a superintendent. My dad did all of our laundry, and I remember him vacuuming and cleaning and dusting. My mother certainly did housework too, but he was very helpful and even nurturing. I remember several times when I was sick, he would be the one to stay up or to lie in bed beside me. He was certainly just as nurturing as my mom.

I'm not an extremely effeminate person but as a boy I probably was more effeminate than some of the other boys in our rural area. Yet I also rode motorcycles and played in the dirt and had a lot of fun and stayed cut up and bruised a lot. Due to our Fundamentalist Baptist religious background we didn't have a TV, so I wouldn't even have known what a gay person was. I didn't know what gay was until I was about fifteen. I recall seeing something in the paper about the Gay Pride Parade in Dallas, and Dallas was pretty far away from us. I saw the pictures and I remember feeling relief because I thought, "At least I know I'm not gay because I would never want to be like these people…" There were certainly no role models in my immediate world and it wasn't a topic that was ever discussed. I knew I wanted to be married and I wanted to have kids and I remember daydreaming sometimes that that would be with a man, but I didn't think that would be possible.

Our family was at church Sunday morning, Sunday night, Tuesday night, Wednesday night, and I loved it. I loved the structure and I loved the music. I was certainly "drug" to church, but I loved it.

My dad had the birds and the bees talk with me when I was nine years old. Now I grew up on a farm so I probably already had a concept, but the talk went like this: "There's a cow and there's a bull, and when the bull gets excited he puts his shaft into the cow, and she gets pregnant and that's how you have babies." I was somewhat confused but I had seen it happen, so I guess I got a concept of it. It's a topic my parents would have never talked about, since they were very modest about sex.

When I was fourteen my parents threatened to put me in military school. I had a lot of questions about life and about faith and I really did not want to live in the country. I did *not* want to be a farmer. So I guess I was what would today be considered mildly rebellious, and it kind of hurts me to think back on some of the things I said to my parents during those years. I made my parents miserable. I was unhappy and I made it known. I would talk back and I wouldn't just take their answers, his especially. I truly thought that he was the dumbest person ever. I hated that he was a farmer and that he always smelled like cow shit. It was just extremely embarrassing to me that my dad was a farmer and I, especially at that time, took it out on him. We became more distant.

During that same time he and my brother really bonded. My brother was really favored because he wanted that life and wanted to be just like my dad. I wanted to be anything other than my dad. That time period really changed my dad's and my relationship and also my dad and my brother's relationship. My brother became the good kid.

At seventeen I knew for sure that I was gay and I knew that I could never tell anybody that. I also knew that, according to our faith, if I were ever to admit that, not only would I lose my family but I most assuredly would end up in hell. So since I wanted to make sure that I would never even *consider* coming out, I decided that I wanted to be in the ministry. I started taking some seminary classes through the mail—at that time they would mail you tapes—and then I simultaneously worked on a real degree at Tarleton, in education.

At twenty I got married to my kid's mom, and the first time I actually had sex with anyone was on my wedding night. We were married for nine years before my wife and I decided to get divorced. I'd never even had sex with anybody but my wife and it wasn't like I was dating anybody, so I was not going to come out of the closet. I really wasn't even sure what I was at that time. But since she had met the guy she ended up marrying anyway, I knew that it was OK for us to split up. I just didn't plan to come out to anybody right at that time since there was nothing to tell.

So my mother, being in a small town, decided to start saying things that weren't too nice about my ex-wife, basically blaming her for the divorce. It got a little ugly. I'd already moved into Fort Worth, which was about an hour from my parents' place, and I went to their house and I said, "You know, it's not her fault. I am gay, and she's put up with it for all this time and now she has a chance to have a happier life." And oh my goodness… My mother collapsed, and I've never really seen my dad that angry before. He told me that I was no longer their son and that he never wanted to speak with me again. He demanded that I leave their property, so I did. I left.

It was really rough. I had no contact with anybody except my ex-wife, but it did take the pressure off her. Suddenly she became the saint to my family for having put up with this horrible person, this terrible liar. My ex and I had done a non-contested divorce, and I said that she could keep the house and savings and everything. I would pay child support. I really didn't care; I just wanted them all to be OK. Then my parents cross-filed against both of us. The only way they wanted me to see my kids was if they were present. It got thrown out, because my wife said, "This is ridiculous. He's a good father." She was the beacon of sanity in the whole nightmare.

My brother was the associate pastor at our church at that time, and all of my family was there: my parents, my brother, my sister-in-law, his four kids, my two kids, my ex-wife… He had become the associate pastor because the original pastor was about to retire, and then my brother would take that position over, which he did. So they held a business meeting and they removed me from the church membership. I got a letter in the mail about that. That's when my ex-wife left that congregation and denomination, when she and my kids had to sit through that meeting and watch my parents and my brother stand to vote against me. And remember, through all of this time I still had not even been with anyone of the same sex! All I had done was to say, "This is something that I have struggled with, and I want to deal with it in an authentic way by being honest." So I was removed from the church. My ordination was removed, my ministerial license. All of that. All of that in front of my kids who at that time were seven and eight years old. So that was rough. I don't know that I've ever faced anything harder.

By that point I had re-established myself. I had rented a house, a place for the kids to come. At that time my son was just determined to live with me, and his mom said that was fine. So I've had him with me since he was nine, and my daughter has stayed with her mom and been back and forth.

With my parents, my mother softened a little over time, so we talk on the phone probably a couple times a month. She doesn't want to hear about anyone I'm dating but she asks about the kids and lets me know she's praying for me. But it's not awful. I've seen my dad at a couple of funerals that I went back home for, but we've not spoken since he told me to get out of their house. I have written him a few letters throughout the years to tell him how much I appreciate him and that I love him and that I can respect and honor his convictions, and that's the honest truth. I honor the fact that both my parents have lived the faith that they espouse. They're not hypocrites. At this point—ten years later—I don't really need acceptance, so much as I just want him to know that I don't hold any of it against him. But I've had no response. Same with my brother; we haven't spoken in over eight years. I do send his kids Christmas gifts and things but I don't know if they get them or not.

Probably the best thing my mom said to me, which at least gave me some peace was, "You know, you're thirty-five years old. You don't have to please us." I think that's the most I will ever get out of her. She'll never be happy about things but I think she's accepted that I'm not going to remarry the kids' mom and fix all of those things that I ruined in her world. She has tried to get me to come to Christmas and different things, and I've said, "No. Dad said that I'm not welcome, and I'm fine with that. But if he wants to call and invite me, I'll be glad to show up." I've not been ugly about that but I've held firm about it. When he wants me there, then I will be there. And until then I will honor that he doesn't want me there.

This sounds really harsh, but I'm guessing that my father would prefer that I be dead. I'm not saying he would like to kill me, but I think that for him that would be an easier situation than knowing that I'm still out here carrying his name. I think he would tell you that Satan has taken over my life, that he taught me the right way to live and the right way to be, and that I've chosen a different path. Also that if I were to repent of all that and come back, that he would be there with open arms. I'm fairly certain that that's what's in his mind, and he's self-assured that he's right. I'm OK with that. It took me a while to get there. That we can even be having this discussion and I'm not in tears, weeping in the corner is actually making me kind of proud. I couldn't have said this five years ago. I simply could not have talked about it.

I think the great equalizer may be that as my parents' age, my dad may need me at some point. I am a nurse, and when he had colon cancer—before I divorced—he relied heavily on me for a year because he was so sick. At some point he might have to live with me, and I would agree to that in a heartbeat. I still don't think we would agree but I think it would be OK. I think that would be the only chance, if he were to need me, or if something were to happen to my mother or him, and they needed me. My dad is not in great health. He has diabetes. I really don't know how he would cope if one of us didn't take care of him.

In the South, and this is fairly common, I thought I was all alone in what I was going though. Then I found so many people like myself who had kids and got married and then came out later in life, so I've found my community. I've given this advice to more than a few guys right after they come out… Don't react. Even though internally I've reacted and been hurt, I think the one thing I'm very proud of myself for is that I've not said things I regret to my dad. There's nothing I've said since I came out that I regret. I've always been authentic and honest with him and even when I felt hurt I didn't lash out at him. Like I've told a million people, don't fight back. Say what you need to say and be honest and be real, but there's no reason to fight and scream and yell and to try to change somebody's mind.

I'd like to think that I've done OK, but I'm tellin' ya… The first year was really bad. I went to counseling every week for the first year and a half after I came out, and then throughout the years I've gone back just to have a refresher. It's been very helpful. I told my counselor, "I've spent thirty years not telling anybody anything, so get ready. I'm about to talk."

The second thing that was really helpful for me was finding a church and finding other people, finding a community, and rebuilding a family of sorts. I felt very lost and alone without my church group and my family, so I needed strong connections. In the abstract I knew that there is a family of blood as well as a family of choice, but until you live it you don't even understand how much that matters. For me finding my family of choice has really helped me re-center and not go crazy.

I always wanted to be a dad, and there are two things that I've wanted to do differently and that I hope I've done well with my kids. One is that I did not want my kids to be afraid of me. I was afraid of my dad and not because he was mean or violent but because he was quick to anger. I did not want my kids to feel like they had to walk on eggshells around me. The other thing is that since my dad never told me he loved me, I wanted to make sure that my kids always knew that I loved them. Even when I was angry I wanted them to know that underneath my being upset about a situation I still always loved them.

But certainly my dad was a major influence on my wanting to be a father. He was an amazing provider and made sure that we had everything that we could have wanted. He influenced me as far as faith, and I've always made sure my kids were in church and that they realize that I have a deep faith base. So many of the values that he instilled in me are things that I've wanted to instill in my kids. I've also realized, as I'm about to turn forty, that I'm actually a whole lot more like him than I ever thought I would be. So my dad has had a tremendous influence, mostly positive, on my life.

I have seen really bad parents. I was an ER nurse for a long time before I moved over into sales and healthcare, and I have seen some *really* bad parents. My dad was certainly not that.

Chapter 23
Johnny George

Johnny is a nursing student studying Diagnostic Cardiovascular Sonography. He lives in Charlotte, North Carolina.

I was born in Mullins, South Carolina on June 10th, 1963. Mullins is a very small tobacco town. They still have a Golden Leaf Festival, golden leaf referring to the tobacco leaf once it's cured. It's really pretty. So I grew up with the smells of cured tobacco wafting through the air. All the major tobacco houses were in my town, where Phillip Morris and all the big names would come and they would have auctioneers there who would auction off the tobacco to the highest bidder... It was a pretty unique experience growing up there.

My mother told me the whole story about my father's death once I was a young adult and was old enough to understand. The story I had been told growing up was that my dad was killed by a drunk driver, but that was pretty much all I knew. I was shown the tree they had hit. He was heading back home when it happened. My mother was actually at the doctor's office at the time and that's when she found out she was pregnant with me. When she got home the sheriff was standing on her porch, and that's when he told her my daddy had been killed in a car accident.

My mom has eleven siblings. She's the twelfth in her family and comes from a sharecropper family, so they were brought up on a farm. I credited her not miscarrying me right there on the front porch when she got the news to her being a strong, resilient country woman. She still lived in the community she was born and raised in, so grandparents on both sides and aunts and uncles all came to help. Until she married my stepfather when I was six years old, I remember my mother's younger brother and younger sister helping out a lot with me and my sister.

My stepfather did not adopt my older sister and me, so we did not carry his name. We carried our daddy's name, and I think my mother wanted it that way. It wasn't like they had gone through a divorce; they were high school sweethearts and they had been married for a while. It must be really hard to have someone taken from you that way, so I think she wanted us to carry our daddy's name. I appreciate being named after him too.

Later in life I found out that my stepfather actually knew my father, which I hadn't known until then. My stepfather owned a restaurant so he wasn't at home a lot. If my mom wasn't at the restaurant helping him she was with us. If both of them were at the restaurant, we had a babysitter/maid who would keep us and watch over us until Mom and Dad got home. She was a small black lady, and we called her Grandma.

I had such a strong family around. My daddy's relatives were in my life, and they came over or they kept us. We'd spend summers with Grandma George and Grandaddy George. Sometime before my mother married my stepfather my Grandfather George died, and that was really hard on me. I do remember my mother holding me at the casket and me screaming like a banshee because I had always been so close to him.

I didn't feel like I was missing anything especially growing up without my dad. It's almost like if you never had a TV you don't really miss it because you've never had one in the first place. I had a lot of women help raise me—an older sister, a mother, and a lot of aunts—so I didn't necessarily feel like I was missing anything and I was close with my grandfathers and grandmothers on both sides of the family too.

I called my stepfather Daddy—all of us did—even my older sister, even though they didn't get along very well. She would backtalk him. I never did, but that's probably just my nature. I always respected him, and we had a good life because of him. We never wanted for anything. He just wasn't around a lot, so I could say we were raised by the strong women in our family. My stepfather used to be mistaken for Andy Griffith because he really looked a lot like him, especially when he was younger, with that jet black hair. I think I reminded him of my daddy a lot because I often got the brunt of his anger, which wasn't physical, but more verbal. He would say degrading things to me when I was younger like, "You'll never amount to anything," and all kinds of stuff like that. When I got to be a teenager, it seemed to get worse, maybe because I started looking more like my father.

I remember I scared my stepfather and my mother one time because they thought I had run away. I was just very good at hiding and, of course, when I came out of hiding I got a whipping. My mother had to make him stop. That was the one and only time he did beat me, but I'll never forget it. He was a big guy and had formerly been a policeman and had also been in the Army Air Corps.

My real daddy had been in the Army, and because of that, the VA had been paying my mother for my sister and me. She'd been getting a stipend to put away for our education or to support us while we were growing up. That could have been another reason why they didn't change our names. I was going to use the money for college and unbeknownst to me, my mother signed my money over to my stepfather when I turned eighteen, and he went out and bought a car, about which I had no say so. I didn't know it was happening until he showed up with the car, and when I found out that he had used my college money to buy it I was not happy. He pretty much made it known to me that he didn't want me to go to college. I don't know what it was with him and me trying to better myself; he wanted me to stay "beneath" him. I think he just had a problem with me because I looked so much like my daddy, with all the negative things he would say to me.

I got accepted to the American College in London, England, which was still around at that time. After I graduated high school I was still living at home, trying to decide what I wanted to do. I was working part-time and attending the local community college, which I was driving back and forth to. Apparently one of my art teachers sent some of my drawings to someone at the American College in London, and it turned out they were going to pay for my schooling for four years—a full scholarship—for me to get my design degree. For some reason even though I was nineteen I couldn't just go of my own accord, something I still don't understand to this day. I gathered that it was something to do with my still living at home and my parents still claiming me as a dependent. The college had to have at least one parent's signature to OK me going, so my mother was going to sign. I asked my stepfather to sign as well because I thought he'd be proud and happy, and he had a fit. He said, "I'm not signing anything."

He had it set in his mind that there was no way somebody would actually be paying for my schooling. He couldn't wrap his head around that. I don't know if it was his upbringing or what, but my mother tried to explain it to him. The financial aid officer from the Atlanta location of the college called and tried to talk to him, and he practically hung up on the guy. "Somewhere along the line it's going to come back to bite me on the ass and I'm going to have to pay for it. I'm not paying for you to go to school. Period." I argued with him. I said, "I've been going to school for a year and a half, Daddy, and you've not paid for me to go. I've been paying that by working part-time, since you took my money and bought a car with it that I did not want." Of course, I had to drive the car to get back and forth to school but I wouldn't need the car in London so I could have sold it. Then my mother said to him, "That's fine, Winston. I will sign the papers with or without your blessings because my son is getting an education." She didn't want me to go to London but she was very happy and ecstatic for me. And then he dropped the hammer. He said, "That's fine, Rosemary. You go ahead and sign the papers for that boy. You'll have my divorce papers in your hands the next day as soon as you sign them." I was like, "*WHAT????*" I was just floored. For him to threaten my mother with something like that, I was crushed. My mother was speechless as well. She turned white as a ghost.

After that I didn't even bat an eye, and the next day I went and joined the military. I actually wasn't going to tell them until I was walking out the door, I was so angry at him. For him to be so resentful of me that he would go to that length just to hold me back floored me. I was also angry at my mother because she didn't stand up to him and call him on his bluff. She has told me since that she wished she had. She said, "That was not fair to you and that was really very ugly of him." As it stands now I'm still the only one in the family who has gone to college. I was the only one to join the military, which seemed to make him happy. And not that I was trying to make him happy. I was trying to get away from him to be honest. The military got me out of that small town and the military is actually where I had my first sexual experience with another man, which was actually my first sexual experience with anybody. I was then twenty-one.

My sister and I had been brought up in a Christian household. We went to church every Sunday and sometimes on Wednesday and Sunday nights. I had also been a missionary for two years for the Baptist Church. In my teen years I was very aware of my feelings toward guys and I was lucky not to have had a fire and brimstone preacher and I never heard the words homosexual or gay. I never got picked on in high school and was never bullied. I was one of those lucky kids who, even though I was a nerd, nobody shunned and everyone welcomed. My best friend was the quarterback of the high school football team. We went to church together. So a lot of my male friends were football players I looked up to and who I also thought were cute. Their girlfriends were friends of mine. So I knew I was gay but I had never acted on it and I really didn't come out until I was in the military.

After getting out of the military, my mother took it pretty well when I first tried to talk to her about it. She said, "But I still want grandchildren," and I said, "Well, I don't know how that's going to happen…" I had dated girls but never had a serious relationship with a girl. Mother comes from that generation where the men would marry and have kids but they were in the closet and having sex with guys behind their wife's back, and she pretty much told me she had friends who were like that. That kind of took me aback, and I was basically closing my ears going, "I don't want to hear this! Don't say any names…" I said, "Mom, I don't think I could love someone and do that to them."

I didn't tell my stepfather until I was probably twenty-nine, and I wrote him a letter. By that time I was living in Dallas and I had gone through The Experience weekend. I had moved to Dallas after the military at age twenty-four. My friends in Dallas wanted me to go to this weekend retreat thing that was being held there. Basically it was a weekend for gay men and lesbian women where we would come to terms with our sexuality. Essentially it taught us to trust and forgive. I forgave my stepfather for a lot there and I also had an epiphany—it was like a bring me to the knees experience—it was, "Oh my God… I'm responsible for all the shit that's happened to me in my life and I've been blaming my stepfather all these years, using him as a scapegoat…" So The Experience taught me forgiveness and also to be responsible for the road that I was on at the time and to take ownership of that, and from that point forward, things were better for me because I wasn't carrying around that hatred anymore. I'd had a lot of hate, a lot of unforgiveness for my stepfather that I had been carrying around with me, and that weekend I was able to truly forgive him. It was a big load off of me and it really changed me as a person.

I was close with my mom and we talked all the time and I told her that I was afraid to tell my stepfather. I'd talk with him on the phone and he'd joke with me, even when I'd come to visit: "Have you married any of these older rich ladies in Dallas yet?" But after going through The Experience weekend I wrote him a letter and forgave him and told him that I was a gay man living in Dallas as a gay man. After mailing the letter I said to my mother on the phone, "Oh my lord, he's going to show up at my door with a straight-jacket and a shotgun. I just know it!" She said, "Well, let's just wait and see…" She wasn't sure how he'd take it either, but he surprised both of us.

Actually our relationship improved a lot. Whenever I'd go home after I came out to him, he seemed to have a lot more respect for me. We would actually have conversations instead of yelling matches. Instead of lecturing, he talked to me like an adult, and I could see the difference. He would still talk to my brothers and sisters condescendingly and say negative things about them but he would speak to me like an adult or friend. He'd say, "I don't know what I'm going to do with Ricky…" And even though I didn't like him talking down about my siblings, it still made me feel like, "Wow, he's actually talking to me and listening to my input. Wow!" In the letter he replied to my letter with he said, "I've always thought of you as my son"— which I found surprising—"and I still love you." So that was very moving for me and a big load off my shoulders and a big relief.

My stepfather did not express his emotions much. Only once did I see my stepfather cry. My older sister lost her first-born, and that was the first time I ever saw him cry, when he lost his grandson. Seeing him cry made me cry.

When my mother had a stroke several years ago, I came back from Dallas to be with her. She's still in a nursing home now. Her left side is paralyzed and she has aphasia, which is a difficulty in getting her words out, so it is hard for her to speak. My stepfather had a heart attack two weeks after my mother had her stroke. I had just gotten in from Dallas prior to that and had taken him to the cardiologist, so I was in the cardiologist's office when it happened, thank God. I was in the waiting room, and they came running out saying, "Johnny! Johnny, come back here with us!" They called the ambulance and I accompanied him to the hospital. After his heart attack he lingered on for a while but passed after about eight months. He was in the hospital a lot. The last time he was hospitalized he suffered from what the doctors called "hospitalized dementia," and he wasn't always cognizant of who I was.

He never brought up the whole college situation. I brought it up originally in the letter I wrote, but he never mentioned it when he wrote me back or anytime later. I think he regretted how he handled that situation, and I thought that was the case long before he died because of the way he treated me; he treated me with more respect than my other siblings. I think he felt bad about what he'd done.

Once you forgive somebody, it's kind of like having a veil lifted off your eyes. With my stepfather I realized that some of the things he'd told me over the years were true. I credit him with teaching me things like "You're only as good as your word." If you tell somebody you're going to do something you'd better do it. I think a lot of people forget that. Some of my friends have said, "If Johnny ever says he's going to do something, he will do it." Winston tried to teach us to always tell the truth, because if you don't it's going to come back and bite you in the butt. And that's true.

After Winston died, this blackbird kept showing up repeatedly. It was always the same bird, and not only has it shown up for me, it has shown up at my sister's house and my baby sister's house and in my baby brother's yard. It's always the same bird and it has always freaked us out. When we were at his grave not too long after his death, that's the first time it showed up, and it actually flew directly—I mean I could have reached up and grabbed it, it was that close to us—and landed on a tombstone right next to where we were. It was like it wasn't even afraid of us, and it kept cawing at us. We named it Winston.

The thought of "How would my life have been different if my real dad wasn't in that car accident?" has certainly crossed my mind before, especially when I was a teenager. Of course, you can speculate all day long, and as I've gotten older I just want to be grateful for what I've been given. Things probably work out the way they do for a reason. I've had terminal cancer and I've been in two very bad car accidents and I'm still here. So I think I'm here for a reason and I just want to make the world a better place than what I grew up in.

My aunts and uncles and my grandmother on my birth father's side of the family would regale me with stories about my dad. Mama would talk about him too, so nothing was ever hidden from me. They spoke very highly of him, though he was human and had his faults like everyone else. He was 6'1 and had auburn hair. My older sister has the auburn hair, but I don't. My beard when I was younger would be red, which was funny. I have pictures of my dad. He was a handsome man, so when people say I look like him I take it as a compliment. One of the photos is a really beautiful one of him in Mexico. He has a white dinner jacket on. People see it and they think it's me, and I say, "That's not me. That's my dad." I have been to his grave-site a number of times. My sister and I still go and put flowers on it.

When dealing with your father my advice is to be forgiving. Fathers try to do their best even if sometimes it's not good enough. If you don't learn to forgive, your anger can eat you up. That doesn't mean that what your father did was necessarily right; it means you can go and be free and be a better person. Carrying all that resentment and hurt is a big load to carry around.

When I was going through a lot as a teenager I would try to talk to my real dad because I felt so alone, even though I was in a family of five. I guess when you're having feelings you don't understand and then you have a stepfather who's berating you with negativity it can make life difficult. I used to call out to my real dad to protect me and help me, and I think he did.

I've often thought it would be nice to be a father. I still feel kind of empty. My heart swells whenever I see gay dads with their kids. Two of my friends in Dallas adopted a little girl from China, and she's just the cutest little kid you've ever seen.

Chapter 24
Dennis

Dennis lives in California where he works as an over the road truck driver.

I was born in Arlington, Virginia in June of 1962, where we lived until I was eight years old. I'm the oldest and I have two younger brothers. We moved to San Diego and then Portland, Oregon before settling in Tucson in 1975. I went to junior high and high school in Tucson. My dad worked long hours in the transportation industry and moved up over the years and became a big-wig. He was always more of a strict father. Any time we got out of line we'd get sent to our room or we'd get a whipping. His whippings weren't abusive and he didn't drink or just fly off the handle for no reason. My mom was always the softie, so we always used to run to her. Dad wasn't affectionate or much for hugging, and saying "I love you" wasn't something we would really say in our family.

My dad always wanted us to do well and be successful. He used to take us camping and fishing and stuff like that, so it was always all about doing activities together. I was in baseball and football, and he was assistant coach. My mom had been a cheerleader. I was always closer to her and kind of avoided my dad at times. My mom was always there for us and she'd bend over backwards to get us anything we needed.

When I was around sixteen, Dad and I would drive up to Oregon to go salmon fishing. That was a big thrill for me. Just me and him would drive up there and we'd meet some old friends and would charter a boat and go out on the ocean to do some deep sea salmon fishing. I remember one time too, Elvis Presley was playing in concert in Tucson, and Dad asked me if

I wanted to go. I kind of chuckled and said, "Why would I want to go to an Elvis Presley concert?" So I didn't go but to this day I kind of regret it. That would have been something to really cherish, seeing an Elvis Presley concert.

When I was six years old this other six year old kid and I went down in the basement and pulled our pants down and kind of just hugged each other. When I was eleven or twelve I was already giving blowjobs to other kids in the neighborhood. I remember we'd all play hide and seek and everyone would take turns hiding with me in the closet. It was funny that everybody knew where I was hiding and since everyone took turns with me, of course, nobody would find me and the kid I was giving a blowjob to. A kid about the same age as me named Curt had a fort up in the rafters of his garage, and we used to go up there and suck each other. This was around 1973 or '74, when we were eleven or twelve.

Then we moved from Oregon to Tucson and I started seventh grade down there. I didn't know anyone who was gay there so I was totally in the closet all through high school. I was religious when I was around sixteen years old and I remember days and nights sitting in my bedroom by myself crying and praying to God, "Why can't I be like everybody else?" I remember those times very well.

In 1980, the local newspaper had a week-long series on homosexuality. I remember waiting each day until my parents had thrown the paper in the trash and then I'd go out to the trashcan and dig it out so I could read it. I didn't want any suspicion that I was reading this series on homosexuality. On the last day of the series they listed all the gay bars in town, and that was when I took the big step to go to a gay bar. Drinking age was nineteen at the time, and I was eighteen, so I was sneaking in. I remember the first time I went I drove back and forth for like forty-five minutes before I had the courage to pull into the parking lot. The gay bars were the only place we could go at that time and feel safe. There really weren't gay organizations that you could easily look up, and, of course, we didn't have the Internet back then.

When I was eighteen I was pretty much forced out of the closet. I used to keep gay porn magazines in the bottom of my dresser. Of course, brothers like to snoop, and my middle brother found my gay porn magazines. He kept it quiet for a while until one day when we were fighting. My parents were sitting in the kitchen, and he went up to them and said, "Mom, Dad, guess what? Dennis is a fag." I was standing there, and my parents were like, "Is this true?" I knew at that point that I could just deny it for who knows how long, but I just thought to myself, "To hell with it. I'm not going to deny it any more," and I said, "Yes." My mom cried and said that's what she had thought. My dad was furious and disgusted. They sent me to a psychiatrist for a couple of months after that. The psychiatrist told me, "Be however you want to be."

Over the course of the next several months my relationship with my dad seriously deteriorated. I remember one time sitting in front of the TV and I don't recall what was on that brought up the conversation—maybe a news report on AIDS, which they then called the gay cancer—but my dad said to me, "If you ever turn your brothers gay, I'll kill you." I didn't reply.

A few weeks after that something got set off and we were arguing and he started to charge at me, so I ran into my room and slammed and locked the door. He was pounding on the door, and it finally came open and we just started fist-fighting each other. I think he was shocked that I was actually hitting him, but that's what I needed to do at the time. Finally he backed off, and I grabbed whatever I could at the spur of the moment and threw everything in my car. As I was backing out the driveway he came running out, yelling at me through the driver's window. I spit right in his face and slammed on the gas pedal backwards, and moved one hundred twenty miles away to Phoenix, with five days worth of clothes and about a hundred bucks. That was early in 1981. From the moment I peeled out of the driveway I didn't hear from him for sixteen or seventeen years. I did keep in touch with my mom. My parents got divorced shortly after that, though for reasons other than that. I basically wrote my dad off. I had no interest in ever talking to him again. After I came out, he was a negative force in my life, and I just had to leave. I wish things had been different but they weren't.

Looking back now, I'm so glad my brother outed me. I probably never would have had the courage to come out on my own. After I came out, all that pressure was just lifted off of me. I am really thankful that he did, though I was not thankful when it happened!

I knew one person in Phoenix, and he let me stay at his place until I got kind of settled. The first couple years there were pretty tough. I was actually an escort for a while living in an escort house. We had hallway cupboards there with locks on them, and you'd pick a cupboard and put your stuff in it. That way you could keep your stuff safe from the other escorts. I lived there for about six months in 1982. It wasn't too bad. I made friends with the other escorts; we were like a little family. Then I moved out and moved in with some friends after that, and things kind of took off from there.

My younger brother's wedding was the first time my dad and I were going to see each other. The whole family was going to be there and everybody was curious how it was going to be with both me and my dad at the wedding. From what everyone else had been telling me, he was regretting how he'd treated me and was sorry about it. I was the DJ at the wedding. I remember shaking my dad's hand and, "Hi, how are you?" Basically small talk. It went fine. It was like we had never fought but it wasn't like we were sitting down being buddy-buddies either. He looked like he was aging faster than my mom. Even nowadays my mom still looks pretty young at seventy-four. My dad is seventy-eight and looks like he could be my grandfather.

In the late '80s and early '90s I'd go visit my brothers or they'd visit me and I'd take them out to the gay bars. We'd dance together and stuff like that. No big deal. With my youngest brother, when I used to visit I'd take him to the gay bar down there, and my sister-in-law loved it because she knew that he could go out and have a fun time and drink and party and he wouldn't pick up anybody. She'd kid me and say, "At least I know Greg's not going to pick up some girl with you!"

Pretty much from the time of my brother's wedding the only contact I have with my dad is about once a year. Every once in a while I might give him a call on his birthday. My birthday is a month before his, and he usually sends me $150 for a birthday present now, so I kind of feel obligated to at least call him. When my ex and I were living in Arizona together, he would see us maybe once a year or so and he treated my ex like part of the family. He was very friendly and open and supportive, so he totally did a

180 degree turn. But I still have a hard time forgiving him. I guess that's why I don't call him all that often. I've heard through other family members that he regrets what happened. But I don't really care for any in-person apologies because that's not going to do anything for me. Like I said, he's treated my ex like part of the family, which to me is better than an apology. Even when I've been out of town and he's come up to visit my mom and brother in Phoenix—when my ex was still living there—he'd take my ex out with him and buy everybody lunch, even though I wasn't around. And that's not his attempt to apologize; that's just how he is now. From what I understand from other family members, his ex-wife, who he married after my mom, was supportive of gay people. I guess she kind of turned him around. I met her a few times. She died a few years ago.

My dad was in the military for about four years. I think I remember him telling me a story—this was before I came out to him—when he was like eighteen or nineteen and was thumbing a ride in his military outfit, this guy in a truck picked him up and was a "little too friendly." That's all he said. I can kind of imagine what he meant by that, that the driver was trying to pick him up.

My dad has been out of my life for so long that he's pretty much just a stranger with a familiar face. My relationship with him could be better if I would participate in it, but for me it's basically "too little too late." I don't know if I would attend my father's funeral or not. If I was in town I probably would. But if he's dead he's dead, and there's nothing I can do by showing up at his funeral. I'm not particularly looking forward to that day though either.

Chapter 25
Matthew Shurka

Matthew is a prominent activist working to outlaw the practice of conversion therapy. His efforts have resulted in important legislation being passed in a number of states and major cities. Matthew lives in Brooklyn, New York.

I was born in Great Neck, New York in May of 1988. I'm the youngest of three and have two older sisters. My father worked in commercial real estate in New York City. I remember that when I was in Kindergarten I just wanted to be with him and I went to work with my dad most every Friday instead of going to school. I don't know how I got permission to do that or how it even happened. I would just play in the office all day because his office was like an amusement park to me. In the middle of the day we'd leave the office and go have lunch, and since my dad is Israeli we'd go to some Israeli falafel shop or something. I just really enjoyed being with him. Spending the whole day with him and seeing what his workday was like was an exciting adventure for me as a kid. Retelling it now I felt like I was very close to my dad but I was always closer to my mom.

It's interesting that there was a real yin and yang with my father. He was definitely a very affectionate man. He worked a lot so he wasn't around as much as my mom was. He'd come home late from work, but I'd always wait for him to come home. My dad was certainly affectionate with us. My dad is a very strong man and he's a little bit of a hard man. He was a New York City cab driver with no money and he lived in a garage because that's all he could afford. After he met my mom he ended up becoming a very successful commercial real estate developer. My father has a hustler type mentality. He could be tough as a dad in terms of "Get good grades," but he definitely was affectionate with us as well.

I didn't feel I was a disappointment to my dad until I got older. I didn't feel that way as a kid. During my school years my dad did not go to sporting events with me. He refused. He hates that stuff. I think if he had attended I would have felt more supported in the sports I played. I was on a soccer team for a while though I wasn't very good. When I became a swimmer I was an athlete and was undefeated in my high school in swimming actually. The funny thing is that my dad didn't come to a single swim meet yet he was the one who taught me how to swim. So there was this irony there.

When I was growing up, he was the type of father to teach hard lessons. We had a pool in our home, and I always swam sitting in a tube. I didn't want to get out of the tube and it was my favorite one, with a horse head sticking out in front. I was probably around five or six at the time, and my parents were arguing about how I didn't need to be in the tube anymore and that they thought it was ridiculous. I was in the tube in the pool, and my mother slowly brought me closer to the wall. My father was standing beside the pool and he reached down with both his hands and scooped me out of the tube and threw me into the deep end of the pool. It was very traumatic for me. I was under the water for a bit and I got to the wall as soon as possible and jumped out of the pool screaming and kicking at my father's legs for doing that. All my aunts and uncles were there and laughing, and I was crying and yelling and kicking him, and he said, "What's the problem? Look. You swam! You actually did it…" —which was the truth. By getting thrown into the twelve-foot deep end of the pool, I somehow swam to the edge and got out. I looked up at him realizing that that actually did just happen; I just swam. But I was so upset when he said that that I ran to my mom for comfort. That's sort of how my dad is; he's the kind of guy who likes to give hard lessons. And he made his point: because of that lesson I never used the tube again, and he started teaching me how to swim, where he was actually in the pool with me and instructing me how to swim. So something great did come out of it.

During my growing up years there was no example of anyone gay in my life. There was no out person. Everything was heteronormative. My father has always been super-masculine and even though he's shorter in height he's always been the definition of a strong man. He's definitely an alpha male type. His presence was always very strong and he was definitely the dominating parent. My father would always ask me about girls while I secretly knew that my attractions were different. So even if there were never any gay-related conversations, the heteronormative conversation certainly made a strong impression on me.

My dad was hard about everything. He was not born in the states, and because I was a swimmer he never understood the whole idea that American boys would wear short bathing suits. He thought you were supposed to wear a Speedo because that's what every young man in Europe and in the Middle East wears when they're at the pool. My dad said, "This is the dumbest thing ever. I don't understand why you'd want to change that. The whole point of a Speedo is that you can swim and be comfortable in the water."

My mom was American, and I understood that my dad was Israeli. But I went to my mom for all those things in my life where I knew she'd be understanding. My dad was very attached to certain things and to how they should be, and my mom wasn't, so I always confided in my mom far more than I did my dad.

I think my dad had two talks with me about the birds and the bees. The first time was when I started sleeping with women and I think it started again when he knew I was sleeping with men. I was probably sixteen or so when I started sleeping with women, and his talk was simply about being safe. There was no "how to." It was just "be safe and be respectful." My dad had a big thing about respecting women, though my mom would probably argue that now because their marriage ended in divorce.

I started fooling around with boys as early as age twelve. By the time I was sixteen I was in denial that I was gay but I knew the attractions were all there. I did everything I could to fit in at school by acting like the other guys. In those years as a high school student on Long Island, phrases like "Bro" and "Oh man, don't be so gay" were very common and popular. "Don't be so gay" had nothing to do with homosexuality. Gay was a word synonymous with loser, so to say "that's so gay" meant so not cool or so corny or so cheesy, and everyone spoke like that, so I would talk like that and I did it purposely to fit in. The fear in me was so strong because what gay meant to me was something so different and I knew that there was a part of me that actually was a homosexual male. So what I did to stand out was I became the guy in high school who started throwing the biggest parties and I did that behind my parents' back. My parents are very outgoing people and on a typical Saturday night they might easily be out 'til three or four in the morning. They're not even drinkers; they just loved to go dancing and they used to go out to different jazz and blues clubs on Saturday nights. So I was able to have friends over and have them leave and clean up all before my parents got home and so I was becoming really popular at school. The kids in my grade and the kids in the older grade would come as well, and there was a group of bullies in the grade above me who didn't like this. My parties kept getting bigger—up to two hundred teenagers would show up—but I was always adamant that those boys couldn't be there. Obviously I became one of those people on their "Who-the-hell-does-this-guy-think-he-is" list. They began to harass me, and small fights happened. They really disliked me, and there were two guys who were the leaders of the group.

On the first Friday of my junior year at school I was leaving school, and these same two bullies were crossing the crosswalk and they started to harass and provoke me. Things like, "Oh look, it's Matt Shurka... C'mon bro, you want to hit us with your car? You think you're such hot shit..." In that moment the crossing guard shooed them off out of the crosswalk so that I could drive past, and when I went past them I rolled down the window and said, "That's right, you fucking faggots," and I drove off. If anyone had ever used that word with me I would have killed them and yet in that heated moment of aggravation it came right out of my mouth. I went to the barbershop. They followed me, and when I walked out of the barbershop I got attacked by all ten of them. I was hospitalized and in the ER. The two boys got arrested that night and also ended up getting expelled from school.

It was traumatic. That was on Friday. On Monday I thought I was going to be a man and be tough and I went back to school with my face swollen and black and blue. But the thing that really scared me was, "My God, if they only knew I was gay..." I started cutting school almost every day for the next two months and I was acting out at home, and my parents were like, "What the hell is wrong with you? You're not being yourself." I finally went for a ride with my dad and sat in the car and shared with him, "I'm confused. I've been hooking up with boys. I've been with girls—it's happened—but I just don't know where I'm at with all of it." My dad was amazing. He was so loving and told me that he was there for me and he's always my father and nothing's going to change. I felt very comforted. But that whole next week he began to panic. His attitude was shock and, "What do I do? My only son is gay…" He began looking for a therapist for me and in his search he met a licensed therapist who said, "There's no such thing. It all goes back to childhood traumas and if you heal those traumas—because every person is born heterosexual—the attraction to the opposite sex will come back all by itself." That's the theory of conversion therapy.

My dad explained to me what the therapy was and said how important it was that I try this. More or less it was like, "You have to do anything and everything you can to not live a gay life." It really was his fear that I was going to live a horrible life if I were an out gay man in this world. He said, "If there's really something to it psychologically and there's a cure, you need to go for it." So no one held a gun to my head and dropped me in a therapist's office, but I had a fear. I was terrified and I thought, "Yes, I'm going to do anything and everything I can." I began conversion therapy here in New York City and I really gave it my best. I believed in it one hundred percent. That was the beginning of five years of conversion therapy.

It's interesting that I felt much closer to my mom overall but I felt that my dad was a stronger person because of who he is in our community and who he's been as a businessman. I thought, "If there's any person here who is going to help me it's going to be my father," even though he was the scarier parent to go to. So he updated my mom on what was going on. Both my parents were very naive and they didn't know anything about being gay but they were all for me working with a professional. In the beginning my mom had no issue with it because it was so important to my father that I went through this process. When she saw what it was doing to me—already in the first month—she became very opposed and would have arguments with my father: "What are we doing? This is crazy…"

The first steps in the therapy were that I had to spend as much time with other males as possible to confront any issues I had with men. At the same time I was to avoid women at all costs because they didn't want me to learn effeminate behavior. They didn't want me to associate with "the female"; they wanted me to keep females as the mysterious, opposite sex. It was a very Freudian model for the therapy. So that was the beginning of three years of not speaking to my mother and my two sisters. My mother was never going to agree to physically separate—as in move out of the house—so what that meant was I didn't talk to my mom for three years while living in the same house. I believed in the therapy so much that she lost me in it. She would approach me and say, "You know if you're gay it's OK," or she would try to talk to me about it, and I would just get furious. I was working so hard and I saw that she was trying to ruin it—how *DARE* you even say such a thing to me—so I became pretty much the police in my own home.

I was in and out of the therapy for a total of five years. This is something that's very common among teenagers who do conversion therapy; they end up being in the therapy on and off for a while, and the reason is because they believe they failed the therapy. So many times they'll put themselves back into it or keep trying, thinking that maybe they didn't try hard enough in the past, and I definitely was in that category. Over time the conversion therapy ended up splitting our family apart, and after three years I had stopped speaking to my father. My mom started to come back into my life at the time my parents were beginning their divorce. It was a transition for me to have my mom back in my life and to be speaking to her regularly, and she was the one who advocated for me to see a general psychotherapist, so it was the first time I was doing that. It was great but regardless, I kept thinking that I had failed conversion therapy so I put myself back into it and I was on and off with it for another two years.

It was becoming clearer and clearer to me that in the five years nothing was really changing. If anything I was only becoming stronger and I became more of a man and grew into myself. I was also noticing all the patterns among the psychotherapists I was seeing. Many of them claimed to be former gay men who had cured themselves and that's how they had gotten into the practice. But at some point or other every one of them admitted that the attractions are not ever going to go away; it's just something you learn how to not act upon. When I started to notice that pattern I started to really question them more, asking about their life and their own story and what they were personally dealing with now, and they all still had their own issues. They still had same sex attractions and if they were married they were troubled by still having to deal with their attractions. I kept asking to meet and talk with someone who now has no same sex attractions whatsoever and in all my years I never met a single individual who could truthfully say that was the case. In the end they said it's more of a practice, like fighting alcoholism—that was an example they gave—just knowing not to have one more drink. That's what they compared it to. I was told I would never experience love until I met a woman and had a child and that's how God intended it to be. It was the same thing with every therapist, and I wasn't seeing any proof for the therapy working. For myself I gave it my best, and since it wasn't going anywhere I exited conversion therapy when I was twenty-one.

Just being out and living my life in New York was freeing. I got a job as a server in a restaurant in Soho with a gay clientele and I had a lesbian boss who was married with kids. I was witnessing all these different individuals going about their lives and being gay wasn't something they even thought twice about. They were being exactly who they were, and that impressed me. It took me another two years to have the courage to come out at twenty-three and I began advocating when I was twenty-four.

In the midst of this period my dad moved to Israel, in 2010. I came out of the closet in 2012 when he was already living there. He and I were really not in communication for a total of about five years. During my parent's divorce I had to support my mom in certain things so if I had seen him during those five years it was in a courtroom from the other side of the room. My parent's divorce was really an ordeal for all of us, and since I sided with my mother I was against my father and I even had representation and went as far as legally suing him. It was all because there were assets in my name as their child and legally I had to be involved as a party because they were ruling what to do with these assets. I didn't really care about the assets; whatever my parents wanted to do is whatever they wanted to do. But my drive and motivation was pure resentment and upset with my father for what he had put me through during those years.

I took a course called The Landmark Forum which had a dramatic impact on me. The ironic thing is that it was my lawyer's secretary who recommended it to me, and I really didn't think anything of it. I thought it was stupid. But I eventually did it, and it had a really powerful impact on my life. It was after I did the course that I chose to reach out to my father.

No one at Landmark promises you a happily-ever-after life. During the three-day course there's a leader in the room and he or she is just teaching you a set of tools to use in life. That's all it is, and then no matter what happens in your life, positive or negative, you have new tools to take situations on effectively. One of the things they talked about was that we all have "filters" in our mind about everything, like I have an opinion or judgment about my mom or my dad or about L.A. or New York or about friends of mine or about communities of people like the black community or the Jewish community… We all have these filters or preconceptions and everything that happens in our life goes through these filters. I really saw that I had a filter about my father and the filter I'd created for him was "he doesn't love me." So all of my actions and reactions and behavior were always according to that filter. Even if my father said the words "I love you," my reaction would be like, "What an asshole. I can't believe you'd use those words with me," because the filter is that strong and powerful.

If I really looked at my father, he never disowned me and never said he didn't love me. So I had to start realizing, wow… I created this filter, this "What an asshole. He put me through all this. There's no way he loves me…" That is what I had going on in my head. So that tool specifically had a huge impact on me and when I completed the course—my sisters had completed the course prior to me—we bought a plane ticket to Israel. I was a server at the time and was only able to get three days off work, not including the flight, and I called my dad the night before and I said, "Hey Dad, how are you?" We spoke and I said, "I bought a plane ticket. I only have a couple days off work and I'm coming with my sisters to see you." Now, mind you, we hadn't spoken to each other in five years. I'm in a law suit against him and I'm coming to see him for three days. And my dad's like, "O…K…" One of my sisters lived in Israel at the time, and he said, "Why don't you just go to Nancy's apartment and we'll meet for dinner.

How 'bout we do that?" I said, "Great. I'll see you tomorrow." So me and my other sister flew to Israel from New York and we saw my dad for dinner, and it was incredible. Because I'd done the Landmark course I was light. I was free. We were all sitting together and we laughed and we cried. We said, "Dad, how are you? We hear you have a girlfriend. What does your home look like?" It was remarkable to have my dad and his three kids all sitting together.

The next day we went hiking and my dad grabbed my hand, and I don't even remember the last time my father ever held my hand. The second night we were out to dinner again and this time it was my two sisters and I, my father and his girlfriend. So we're sitting at the table enjoying the evening—it's a beautiful spring night in Tel Aviv—and I made some gay joke at the table, and everyone laughed. My father laughed but he laughed awkwardly. He said, "Let's leave the girls at the table and take a walk," and I said, "Sure, let's do it." We took a walk and we had probably walked about two blocks from the restaurant when my father looked at me and said, "So… Whatever happened to conversion therapy?" The last time my dad spoke to me I was eighteen or nineteen and in the middle of conversion therapy. He said, "Are you gay? It sounds like you might be openly gay…" I mean, he had no idea. So I said, "Dad, yeah. I met some really inspiring people and people I look up to and I'm out and this is who I am and who I've always been." And in that moment my father started the same speech he'd always given which was, "You can't be gay. You don't know what you're doing…" I was shocked, like, "Oh my God. After five years he's going to repeat the exact same thing that he's been saying this whole time."

Now my old reaction would have been to start to throw a fit and argue back with him verbally. I had just done this course at Landmark and I remembered the filter I had and so I held back my reaction and just *listened*. I thought, "Whatever my filter is, whatever I think he's doing, put it aside and just listen…" He went on for maybe ten minutes, and even though I had his speech memorized it was like I was hearing it for the first time. It was the first time I noticed that my father was absolutely terrified about his only son being gay and he had no idea what to do about it, and he was literally standing there pleading with me to listen to him: "Let me help save you!"

I never saw it that way before and I could also see how much he loved me. That was the remarkable part, to see my father have concern for me. He rambled for ten minutes like this, and I literally stopped him and I gave him a big hug and a kiss on the cheek and I looked at him right in the eye and said, "Dad, there is NOTHING to worry about."

Now, mind you, I've never told my father not to worry and that's not something I would ever say to him. He looked at me and said, "What are you talking about? What do you mean don't worry?" I said, "Dad. There's nothing to worry about. Look around. We're all together. Me and my sisters and you, we're all together for the first time in five years. It's a beautiful spring night. And I heard what you said. I know exactly what the world is and I know exactly who I am and my promise is that I'm going to take it exactly as it comes and I'm going to live a really, really beautiful life. And that's what I'm telling you; there's actually nothing to worry about." My father's mouth was wide open in pure shock that I had said something like that to him and he's staring at me and finally he just said, "OK." And I looked at him and I said, "OK!"

He had to let it sink in for a little bit. I was just telling him, "This is not a big deal. It's OK." For me what was so big in that moment was that I got my father back in my life. My sisters had their own upset with our father, and during those five years we'd had conversations about him getting older and if he had passed whether we would have gone to his funeral; that's how much resentment and anger we had towards him. And here I am making peace with him and I can hardly fathom the fact that he wasn't in my life for the last five years and how on earth did that happen? It was such a shift.

The next day was my last day there before I flew back to New York. He wanted me to stay, and I said, "I have a job and I gave a promise to go back." When he drove me to the airport I apologized. I apologized for suing him. Yes, it was my mother and father's divorce, but I blatantly went after him. I helped the lawyers and my mother. I was like a soldier searching for whatever sneaky information I could find out about the property or the assets and I apologized to my father for doing that. I told him how painful that was for me and that I was sorry that I wasn't there for him. I subsequently dropped the lawsuit, of course.

So we're sitting in the car outside the airport and he's dropping me off. It was just the two of us and we're holding each other and sobbing for what seemed like twenty-five minutes, both of us apologizing to each other. It was such a profound experience. I got out and walked toward the airport and we said goodbye again and said, "We'll figure this out. Whatever needs to be figured out going forward, we'll work it out." As I walked toward the terminal, my father was staring at me and he doesn't usually do that. My dad's the kind of guy to just drop you off and go, but I remember him staring at me the whole walk into the terminal. I cried through security. When you fly to Israel you have to go through security questions before you can actually check-in your suitcase, and they thought that there was something wrong with me. I was crying out of joy and also sadness: sadness that I had helped create the issues between my father and me, and joy at this one conversation with him that had shifted everything during these three days that I had just spent with him.

This doesn't mean that my father is now a gay rights activist or that he's marching down Fifth Avenue during Pride. He's not. But we have our father/son relationship back. At Landmark we use the word "complete," which means we're both completely settled about everything that has happened in the past. It doesn't mean the past goes away. It's there. It's what happened. My father has said everything he needed to say about conversion therapy, and I said everything I had to say. We're not even bothered by it anymore. My father really got "complete" about everything we've been through, and we have this incredible father/son relationship today. And yes, things come up that he still doesn't like. He doesn't really think I should be an advocate; he wants me to pursue other goals now. If we have our arguments we have our arguments, but the essence of our father/son bond has never gone away and I don't think it ever will. He's one of the closest people in my life today. My father still lives in Israel and we talk every couple of days. He comes here a few times a year, and I go there a few times a year.

I'm definitely interested in being a father. I do know gay couples who have kids so I have some examples of what it could be like. I think it all depends on my future partner. Would I have a child from birth? Would I adopt? Time will tell. Depending on who my future partner is, what we choose to create together will dictate more what will happen in the future. But it's exciting to think about being a father and raising a child and about the kind of father I could be. I think I would love being a parent.

My father and I share some features. People in general think I look Middle Eastern, so I definitely got that from him, though he's much darker skinned than I am. We have similarities in personality. My father is hardworking and he's a hustler. He has balls, as they say. My father's almost like a little Napoleon because he's about 5'8" and he's a very typical driven businessman. He's a very, very strong willed person, and I definitely have that in my personality. I'm a very confident person and I definitely have a strong presence like he does. I have chutzpah or balls like he does, so needless to say our arguments together are pretty strong ones. I'm a go-getter and if I really want something I will make it happen.

My advice? Get to know your father. Get to know him in terms of all the things he is and also all the things he is not, and respect and accept that. A big reason we may suffer as sons is that we really wish our father was this way or that way and we may be trying to change something about our father that is not changeable. I believe that people can transform or shift areas of their life, but you have to just accept who they are right now before anything can change or shift in your relationship. A lot of suffering really comes from wishing or wanting this or that to be different, when in reality, this is how it is. Your father is this way. He's not that way. He's this way, and we are so upset about it that we want to reject and argue and fight. So first, it's really important to really understand who your father is and who he is not. That's him. That's the whole picture. I think when you get to that place first, the conversation will then be different. You'll be accepting and you will be talking to the person that he is instead of the person you wish he was.

*Postscript: five months after this interview....

Matthew's June 25, 2017 post on Instagram, the day of the New York Pride parade:

It has been a long month of hard work, new projects, and big challenges. Each year, I always get a little emotional when the parade starts on Sunday morning. The excitement, the noise, all the faces of happy families, parents, men and women who relocated or traveled to New York to find their own freedom, self-expression, and peace of mind. For the first time since I have come out, and just this morning, I got a phone call from my dad who said he will join me at the parade. He said "I'll be looking for you in the March, is that okay with you? See you there!" Don't ever stop believing what you stand for. I'm incredibly grateful, and completely beside myself. Happy Pride!

Matthew and his dad
June 25, 2017

Also by Tim Clausen:

Love Together: Longtime Male Couples on Healthy Intimacy and Communication

Longtime male couples share candidly in *Love Together* how they navigate issues of monogamy, intimacy, affection, communication, money, spirituality, marriage, and parenting. Included here are the first same-sex military couple in America to legally marry, a Catholic theologian, a pioneering Texas pair featured in a 1996 *Life Magazine* article, a practicing Buddhist couple who recently celebrated their 60th anniversary, two Paris-trained chefs turned international vintners, a Canadian couple who produce a line of gay erotic comics, a Christian pop-singing duo who became parents through surrogacy, a movie industry couple who met the day World War Two ended, and more. With hundreds of years of collective experience, these couples share their life wisdom and offer practical advice for singles who want to find a lasting love relationship.

Out in Print: Queer Book Reviews:

"What you need to do is simply dig in and experience these forty-four lives and how they have come together and stayed together for amazing amounts of time. The similarities will become apparent, as will the differences. Make no mistake, this is an important book if for no other reason than the lack of others like it on the market. And it is even more important as it's largely in the words of the men who live these lives. Highly recommended."

Available on Amazon in both paperback and Kindle

About the Author

Jazz pianist and writer Tim Clausen grew up in Oconomowoc, Wisconsin, where MGM's *The Wizard of Oz* had its world premier in 1939. From an early age he taught himself to to play piano by ear. In addition to recording three solo CD's Tim has played piano engagements at many of Milwaukee's top restaurants and hotels. In his work as a jazz historian he has conducted hundreds of interviews and has had the pleasure of interviewing some of the jazz world's leading artists. A father, Tim founded and facilitated The Milwaukee Gay Fathers Group for its ten-year run from 1995 to 2004. His first book, *Love Together: Longtime Male Couples on Healthy Intimacy and Communication* was published in 2014. *Not the Son He Expected* is the second offering in a planned trilogy of works on gay men's relationships which Tim hopes will help to make life better and easier for gay men and their families. In his spare time Tim enjoys abstract painting, hiking, meditation, cooking, travel, movies, swimming, biking, and spending time with friends.

Made in the USA
Columbia, SC
22 April 2018